Key words in context

Thematischer Mittelstufenwortschatz Englisch

Key words in context

Thematischer Mittelstufenwortschatz Englisch

von
Joanne Popp

Ernst Klett Sprachen
Stuttgart

Picture credits

12 iStockphoto (Alex Belomlinsky), Calgary, Alberta; 26 Shutterstock (Visual Generation), New York; 32 Shutterstock (freelanceartist), New York; 38 Shutterstock (newcorner), New York; 52 Fotolia (Jim Vallee), New York; 66 Shutterstock (Radu Bercan), New York; 76 Shutterstock (Chistoprudnaya), New York; 80 Shutterstock (ducu59us), New York; 88 Thinkstock (PennaPazza), München; 90 Shutterstock (Aquir), New York; 98 Shutterstock (Naturespixel), New York; 100 Shutterstock (ju.grozyan), New York; 120 Shutterstock (Yelena Jumelya), New York; 128 Shutterstock (Katyr), New York; 150 Thinkstock (Bonilla1879), München; 154 Shutterstock (Anabela88), New York; 172 Shutterstock (Fandorina Liza), New York; 190 Bigstock (Sasha_Petra), New York, NY; 192 Shutterstock (Evgenii Matrosov), New York; 196 Shutterstock (patrimonio designs ltd), New York; 200 Bigstock (Tupungato), New York, NY; 208 Shutterstock (Myimagine), New York; 214 Shutterstock (squarelogo), New York; 218 Shutterstock (Art'nLera), New York; Kapitel 6 Shutterstock (Vitezslav Valka), New York

1. Auflage 1 8 7 6 5 4 | 2024 23 22 21 20

Nachfolger von 978-3-12-519702-2

Alle Drucke dieser Auflage sind unverändert und können im Unterricht nebeneinander verwendet werden.
Die letzte Zahl bezeichnet das Jahr des Druckes.
www.klett-sprachen.de

Redaktion: Wolfgang Volz
Layoutkonzeption: Elmar Feuerbach, Sandra Vrabec
Gestaltung und Satz: Datagroup Int. SRL, Timisoara, Rumänien
Umschlaggestaltung: Maja Merz
Druck und Bindung: Medienhaus Plump GmbH, Rheinbreitbach

Printed in Germany

ISBN 978-3-12-519770-1

9 783125 197701

Contents

A note from the author

Dear pupils,

Learning new words isn't easy and you can probably always find something better to do. The problem is: A language lives on words and without them you will be lost and cannot speak or understand the language. With any language it is a problem, but with English it makes life even harder as it is spoken by so many people in so many places and situations.

You may go on a school trip to the UK or a family holiday, you may watch a film in English or read an English book or you may even want to revise certain topics before an English exam - either a written one or an oral exam. Key words in context can help you with all these things and also provides you with the most important key words and expressions for a variety of topics. You may notice that certain words and phrases appear in different chapters. This goes to show that the same words are needed to talk about different topics and helps when you are learning the words.

I hope you enjoy using this book and that it helps you with your English wherever you use it.

Joanne Popp

How to work with *Key words in context*

Why is it easier to learn words when they are in a text?

A text shows you how the words are used and the context you can use them in. This helps you understand the meaning of the words. The texts also give you important and useful information on these topics and reading texts is always good practise for class tests and exams.

Why are some words green/bold?

They are the words which are translated into German on the right-hand side. Some of them have help for the pronunciation, too.

Why are some words highlighted more than once in a chapter?

The key words and phrases are explained each time they are in a new main section. This means you don't have to read all the texts in a chapter but can pick out the sections you need.

If you go to the index at the back of the book, you can see where each word appears and also when the same word is in more than one chapter.

Why is there sometimes additional information?

Sometimes there are opposites, similar words or words from the same word family given. It is easier to learn 'new' words if you can make a connection to 'old' words.

Do I need to learn all the words in *Key words in context*?

The texts have been written to include the most important key words and phrases for the topics. You have to decide which of them are important for your next test, exam or presentation and learn them. Try to use them where you can so that they become part of your active vocabulary.

Why is there a QR code?

This is so that you can listen to native speakers reading the texts and hear the key words and phrases in context. Just scan the QR code and you can listen to the texts in the chapter or download them. Alternatively, go to www.klett-sprachen.de and enter the 6-digit code (underneath the QR code) in the search field. You'll then be taken to the 'Key words in context – audio online' page where you can listen to the texts or download them.

How can I use the chapter on skills? It is different to the rest of the book.

This chapter contains a lot of tips and advice that are useful when you are writing texts or preparing yourself for an oral exam or a presentation. Last but not least they are useful in everyday communication. You can look something up if you aren't sure or you can use it to check your texts when you have written them.

What do the symbols and abbreviations mean?

▸	words in the same word family	*sb*	somebody
=	synonym	*sth*	something
≠	antonym	*etw.*	etwas
AE	American English	*jmd.*	jemand
AusE	Australian English	*jds.*	jemandes
BE	British English	*jdn.*	jemanden
GB	specifically British phenomenon	*jdm.*	jemandem
US	specifically American phenomenon	*ugs.*	umgangssprachlich

Words in context **at a glance**

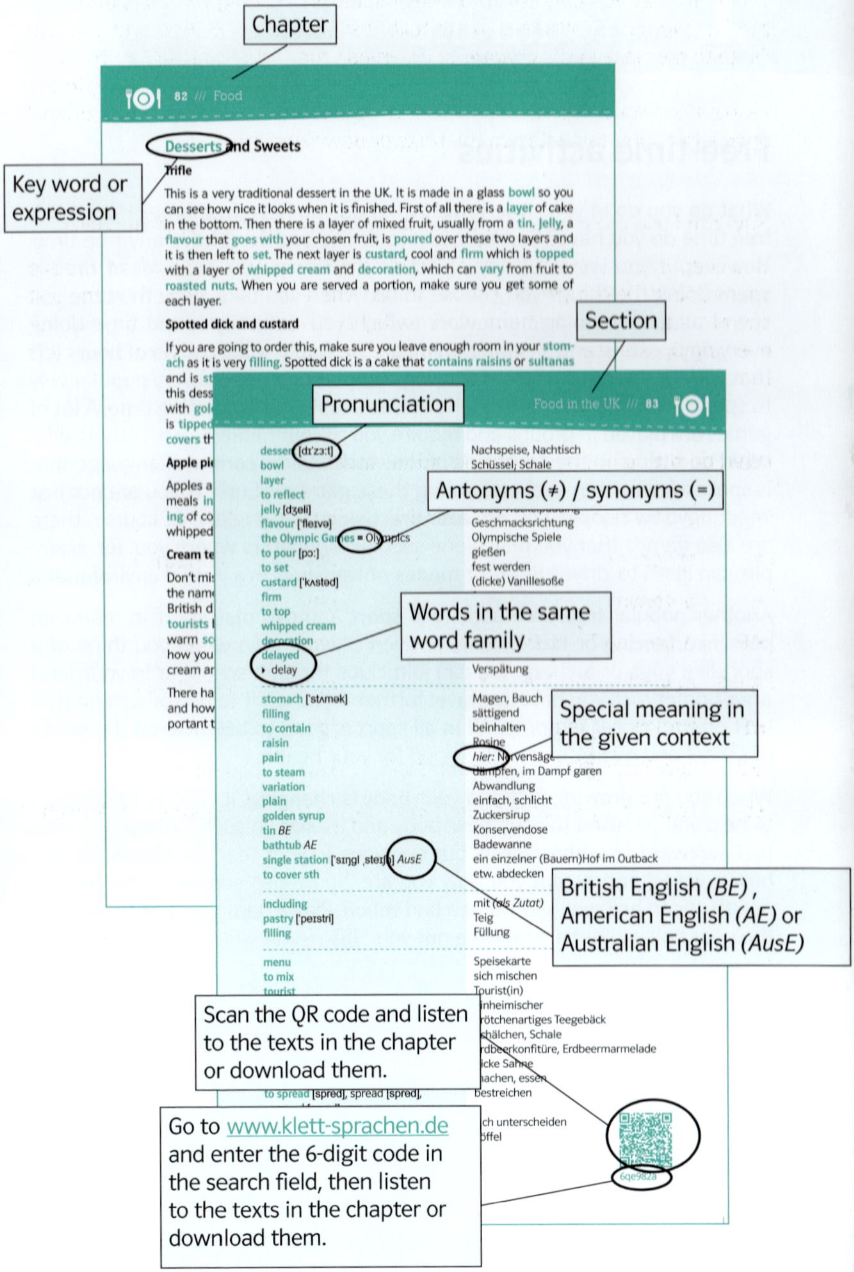

1 Youth life

Free-time activities

What do you do in your free time? When do you have free time? How much free time do you have? Sometimes it feels like you don't have any free time. However, if you were to make a list of the things you do, a lot of time is spent doing the things you choose to do. When you take away the time you spend at school, doing homework (which you naturally spend time doing every day), eating and sleeping, there are probably still a couple of hours left that you choose how to spend. Playing computer games is a very popular way to spend your free time, although parents usually call it wasting time. A lot of games are played in groups and require you to communicate with others who could be sitting on the other side of the world. As the common language that is spoken (or written in chats) during these games is English, you are not just 'meeting' new people, you are also practising your English. Of course, there are also games that you play alone such as simulators where you, for example, can learn to 'drive' different modes of transport in a virtual environment.

Another popular free time activity is sport. You can play sport in teams, in pairs like fencing or kick-boxing, or even on your own when you think of a sport like yoga or archery. You can join clubs through school or in your local area. Sometimes you have to travel further if you want to do something that isn't offered closer to home. All in all sport is good to balance out the stress of school and exams and is also good for your health.

When you are growing fast and your body is changing, it is good to do sport to help you get used to your 'new' body and its size. In such a phase you may feel awkward or embarrassed, but everyone in your team or club will know how you feel and accept you how you are. Sport also supports your mental health, it can help you get rid of a bad mood. Play a hard game of tennis and the poor ball will get a headache not you. »»

free time	Freizeit
however	jedoch
to spend [spend], spent [spent], spent [spent]	*(Zeit)* verbringen
to take away	abziehen
naturally ['nætʃrli]	natürlich, selbstverständlich
probably ['prɒbəbli]	wahrscheinlich
a couple of	ein paar
popular	beliebt
to waste	verschwenden
to communicate [kə'mju:nɪkeɪt]	kommunizieren, sich austauschen
common	üblich, normal
to practise	üben, trainieren
simulator ['sɪmjəleɪtə]	Simulator *(Computerspiel)*
mode of transport [træns'pɔ:t]	Verkehrsmittel, Fahrzeug
virtual ['vɜ:tʃuəl]	virtuell
environment [ɪn'vaɪrənmənt]	*hier:* Umgebung

sport [spɔ:t]	Sport, Sportart
to play	*hier:* (be)treiben
fencing	Fechten
kick-boxing	Kick-boxen
yoga	Yoga
archery ['ɑ:tʃərɪ]	Bogenschießen
local area	nähere Umgebung
to travel	fahren, reisen
all in all	alles in allem, insgesamt
to balance out	ausgleichen
stress	Stress
exam	(Abschluss)Klausur, Prüfung
health	Gesundheit

to grow [grəʊ], grew [gru:], grown [grəʊn]	wachsen, größer werden
body	Körper
to change [tʃeɪndʒ]	sich (ver)ändern
size	Größe
phase	Lebensabschnitt, Phase
awkward	ungeschickt
embarrassed	verlegen, peinlich berührt
to accept	akzeptieren, annehmen
to support	unterstützen
mental	geistig, mental, psychisch
to get rid of sth	etw. los werden
mood	Stimmung, Laune
headache	Kopfschmerzen

972a4a8

There are also other great ways to spend your free time, that depend on if you prefer being indoors or outdoors. You can hang out with your friends, go shopping (or just window-shopping if you have spent all your pocket money already), go to the swimming pool, go on a bike tour, watch the latest film at the cinema or just go for a snack and a game of darts or pool at the local youth club. If you are lucky and live near a bigger town or city, you can go to concerts by your favourite band or even watch musicals and plays. If you don't feel like going out, you can always pick up a good book (one with paper pages or an e-book) and make yourself comfortable on the sofa.

There are also lots of opportunities to do things for others, too. If you live near an animal home, you can help at weekends cleaning the cages or taking the dogs for a walk. There are places where homeless people or refugees live. The volunteers there are always happy when there is an extra pair of hands to help them at the weekend. Charity events to raise money like runs, sporting events run by your local club, as well as activities like keeping your town and countryside tidy are all things you can do to help others. You can even go to visit old people who either live in a care home or in their own home but can't get out. Read them the newspaper, tell them what you have been doing or go shopping for them. Some of these social activities you can also include in your CV when applying for a job.

Relationships

Gender and inter-generational problems

So what am I? In Biology we have talked all about the birds and the bees, plants and reproduction and also the human body. Our parents and even grandparents ask us if we have boyfriends or girlfriends. They warn us against unwanted pregnancies and tell us about contraception like taking the pill or using condoms.

My body feels strange sometimes, I have grown so quickly in all directions. Sometimes I could eat a horse, and at other times I don't want to even come out of my bedroom. Do I have a girlfriend? – No. Do I want a girlfriend? – I'm not sure. Do I want a boyfriend? – I'm not sure about that either, although I think I like the look of girls better. Is it wrong to like people of the same sex? ⟫

to prefer	(etw.) vorziehen, lieber tun
indoors	drinnen, in einem Gebäude
outdoors	draußen, im Freien
to hang out	abhängen, gemeinsam Zeit verbringen
window-shopping	Schaufensterbummeln
pocket money *BE*	Taschengeld
swimming pool	Schwimmbad
darts	Darts *(Wurfpfeilspiel)*
pool	(Pool)Billiard
▸ a game of pool	eine Partie Billard, eine Runde Billard
youth club *BE*	Jugendklub, Jugendhaus
concert	Konzert
musical	Musical
play	Theaterstück
comfortable ['kʌmftəbl]	bequem

opportunity	Möglichkeit
animal home	Tierheim
to clean a cage	einen Käfig sauber machen
to take a dog for a walk	einen Hund ausführen
homeless	obdachlos
refugee	Flüchtling
volunteer	Freiwillige(r)
charity event	Wohltätigkeitsveranstaltung
to raise money	(Geld)Spenden sammeln
run	Rennen, Laufveranstaltung
to keep tidy	sauber machen, sauber halten
countryside	Landschaft
care home	Pflegeheim, Altenheim
social [ˌsəʊʃl]	sozial
to include	aufnehmen
CV [siːˈviː]	Lebenslauf
to apply	sich bewerben

the birds and the bees	*(sexuelle)* Aufklärung, die Bienen und Blumen
reproduction	Fortpflanzung
human body	der menschliche Körper
to warn sb against sth	jdn. vor etw. warnen
unwanted pregnancy	ungewollte Schwangerschaft
contraception	Verhütung
▸ contraceptive	Verhütungsmittel
the pill	die (Antibaby)Pille
condom	Kondom

strange [streɪndʒ]	seltsam, eigenartig
direction [dɪˈrekʃən]	Richtung
same sex	das gleiche Geschlecht

972a4a8

Everyone **makes fun of** Kevin and Jane because they are **going out with** each other. They look happy enough; and at least he still has time to come to football practice on Thursdays.

Parents tell us all about getting **qualifications** and thinking about our future. I'm 16, my biggest problem is if my favourite rugby team is going to win its next **match** or if I can smell my **favourite meal** when I get home. Why do my parents want me to go on holiday with them again in the summer? It's **cheaper**, that's **fair enough**. But what is **getting on my nerves**, they always want to know where I am and who I'm with. Well, I don't understand the **pressure** that parents put us under. I know one thing, I need to pass my Maths test at the end of the week, **otherwise** I don't **stand a chance** of **passing** my GCSE in Maths in three months time.

What is your family like?

*I **interviewed** three different families to get an idea of what modern families are like. As I live **alone** and my parents **split up** when I was ten, I wanted to see what families are like today. I'd like you to meet the Davis family from Taunton in Somerset, the Singh family from West Bromwich in Birmingham and the Chong family from Harrow in London.*

*I'm Rachel Davis and I'd like to **introduce** my family. We are what is called a **blended family** and I love it. I am 17 years old and I have a younger brother who is 14. He is a **pain**, but we **have been through a lot** together. My dad died in a car **accident** when I was four, so my brother doesn't really know much about him – I don't either really, but I have a few **faint memories**. On my tenth birthday we went **bowling** at the 'Silver Pin', my favourite place. I was **allowed to invite** two friends, and I let my brother take a friend, too. We had great fun and on the **bowling alley** next to ours there was another birthday group; there was only a dad with the other group. Anyway you can guess what happened next. We all had a meal together in the restaurant and my mum and my now **stepfather swapped** numbers, and **the rest is history**.*
*We live in a large house in Taunton which is quite a large town in Somerset. My stepfather also has two children who are **both** younger than me and my brother. They are eight-year-old **twin girls**. Every second weekend they visit their mum at her **flat**. They can't live with her all the time though as she isn't very well, that's why we all live together. We have a dog, Sam, and two cats, Thomas and Daisy. I can walk to school as it isn't far. My mum is a **part-time teaching assistant** at a **primary school** and my (step)dad works for a **transport company**.* »»

to make fun of sb	sich über jdn. lustig machen
to go out with sb [ˌgəʊˈaʊt]	mit jdm. ausgehen, sich mit jdm. verabreden
qualification [ˌkwɒlɪfɪˈkeɪʃn]	(Bildungs)Abschluss, Qualifikation
match	Spiel
favourite meal	Lieblingsessen, Lieblingsgericht
cheap	billig, preiswert
fair enough	in Ordnung, schön und gut
to get on sb's nerves	jdm. auf die Nerven gehen
pressure [ˈpreʃə]	Druck
otherwise	sonst
to stand a chance	eine Chance haben
to pass	bestehen
to interview	befragen, interviewen
alone	allein
to split up with sb	sich von jdm. trennen
to introduce sb [ˌɪntrəˈdjuːs]	jdn. vorstellen
▸ to introduce oneself	sich (selbst) vorstellen
blended family	Patchworkfamilie
pain	*hier:* Nervensäge
to be through a lot together	zusammen viel durch machen
accident	Unfall
faint	blass
memory	Erinnerung
bowling	Bowling, Kegeln
to allow	erlauben
to invite	einladen
bowling alley	Bowlingbahn, Kegelbahn
stepfather	Stiefvater
▸ step sister	Stiefschwester
to swap	tauschen
the rest is history	der Rest ist Geschichte; was dann kam, kann man sich vorstellen
both	beide
twin girls	Zwillingsmädchen, Zwillingsschwestern
▸ twins	Zwillinge
flat	Wohnung
part-time	in Teilzeit, Teilzeit-
teaching assistant	Lehrassistent(in)
primary school *GB*	Grundschule
transport company	Logistikfirma, Transportunternehmen

972a4a8

*He works **full-time** and he has got to start work really early in the morning but gets home at the same time as we do from school. He has to go to bed early as he gets up so early in the morning, that **means** we have to be quiet in the evenings. We always go on holiday together in the summer. One year we stay in England and the next year we go **abroad**. We have been to France, Germany and Italy.*

*My name is Farah Singh. I live with my family in West Bromwich which is part of Birmingham in the West Midlands. We live in a flat above my parents' shop. My **grandparents** came to England as **immigrants** in 1947 when India was **divided**. My parents were born and **raised** in England and we all live together with my grandparents. There isn't much room and I have to **share** a bedroom with my two sisters. My parents **work** very **long hours** so my grandparents **look after** us most of the time. At home we don't speak much English, and we always eat Indian food that my **grandmother** cooks. My friends love eating at our house, and I like going to their houses for real English food like **casserole** or **roast beef**.*
*I have an older sister who is just doing her **A levels** and will be going to university to **study** to be a **pharmacist** in September if she **passes** her **exams** which I'm sure she will. My younger sister is only ten and I often have to help her with her **homework**. As money is a bit **tight**, we can't **afford** to pay for **extra tuition**. I'm doing my GCSEs in the summer and then I'm going to **sixth form college** for my A levels. I want to study **pharmacy** the same as my sister.*

*Hi, my name is Ana Chong. I live with my **single parent** dad, my brother and my **grandad** in Harrow in London. It can be a **struggle** for me living in a house full of men. I have to do a lot of the **housekeeping**. As my father works hard every day and my brother is studying at university, they have no time to help. My grandfather helps me, but I always have to tell him what to do while I'm at school, **otherwise** he forgets. My dad is a **chef** at a big hotel in London. He works so hard, but when he is home he **cooks** us **delicious** food. I try hard at school, but I'm not very good. I think I'm going to do a **hairdressing course** at college when I pass my GCSEs as I love chatting with people and I'm always **styling** my friend's hair. My mum lives in Liverpool with her new family. She has a new **husband** and two small children. We do video calls **at weekends** and I visit her in the holidays, but I like our life in London better. I would love to go to China one day and see where my grandparents came from and where some of my family still lives. One day my **dream** will **come true**, I'm sure.* »

full-time	ganztags, Vollzeit-
to mean	bedeuten, heißen
abroad	im Ausland

grandparents	Großeltern
immigrant	Einwanderer
to divide	teilen
to raise	aufziehen, großziehen
to share	teilen, zusammen bewohnen
to work long hours	lange arbeiten *(viele Stunden am Tag)*
to look after sb	sich um jdn. kümmern, jdn. versorgen
grandmother	Großmutter
casserole	Auflauf
roast beef	Rinderbraten

A levels *(short for: advanced levels)*	Abitur
to study	studieren
pharmacist ['fɑːməsɪst]	Apotheker(in), Pharmazeut(in)
to pass an exam	eine Prüfung bestehen
homework	Hausaufgabe(n)
tight	*hier:* knapp
to afford sth	sich etw. leisten
extra tuition [tju'ɪʃn]	Nachhilfe(unterricht)
sixth form college	Oberstufenschule
pharmacy ['fɑːməsi]	Pharmazie, Pharmazeutik *(Wissenschaft von den Arzneimitteln)*

single parent	Alleinerziehende(r)
grandad	Großvater
= grandfather	
struggle	Kampf, Anstrengung
housekeeping	Haushalt(sführung)
otherwise	sonst, andernfalls
chef	Koch, Köchin
to cook	kochen, zubereiten
delicious [dɪ'lɪʃəs]	sehr lecker, köstlich
hairdressing course	Ausbildung zum/zur Friseur(in)
to style [staɪl]	stylen, zurechtmachen
husband	(Ehe)Mann
at weekends	am Wochenende, an den Wochenenden
dream	Traum
to come true	wahr werden

972a4a8

Wow, they are three different families, but they are all families who ***stick together*** *and help each other. They talk about things, they have* ***arguments****, they do things together and they know where they* ***came from****. You will meet* ***more and more*** *people at school or in sports or youth clubs that live* ***separated*** *from their families and maybe don't even know where their families are. They are* ***refugees*** *who have* ***escaped*** *from their country because of* ***war*** *or because their* ***religious beliefs*** *are 'wrong'. These people have to start a new life in a* ***foreign country****, but at least there are people to help them and give them* ***support****.*

Role models

Susi:

I'm 16 years old and live in Manchester. My **bff** has got a **bf** and **all of a sudden** she doesn't **spend** any time with me any more. We still get the bus to school together, only because he lives on a different **estate** I'm sure. We have been bffs since primary school. We did everything together, our homework, going to the cinema, listening to the same music, talking about our **idols**, **absolutely** everything. Now she has M. and all I hear is 'M. says this, M. does that, M. **is fond of** this, M. is so **handsome**, oh isn't M. wonderful?' To be honest: no, he isn't. What makes it even worse is that I had **fancied** him first, and she knew I did. Then I got **flu** and couldn't go to the school disco, and he asked her to dance. She **reckons** she couldn't say no. So now they are a **couple** and I **play gooseberry** whenever we go anywhere together. Judith, please tell me what to do to make me happier. I've tried telling my bff what I think, but she doesn't understand. I don't want to lose **what little friendship** we have as I have **no-one else**.

Yours, in **desperation**
Susi D, Manchester

Judith:

I get lots of letters **similar** to yours and I always give people the same **advice**. At the beginning of any relationship the partners only have eyes for each other. This time **passes** as normal **daily life** takes over. At the moment it is hard as your best friend doesn't have any time for you. **Hang on** in there, when the **novelty** of having a boyfriend **wears off** she will find time for you again. His **mates** probably feel the same as you do. »»

to stick together	zusammenhalten
argument	Streit, Auseinandersetzung
to come from	herkommen
more and more	immer mehr
separated ['sepreɪtɪd]	getrennt
refugee	Flüchtling
to escape	fliehen, entkommen
war	Krieg
religious belief [rɪ'lɪdʒəs]	religiöse Überzeugung, Glaubensvorstellung
foreign country	fremdes Land
support	Unterstützung

---

bff *(best friend forever)*	beste(r) Freund(in) für immer
bf *(boyfriend)*	*(fester)* Freund
all of a sudden	plötzlich
to spend [spend], spent [spent], spent [spent]	*(Zeit)* verbringen
estate [ɪ'steɪt] *BE*	Wohnsiedlung *(mit vielen gleichartigen Häusern)*
idol ['aɪdəl]	Idol, großes Vorbild
absolutely	absolut, komplett
to be fond of sth	etw. gern haben
handsome	gut aussehend, attraktiv
to fancy sb	für jdn. schwärmen
flu	Grippe
to reckon	meinen, behaupten
couple	Paar
to play gooseberry	das fünfte Rad am Wagen sein, sich überflüssig fühlen
what little	das Wenige an
friendship	Freundschaft
no-one else	sonst niemand
desperation	Verzweiflung

similar	ähnlich
advice	Rat(schlag)
to pass	vergehen
daily life	Alltag, tägliches Leben
to hang on	abwarten
novelty	Neuheit, Neuheitseffekt
to wear off	vergehen, sich abnutzen
mate *BE*	*(ugs.)* Freund(in), Kumpel

972a4a8

I assume, at the latest in a month's time you will be back hanging out together and she will tell you everything. Just be patient and show her what a good friend you are.

Fingers crossed,
Judith

Dylan:

I'm in love with a famous model, I can't even write her name it's so embarrassing. All I can think about day and night is how I could meet her. She is so glamorous and stunning ... and she hasn't got a boyfriend at the moment. Can you please help me get her mobile number or address, please? I know you think I'm mad, but I can't stop myself.

Thx a mill,
Dylan

Judith:

Sorry, but even if I knew the name of your model I couldn't help you. I can't pass on anybody's personal information. Look online, I'm sure she has a website and you can write to her manager and tell her your feelings. I'll keep my fingers crossed for you that it works out well.

All the best,
Judith

Denise:

I have done something really awful and don't know what to do. I'm desperate and don't know who to turn to. On Saturday I stole a T-shirt from a department store in town. I didn't mean to do it. It was a gorgeous pink T-shirt and it fitted me perfectly. All the other girls in my class have got T-shirts of the same brand and they always look happy and cool. I had seen it in the window a few times and wanted it for the party on Saturday. I was broke and so when no-one was looking, I put it in my bag and walked out of the shop. I was happy at first, but soon I was so ashamed I didn't wear the T-shirt to the party and don't know what to do. Please help me.

Denise

to assume	annehmen, vermuten
to hang out	abhängen, herumhängen, Zeit verbringen
patient ['peɪʃənt]	geduldig
fingers crossed *(short for: to keep one's fingers crossed)*	jdm. die Daumen drücken
model	Model, Fotomodell
embarrassing	peinlich, unangenehm
glamorous ['glæmərəs]	glamourös, zauberhaft
stunning	umwerfend, atemberaubend
boyfriend	fester Freund
at the moment	im Moment, zur Zeit
mobile number *BE*	Handynummer
thx a mill *(short for: thanks a million)*	tausend Dank, danke vielmals
to pass on	weitergeben
anybody	(irgend)jemand
personal information	private Daten, persönliche Angaben
manager	Manager(in)
feeling	Gefühl
to work out	gut laufen
desperate	verzweifelt
to turn to sb	sich an jdn. wenden
to steal [sti:l], stole [stəʊl], stolen ['stəʊln]	stehlen
department store	Warenhaus, Kaufhaus
gorgeous	wunderschön
to fit	passen
perfectly	*hier:* wie angegossen; ideal, perfekt
brand	Marke
window	(Schau)Fenster
to be broke	Pleite sein, kein Geld haben
to be ashamed	sich schämen

972a4a8

Judith:

Don't panic! You have done something wrong stealing the T-shirt, but you **realise** it was wrong which is good. If you still have the T-shirt and it has got all the **labels** on it, be **brave** and take it back to the shop. Maybe you have a good friend who can go with you, or even tell an older sister or your mum. The important thing is, you made a **mistake** and you want **to make it right**. Go back to the shop with the T-shirt, **explain** what you did and **face the consequences**. One thing I know is that you won't do it again, **no matter** how nice the T-shirts are or who you want to **impress**.
Be strong, I'll be thinking of you,

Judith

Health

Top Ten singer found dead in hotel **bathtub**

Emergency services were called late this morning to room 112 at the Best West Hotel in **downtown** Chicago. **Unfortunately**, they only arrived in time to **confirm** the **death** of Andrea Wearing (25). At the moment there has been no confirmation of the **cause** of death, but it is **rumoured** that Andrea was fighting both a **drug** and an **alcohol** problem. Her manager wasn't **available** for **comment** when this **article** went to **print**.

On Saturday Andrea was out **celebrating** her tenth number one hit with friends. They had a **meal** at the Surf 'n' Turf 51 and then went on to the Warehouse Club Disco. They **partied**, **smoked**, **drank** and **consumed** a **cocktail of drugs**. Andrea left the **bunch** at about 2 a.m. to return to her hotel alone as she had to be in the studio at 10 this morning.

When she didn't **turn up** at the studio, the **sound engineer** called her hotel. There was no **reply** in her room and her manager was informed. He went to the hotel and **persuaded** the hotel manager to open the door of Andrea's **suite**. In the bathroom they made a sad **discovery**.

Andrea was lying **face down** in the bathtub that was still full of water. »»

Don't panic!	Keine Panik!, Immer mit der Ruhe!
to realise	begreifen, verstehen
label	Etikett
brave	mutig, tapfer
mistake	Fehler
to make sth right	etw. in Ordnung bringen
to explain	erklären
to face the consequences	sich den Konsequenzen stellen
no matter	ganz gleich, egal
to impress	beeindrucken
to be strong	stark sein

---

bathtub *AE*	Badewanne
emergency service	Notfalldienst, Notdienst
downtown *AE*	Stadtzentrum, Innenstadt
unfortunately [ʌnˈfɔːtʃnətli]	leider, unglücklicherweise
to confirm	feststellen, bestätigen
death	Tod
cause	Ursache
it is rumoured	es gibt das Gerücht, man munkelt
drug	Droge
alcohol	Alkohol, alkoholische Getränke
available	verfügbar
comment	Kommentar, Meinung
▸ to comment	kommentieren
article	Artikel, Bericht
to go to print	in Druck gehen

to celebrate	feiern
meal	Mahlzeit
to party	feiern, Party machen
to smoke	rauchen
to drink [drɪŋk], drank [dræŋk], drunk [drʌŋk]	trinken *(alkoholische Getränke)*
to consume	konsumieren, zu sich nehmen
a cocktail of drugs	Mischung verschiedener Drogen
bunch	Gruppe, Gesellschaft

to turn up	auftauchen, erscheinen
sound engineer	Toningenieur, Tonmeister
reply	Antwort
to persuade	überreden, überzeugen
suite	Hotelsuite
discovery	Entdeckung

face down	mit dem Gesicht nach unten

972a4a8

The emergency services were called and they took the **body** to the city **morgue** for an **autopsy**. The **results** of which aren't **due** until the end of the week. There will be no **official comment** on the cause of death until this information has been **received**.
Dave Skinner, her current boyfriend, was not available for comment. In the early afternoon he was seen leaving the hotel only ten minutes after his **arrival**. He had not been celebrating with Andrea last night as his flight from Seattle was **delayed** and he didn't arrive in Chicago until **midday**.
Andrea Wearing had spent some time in the Poplars **Rehab Clinic on the outskirts** of New York in **fall** last year. She left the clinic after two weeks **treatment** and spent time writing her last CD **including** songs about her being **clean** and having given up both drugs and alcohol. She really seemed to have found the right path after many wrong ones.
As soon as we have an **update** on the autopsy report or information about the **funeral arrangements**, we will be sure to let you know. Our **thoughts** and **prayers** go out to Andrea's parents and family back in Boston as well as to her friends and fans all over the world. We have sadly lost one of today's **rising stars** far too early in her life and **career**.

Diets and sport

Training, training, training

Training, training, training ... that's all my manager and trainer want me to do. **Watch** what you eat, don't go to bed late, make sure you train enough and try harder. I really didn't know if I could go on **like that** ... I couldn't and didn't. Read on if you want to be a top sportsman or sportswoman, but don't do what I did.
I always loved swimming, and **to be honest** my parents always said it was all **down to** the **waterbirth** that was more of an **accident** than planned. They couldn't get me out of the water right from an early age, and I was always trying to be faster than everyone else and **dive** deeper. Then I was **spotted** at an **inter-school competition** by a sport **scout** who found out who I was while I was still **competing**. He was talking to my parents about my future swimming career even before I could show them my newly won **medals**.

body	Leiche, Leichnam
morgue	Leichenschauhaus
autopsy	Obduktion, Autopsie
result	Ergebnis
due	zu erwarten
official comment	offizielle Aussage *(der Polizei oder Staatsanwaltschaft)*
to receive	bekommen, erhalten
arrival	Ankunft
delayed	verspätet, verzögert
▸ delay	Verspätung
midday	Mittagszeit
rehab clinic	Rehabilitationsklinik *(zur Behandlung von Drogensüchtigen)*
on the outskirts	am Stadtrand
fall *AE*	Herbst
treatment	Behandlung
to include	*hier:* mit; enthalten, einschließen
clean	clean *(nicht mehr drogenabhängig)*; sauber
update	aktueller Bericht
funeral ['fju:nrəl]	Beerdigung, Bestattung
arrangement	Vorkehrung
thought	Gedanke
prayer ['preə]	Gebet
rising star	aufsteigender Stern *(am Musikhimmel)*
career [kə'rɪə]	Laufbahn, Karriere
diet [daɪət]	Ernährung; Diät
training	Training
▸ trainer	Trainer(in)
to watch	aufpassen, schauen
like that	so
to be honest ['ɒnɪst]	um ehrlich zu sein, ehrlich gesagt
to be down to sth	an etwas liegen
waterbirth	Wassergeburt
accident	Zufall, Versehen
to dive	tauchen
spotted	entdeckt, gesehen
inter-school competition	Wettbewerb zwischen Schulen
scout	Talentscout, Talentsucher
to compete	an einem Wettkampf teilnehmen
medal	Medaille

972a4a8

It all went really fast. Of course, they asked me what I wanted, but to me my **whole life revolved around** swimming. If I could spend even more time in the pool, I wasn't going to say no. My mum was given **diet plans** so she knew what she had to **feed** me, how much and when. My dad was given **instructions** when I had to be at which pool for which **training session**.
I think they were **glad** I was an **only child**, but they were also very **proud of** all the trophies and medals I won. I travelled around the world **participating in** different **junior competitions**. At the same time I also had to make sure that my **education** didn't **fall behind**, so I had to **fit in** French, Geography and all the other subjects that people of my age have to learn.
At 17 I was so good I was **selected** for the **Olympic squad**. The diet plans got even **stricter** and the training even harder. I wasn't living at home then, so my parents couldn't **keep an eye on** what I was doing. It started really slowly and almost **unnoticeably**. I would have a piece of chocolate and **suck** it slowly or I would have a **sip** of a **fizzy drink**. My trainer went **mad at me** about my training times which were **fractions** of a second slower, but he had noticed. He **took me aside** and asked me what was going on. I was honest and told him what I had done. The usual **lecture** came, "If you want to do well you have to stick to the diet plans and training sessions. If you don't stick to them, you will be out of the squad and the dream will be over."
One of my **housemates** heard what my trainer said. She talked to me later that night about what was going on. She felt sorry for me that the trainer had been so **harsh**. She told me about something special that would help me keep up my **speed** but **at the same time** allow me to eat a piece of chocolate or take a sip of lemonade **here and there**.
I wasn't sure, but she made it sound so easy and **eventually convinced** me. I was 17, I was **naive** and didn't know much about life as I had always been **protected** by my parents and trainers. I did the one thing that no **athlete** should ever do: I took **tablets** to make me faster – I **doped myself**. I will **regret** the **conversation** with my housemate and the **decision** I made for the rest of my life. »»

whole life	das ganze Leben
to revolve around	(sich) drehen um
diet plan	Ernährungsplan
to feed [fi:d], fed [fed], fed [fed]	zu essen geben
instruction [ɪn'strʌkʃn]	Anweisung
training session	Trainingseinheit
glad	froh
only child	Einzelkind
to be proud of sth	auf etw. stolz sein
to participate in sth [pɑ:'tɪsɪpeɪt]	an etw. teilnehmen
junior competition [ˌdʒu:niə]	Juniorenwettbewerb
education [ˌedʒʊ'keɪʃn]	schulische Bildung
to fall behind	zurückfallen, zurückbleiben
to fit in	hereinschieben
to select	auswählen
Olympic squad	Olympiamannschaft
strict	streng, konsequent
to keep an eye on sth	etw. im Auge behalten
unnoticeable	unmerklich, unbemerkt
to suck	lutschen
sip	Schlückchen
fizzy drink	zuckerhaltiges Getränk
to go mad at sb	auf jdn. wütend sein, wegen jdm. durchdrehen
fraction	Bruchtteil
to take sb aside	jdn. zur Seite nehmen
lecture ['lektʃə]	Vortrag
housemate	Mitbewohner(in)
harsh	hart, scharf
speed	Geschwindigkeit
at the same time	zur gleichen Zeit, gleichzeitig
here and there	ab und zu, hier und dort
eventually [ɪ'ventʃuəli]	endlich, schließlich
to convince [kən'vɪns]	überzeugen
naive	naiv, ahnungslos
protected	geschützt
athlete ['æθli:t]	Athlet(in)
tablet	Tablette
to dope oneself	sich aufputschen
to regret	bereuen, bedauern
conversation	Gespräch, Unterhaltung, Konversation
decision [dɪ'sɪʒn]	Entscheidung

972a4a8

I was found out. No-one ever thinks they will get caught; I thought the same. I was screened for drugs after I had won my three gold medals at the Olympics. One out of the two drug tests was positive. I was re-tested, positive again. I had my medals taken away from me, I had to talk to the press and I denied cheating. I didn't know really what I had been given. I had to look into my parents faces when I told them what had happened. It was my worst nightmare. Thankfully my parents supported me and have helped me get over the worst time of my life. I have learnt a lesson for life: you can't always trust everyone and not everyone is your friend.

Computer games

You may ask yourself why there is a text about computer games in the chapter about health. Unfortunately, computer games are a health risk that a lot of people are unaware of. They see the fun but don't realise how time flies when you're having fun and how addictive games can be, and of course an addiction is a health problem.

A quick game of any computer game can quickly lead to another one; it's easier to keep on playing until you win. This often takes a while even if you are good at a game. Many games can only be played on the internet, some games give penalties if you take a break – if it is to go to bed or even if it is only to get something to eat. These games usually cause trouble in families and also between friends. The game producers aren't bothered.

Nowadays many games can be downloaded free of charge from the internet. They work on all devices and all platforms. Usually you can save the level you are at when you stop, allowing you to continue from that point later. You can play with friends or against them, and you can also meet people from all over the world as a lot of games have their own groups that people can join. You can work together to complete derbies or just switch candies to clear the board, hoping a funny looking character isn't faster.

There are also many simulator games on the market. They are so realistic you actually feel like you are driving a lorry across Europe, flying a plane from one side of the world to the other or ploughing fields on a tractor. »»

to find out	entdecken, etw. herausfinden
to get caught	erwischt werden
to screen sb for drugs	jdn. auf Drogen untersuchen
drug test	Dopingkontrolle
the press	die Presse *(Medien)*
to deny [dɪ'naɪ]	leugnen, bestreiten
to cheat	betrügen, mogeln
nightmare	Albtraum
thankfully	glücklicherweise
to support	unterstützen
to learn a lesson for life	eine Lehre fürs Leben ziehen

chapter	Kapitel
health risk	Gesundheitsrisiko
unaware	nich bewußt
to realise	begreifen, erkennen
how time flies	wie die Zeit vergeht
addictive	süchtig machend, abhängig machend
▸ addiction [ə'dɪkʃn]	Sucht

quick	schnell
while	Weile, kurze Zeitspanne
penalty	Strafe
to take a break	eine Pause machen
to cause trouble	Ärger verursachen
game producer	Spieleentwickler
bothered	beunruhigt

to download	herunterladen
free of charge	kostenlos
device	Gerät
platform	Plattform
to save [seɪv]	speichern, sichern
level	Spielstand, Level
continue [kən'tɪnjuː]	fortsetzen, weitermachen
point	*hier:* aktueller Spielstand
against	gegen
derby ['dɑːbi]	Nachbarschaftsduell
to switch	tauschen
candy *AE*	Süßigkeiten, Bonbons
to clear the board	abräumen
character	Figur, Gestalt

simulator ['sɪmjəleɪtə]	Simulator *(Computerspiel)*
on the market	im Handel, auf dem Markt
realistic	realistisch, wirklichkeitsnah
lorry *BE*	Lastwagen
to plough [plaʊ]	pflügen

972a4a8

You may feel that they aren't games, but you are still spending a long time in the same position. In real life you have to stop for a break as there are working regulations on how long you can drive or fly for without taking a break.

All these games are designed so that you want to and even sometimes have to play regularly to get further. Animals need to be fed, dragons trained or even towns built. This makes you addicted even though you don't think you are. Time passes very quickly and before you realise it, the 20 minutes you intended to spend on playing a quick game as a break is over an hour.

Just take some good advice and set a timer. When it rings, stop playing. Force yourself to stop after that one game and invite and encourage your friends to do the same. Many people don't realise you spend too long staring at a screen, sometimes only the size of a mobile phone, which also damages your eyes in the long run.

Tricky situations

In a lot of big towns and cities youths join together to form groups or gangs. There are three different kinds of groups or gangs. There are peer groups which are small groups of youths with the same background. They aren't usually interested in doing anything criminal. There is often peer pressure within the peer group, but it is usually about wearing the right clothes.

Another group is street gangs who threaten other people or put them under pressure. They usually give their gang a name and carry offensive weapons like knives. There is often rivalry between different street gangs. Crime and violence and even selling drugs are part of their gang life. The last group of gangs are simply criminals who are only interested in getting money through crime. They often carry guns and are organised groups.

Some groups boast and brag about what they do and call themselves gangs, although they are just groups of friends who hang out together and have no interest in committing crimes. Quite often gangs and groups have their own language, too. »»

position [pə'zɪʃən]	Körperhaltung, Position
real life	das wirkliche Leben
break	Pause
working regulation [ˌregjə'leɪʃn]	Arbeitsvorschrift
to design [dɪ'zaɪn]	gestalten, entwerfen
regularly	regelmäßig
further	weiter
to feed [fi:d], fed [fed], fed [fed]	füttern
dragon	Drache
to make sb addicted	jdn. süchtig machen
to pass	vergehen
intended to	beabsichtigt
advice [əd'vaɪs]	Rat(schlag)
timer	Zeituhr
to ring	klingeln
to force	zwingen
to encourage [ɪn'kʌrɪdʒ]	ermutigen, Mut machen
to stare	starren
screen	Bildschirm
to damage ['dæmɪdʒ]	beschädigen
in the long run	langfristig, lange Sicht
tricky	schwierig, heikel
youth	Jugendliche(r)
gang	Bande, Gruppe
peer group	Peergroup, Gruppe Gleichaltriger
background	*(sozialer)* Hintergrund
criminal	strafbar, kriminell
peer pressure	Gruppendruck
street gang	Straßenbande
to threaten	drohen
to put sb under pressure	jdn. unter Druck setzen
offensive weapon [əˌfensɪv 'wepən]	Angriffswaffe
rivalry ['raɪvlrɪ]	Rivalität, Gegnerschaft
crime	Verbrechen
violence ['vaɪəlns]	Gewalt
drug	Droge
gun	Schusswaffe
to boast	angeben
to brag	prahlen
to commit	begehen, ausführen

972a4a8

They talk about being **streetwise** (knowing the **rules** of the street) or being a **sissy** (someone who is **weak**) or a **wannabe** (someone who would like to be part of the gang but isn't accepted into the group).
Sometimes when you join a gang or a group, you cannot leave again. When youths get older, many **begin** to **realise** that some of the things the group does aren't good and don't want to be **connected with** it anymore. Then the **leaders** of the group make it very hard or even **impossible** for them to leave.
Nowadays with everyone using smartphones, a lot of **threats** and **criminal behaviour** is also done online. There is **cyberbullying**, where **innocent** people are threatened **severely** or are sent horrible pictures and videos. Teenagers are at a very **sensitive** age and can't always **brush off** such behaviour and don't know who to **turn to**. Unfortunately, some people don't find people to turn to and can't always find a way out of a situation without taking their lives. There is always someone who will listen and give you the right **advice**, don't **give up**.
Whenever you are out with a gang or a group or just a few friends, don't forget there are rules and **regulations** that are there to make **living together** in **society** more **comfortable** for everyone. If you don't follow these rules, usually the police **get involved**. In the UK in 1998, Tony Blair the **prime minister introduced** the **ASBO** (the **anti-social behaviour order**). This was to **reprimand** people who were **behaving anti-socially** in **public places** and **disturbing** others without having to make a **court case** of it. The order **restricted** people's behaviour, e.g. **prohibiting** them from going to certain shops or areas or restricting their behaviour **in public** – no **swearing** or drinking alcohol.
If you have **gotten yourself into trouble** – **minor** or **major** trouble – you may need help. The most important people in your life will always be your friends and family. They will be with you in both good times and bad. »»

streetwise	gerissen, ausgekocht
rule	Regel
sissy	*(ugs.)* Weichei, Memme
weak	schwach, schwächlich
wannabe	Möchtegern
to begin [bɪ'gɪn], began [bɪ'gæn], begun [bɪ'gʌn]	beginnen, anfangen
to realise	begreifen, erkennen
to connect with	verbinden
leader	Anführer(in)
impossible	unmöglich
threat	Bedrohung
criminal behaviour	kriminelles Verhalten
cyberbullying	Cyber-Mobbing, Internet-Mobbing
innocent ['ɪnəsnt]	unschuldig
severely	ernsthaft
sensitive	empfindlich, empfindsam, sensibel
to brush off [brʌʃ]	wegstecken, verarbeiten
to turn to sb	sich an jdn. wenden
advice	Rat, Ratschlag
to give up	aufgeben, aufhören
whenever	wann (auch) immer
regulation [ˌregjə'leɪʃn]	Vorschrift
living together	Zusammenleben
society [sə'saɪəti]	Gesellschaft
comfortable	angenehm
to get involved	sich einmischen
prime minister [ˌpraɪm'mɪnɪstə]	Premierminister(in)
to introduce [ɪntrə'dju:s]	einführen
ASBO *(anti-social behaviour order) BE*	einstweilige Verfügung wegen antisozialen Verhaltens
to reprimand	zurechtweisen
to behave [bɪ'heɪv]	sich verhalten/benehmen
anti-socially [ˌæntɪ'səʊʃli]	unsozial, gesellschaftsfeindlich
public place	öffentlicher Platz
to disturb	stören
court case	Gerichtsverfahren
to restrict	einschränken, beschneiden
to prohibit	verbieten, untersagen
in public	in der Öffentlichkeit
swearing	Fluchen
to get oneself into trouble	sich in Schwierigkeiten bringen
minor	gering, klein
major ['meɪdʒə]	bedeutend, groß

972a4a8

They will celebrate with you when you do well and they will support you when you have problems.
With more serious or legal problems you can use a crisis line or talk to social workers. Everyone makes mistakes and needs help to make things better. Share your problems, this makes it easier to find a solution. There are phases in your life when everything is hard and everyone seems to be against you, they aren't though. Having good friends helps you through thick and thin, and true friends will always be there for you.

Communication

Smartphones are what everyone has to have nowadays so that they can message their friends, access the internet, write e-mails, watch films, listen to music, take photos, count how many steps they walk everyday, make notes of all their appointments ... oh yes, and now and again make a phone call.

Here is an example of a typical chat dialogue.

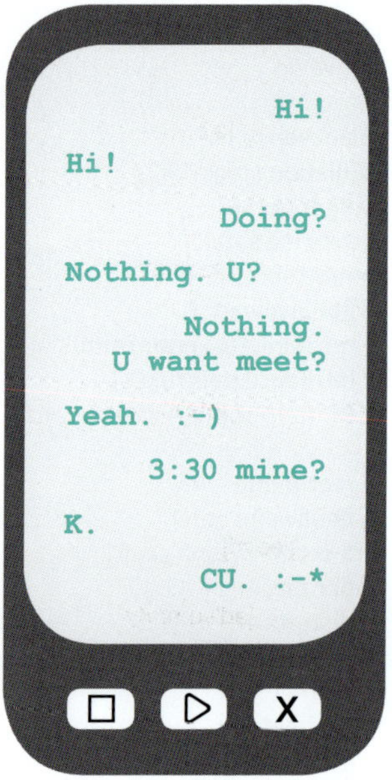

As you can see, there are lots of abbreviations, the grammar isn't correct and nothing is really said. This is an example of a dialogue between two people. More interesting, and complicated, is a conversation between a group. Classes quite often have a class chat or sports groups or other groups of friends set up group chats so that they don't have to write the same things many times. Group chats are also good for passing on information like a meeting point or homework or the date of the next class test.

However, when several people are chatting at the same time, it can get hard to follow what is being 'said'. The advantage is though, you can always read it through again if you have missed something. For many people it is also important to always have an up-to-date profile picture and status. Some people change their pictures many times a day depending on their mood or what they are up to. It can be really hard work.

to celebrate	feiern
to support	unterstützen
serious	ernst, ernsthaft
legal problem	Problem mit dem Gesetz
crisis line	Telefonseelsorge
social worker ['səʊʃl ˌwɜːkə]	Sozialalarbeiter(in)
mistake	Fehler
solution [sə'luːʃn]	Lösung
phase	Phase, Abschnitt
against	gegen
through thick and thin	durch dick und dünn
smartphone	Smartphone
to message	Nachricht schreiben
to access the internet	ins Internet gehen
to count	zählen
appointment	Verabredung, Termin
now and again	hin und wieder
to make a phone call	telefonieren
typical	typisch
chat	Chat *(sich online unterhalten)*
dialogue	Gespräch, Dialog
abbreviation [əˌbriːvi'eɪʃn]	Abkürzung
correct	richtig, korrekt
people	Personen, Menschen; Leute
complicated	kompliziert
conversation [ˌkɒnvə'seɪʃn]	Unterhaltung, Konversation
class chat	Klassenchat
to set up	einrichten, aufsetzen
to pass on	weitergeben
information [ˌɪnfə'meɪʃn]	Information(en)
meeting point	Treffpunkt
however	jedoch
several ['sevrl]	mehrere, einige
to follow	folgen
advantage [əd'vɑːntɪdʒ]	Vorteil
≠ disadvantage	Nachteil
to miss sth	etw. verpassen
up-to-date	aktuell
profile picture	Profilbild
status	Status
to depend on	abhängen von
mood	Stimmung, Laune
to be up to	vorhaben, machen

972a4a8

Music

Everyone's got their own taste in music. What young people like, older people often think is awful and vice versa. However, tastes also change through the years too. And then there are so many different types of music. Pop music, the name is the abbreviation of popular music, is the music that is played most frequently on the most listened to radio stations. It has always been connected with teenagers and young adults. Pop music originated during the 1950s and 1960s and developed out of rock 'n' roll.

When people grow older, their taste in music changes and they turn to other music styles. Not all young people are into pop music, some have specific tastes in music, some like jazz, which was first played by African Americans in the southern states in America in the 19th and 20th century. Others are into hip-hop which is a combination of funk, poetry and mixing music. Classical music is also popular for relaxing to. There is also country music, folk music, swing, heavy metal and … the list goes on and on.

Sometimes on a bus or a train you can't help hearing other people's music, even though they have headphones or earphones on. If their music is very loud, you can even recognise the songs. Then you will appreciate it if you share the same musical taste.

Age restrictions

In all countries the law says how old you have to be to do certain things. Here are a few things you can do in England from different ages.

From the age of 14 you can …

- get a part-time job, for a maximum of two hours on a school day, working sometime between 7:00 a.m. and 8:00 a.m. and 5:00 p.m. and 7:00 p.m. You can work up to five hours on a Saturday between 7:00 a.m. and 7:00 p.m. and you can work on Sundays between 7:00 a.m. and 7:00 p.m., but for no longer than two hours. You can also work five hours a day from Monday to Saturday during the school holidays.
- decide yourself if wearing a seatbelt is a good idea. From the age of 14 it is considered your own personal responsibility, so buckle up.

From the age of 15 …

- working restrictions are the same as 14-year-olds, except you can work up to eight hours on a Saturday between 7:00 a.m. and 7:00 p.m.
- you can watch, rent or buy 15 rated films.

taste	Geschmack
vice versa [ˌvaɪsˈvɜːsə]	umgekehrt
type	Art, Sorte, Typ
abbreviation [əˌbriːviˈeɪʃn]	Abkürzung
frequently	oft, häufig
to connect	in Verbindung bringen, verbinden
to originate	seinen Ursprung haben
to develop	(sich) entwickeln
to grow older	älter werden
style	Stil
to be into sth	etw. mögen
specific [spəˈsɪfɪk]	bestimmt, speziell
African American [ˌəˈmerɪkən]	Afro-Amerikaner(in)
the southern states	die Südstaaten *(in den USA)*
combination [ˌkɒmbɪˈneɪʃn]	Mischung, Kombination
poetry [ˈpəʊɪtri]	Lyrik, Dichtung
to relax	sich entspannen
folk music	Folkmusik, traditionelle Volksmusik
can't help	nicht anders können, nicht vermeiden können
headphones	Kopfhörer
earphones	Ohrhörer
to recognise	erkennen
to appreciate [əˈpriːʃieɪt]	schätzen, zu schätzen wissen
age restriction [rɪˈstrɪkʃn]	Altersbeschränkung, Altersbegrenzung
law	Gesetz
a few	einige
maximum	Maximum, Höchstzahl
considered	angesehen, betrachtet
personal responsibility	Eigenverantwortung
to buckle up	sich anschnallen
except	außer
to rent	ausleihen
rated	freigegeben ab, eingestuft

972a4a8

From the age of 16 you can ...

- have sex, gay or straight, so long as your partner is also 16+ (17+ in Northern Ireland).
- drink a glass of beer, wine or cider with a meal in a pub or restaurant if you are with an adult.
- ride a moped with a maximum engine power of 50cc (and a provisional licence). You can also drive an invalid vehicle (with a licence) and a lawnmower.
- work full time, but not in a bar or a betting shop.
- join the armed forces (so long as that's OK with your parent/s or carer).
- order your own passport.
- play the National Lottery.
- fly a glider.
- get married (with parental consent).
- buy liquor chocolates. At last.

From the age of 17 you can ...

- drive most types of vehicles (with a provisional driving licence and a 21+ adult in the passenger seat who is qualified to drive). If you pass your driving test, and you're properly insured, you can get behind the wheel and take to the road on your own.
- apply for a private pilot's licence for a plane, helicopter, hot air balloon and airship.
- become a blood donor and you can leave your body to medical science.

From the age of 18 you can ...

- vote in local elections and general elections.
- make a will.
- get married without parental permission.
- watch, rent or buy 18 rated films.
- buy fireworks.
- place a bet in a betting shop/casino.
- buy and smoke cigarettes, rolling tobacco and cigarette papers.
- buy and drink any alcoholic drinks in a pub or a bar.
- have a tattoo.
- qualify to drive lorries weighing up to 7.5 tonnes, with a trailer attached.

gay	homosexuell
straight	*hier:* heterosexuell
cider ['saɪdə]	Apfelwein
moped ['məʊped]	Moped *(Kleinkraftrad)*
engine power	Motorleistung
50cc	50 ccm
provisional licence	vorläufiger Führerschein
invalid vehicle	motorisierter Rollstuhl
lawnmower	Rasenmäher(traktor)
betting shop	Wettbüro
the armed forces [ˌɑːmd 'fɔːsɪz]	Militär, Streitkräfte
carer	Erziehungsberechtigte(r)
passport	Reisepass
National Lottery	staatliche Lotterie
glider	Segelflugzeug
to get married	heiraten
parental consent = parental permission	Zustimmung der Erzeihungsberechtigten
liquor	Spirituosen

passenger	Passagier(in)
qualified	*hier:* im Besitz eines Führerscheins
driving test	Fahrprüfung
properly	ordentlich, ordnungsgemäß
insured	versichert
to take to the road	auf Tour gehen
to apply	anmelden
pilot	Pilot(in)
hot air balloon	Heißluftballon
airship	Luftschiff
blood donor	Blutspendenr(in)
to leave [liːv], left [left], left [left]	*hier:* hinterlassen
medical science	medizinische Forschung

to vote	abstimmen, wählen
local election *BE*	Kommunalwahl
general election	Parlamentswahlen
will	Testament, letzter Wille
fireworks	Feuerwerkskörper
casino	Kasino, Spielbank
cigarette [ˌsɪgr'et]	Zigarette
rolling tobacco	Tabak zum Selbstherstellen von Zigaretten
pub	Kneipe
tattoo	Tätowierung
to qualify	*hier:* den Führerschein machen
lorry *BE*	Lastwagen
(metric) **tonne**	Tonne, 1000kg
trailer	Anhänger
attached	angehängt

972a4a8

2 Education

We start learning as soon as we are born. We learn to walk and talk without being taught, we just copy what other people do. Formal education starts when we go to nursery school and finishes for some people when they leave school and for others on graduation from university. Of course, we can continue learning after our formal education has finished at evening classes, further education courses or just by reading articles on the internet.

Education in the UK

All children between 5 and 15 must be given a full-time education, by law. Since 2015, the Education and Skills Act 2008, requires that all young people up until their 18th birthday receive education or training (at least part-time). Primary school is followed by secondary school. Many of them are comprehensive schools and are either run by the state or are privately run (a small minority).

The British school system has a national curriculum which lays down teaching standards, the core subjects (English, Maths and Science) and defines four key stages and the expected standards at each stage. At each stage, tests are taken in order that pupils can be assessed and parents are provided with a written report every year.

Schools in Britain start at about 9 a.m. with registration, then there is sometimes an assembly followed by lessons until about 4 p.m. There are different clubs in either the lunch break or after school. Most schools have a school uniform. »»

to copy	nachmachen, nachahmen
formal	offiziell *(hier: den staatlichen Bildungsvorgaben entsprechend)*
education [ˌedʒʊˈkeɪʃən]	Schulbildung
nursery school	Kindergarten
graduation [ˌgrædʒʊˈeɪʃn]	Universitätsabschluss
university [ˌjuːnɪˈvɜːsəti]	Universität, Hochschule
to continue [kənˈtɪnjuː]	fortsetzen, weitermachen
evening class	Abendkurs
further education	Weiterbildung, Fortbildung
course	Kurs, Lehrgang
article	Artikel

---

full-time	ganztags, Vollzeit-
by law	gesetzlich, von Rechts wegen
act	Gesetz
to require	vorschreiben; erfordern
primary school *GB*	Grundschule
secondary school *GB*	weiterführende Schule
comprehensive school	Gesamtschule
state	Staat
privately	privat
to run [rʌn], ran [ræn], run [rʌn]	betreiben
minority	Minderzahl, Minderheit

---

national curriculum	nationaler Lehrplan/Bildungsplan
to lay down	festlegen
teaching standard	Unterrichtsstandard *(Vorgaben, die die Qualität des Unterrichts sichern sollen)*
core subject	Kernfach
to define	festlegen, bestimmen
key stage	Bildungsniveau *(Wissens- und Kenntnisstand in einer bestimmten Jahrgangsstufe)*
expected	erwartet
to take a test	eine Prüfung machen
in order that	damit
to assess	bewerten, beurteilen
parents	Eltern
to provide sb with sth	jdm. etw. geben, jdm. etw. zukommen lassen
written report	(Schuljahres)Zeugnis

---

registration	*hier:* Anwesenheitsabfrage
assembly	Versammlung, Zusammenkunft
lunch break	Mittagspause

rf5sr3u

The main qualification British pupils take are GCSEs at 16. Most pupils study between five to ten subjects, including the core subjects and a language. All pupils take the same exam and the pass marks start at A* (the best) and go down to G. The final marks are calculated using the exam mark and course-work marks. There are also oral exams for languages. In 2017, this system will be replaced by the English Baccaleureate Certificate (EBacc). The final marks will be based on the final exams at the end of a two-year course.

After taking GCSEs, pupils have a number of choices. They can choose to do A levels in three (or four) subjects which will help them with a degree course at university. They can also do a vocational qualification which is work-related and offers them both job-related skills and practical skills.

Here is an overview of the formal education system in the UK.

UK		
Year		Approximate age
	Nursery	3-4
	Reception	4-5
1	(Infant) Primary School (Junior)	5-6
2		6-7
3		7-8
4		8-9
5		9-10
6		10-11
7	Secondary School	11-12
8		12-13
9		13-14
10		14-15
11	GCSE exams*	15-16
12	(Sixth form = 2 years) AS levels	16-17
13	A-levels or equivalent	17-18
	Higher education - University; graduation after 3 or 4 years depending on degree course	18 - 21

*Some children also take GCSEs a year earlier.

Shaded area = compulsory full-time schooling

qualification	Schulabschluss
GCSE (exams) *(General Certificate of Secondary Education)*	Prüfungen in GB, die man mit etwa 16 Jahren ablegt *(etwa: Mittlerer Abschluss)*
to study	lernen, studieren
pass mark	Note, die zum Bestehen einer Prüfung mindestens notwendig ist
final mark	Endnote
to calculate	rechnen, berechnen
coursework mark	Jahresendnote
oral exam	mündliche Prüfung
to replace	ersetzen
to base on sth	auf etw. beruhen

choice	(Aus)Wahl
A level *(short for: advanced level)*	höherer Schulabschluss in Großbritannien, *(etwa:)* Abitur
vocational qualification [vəʊˌkeɪʃnəl kwɒlɪfɪˈkeɪʃn]	berufliche Qualifikation
work-related	tätigkeitsbezogen
to offer	(an)bieten
job-related skills	berufsspezifische Kenntnisse
practical skills	praktische Fertigkeiten

overview	Überblick, Übersicht
year *BE*	Schuljahr, Klassenstufe
approximate	ungefähr
age	Alter
nursery	Kinderkrippe, Kinderhort
reception	*hier:* Vorschule
infant	Kleinkind (4 bis 7 Jahre)
junior *GB*	*hier*: Kind (7 bis 11 Jahre)
sixth form	*(etwa:)* Oberstufe, Sekundarstufe II
AS levels *(short for: advanced subsidiary levels)*	Prüfungen in GB, die zwischen GCSE und A levels liegen
equivalent	Entsprechung, Äquivalent
higher education	Hochschulbildung
to depend on sth	von etw. abhängen
degree course	Studiengang, Studienfach
compulsory schooling	Schulpflicht

rf5sr3u

Education in the US

Unlike the UK, there is no **national education system** or **national curriculum** in the US, and the schools aren't **operated** by the **government**. Every **state** has its own **Department of Education** which **sets guidelines** for all the schools in the state to follow. In the US parents are **allowed** to teach their children of all ages at home and not send them to school. Only a very small number of students (about 3%) is **homeschooled** although this number is **increasing**. Many have **moral** or **religious reasons** for homeschooling their children. The other main reason for homeschooling is because parents **prefer** a **non-standard approach** to education.

<table>
<tr><th colspan="5">US</th></tr>
<tr><th>Grade</th><th colspan="3"></th><th>Approximate age</th></tr>
<tr><td></td><td colspan="3">Nursery School</td><td>3-4</td></tr>
<tr><td></td><td colspan="3" rowspan="2">Kindergarten</td><td>4-5</td></tr>
<tr><td></td><td>5-6</td></tr>
<tr><td>1</td><td rowspan="6">Elementary School</td><td rowspan="6">Elementary School</td><td rowspan="4">Elementary School</td><td>6-7</td></tr>
<tr><td>2</td><td>7-8</td></tr>
<tr><td>3</td><td>8-9</td></tr>
<tr><td>4</td><td>9-10</td></tr>
<tr><td>5</td><td rowspan="4">Middle School</td><td>10-11</td></tr>
<tr><td>6</td><td>11-12</td></tr>
<tr><td>7</td><td rowspan="3">Junior High School</td><td rowspan="5">Combined Junior-Senior High School</td><td>12-13</td></tr>
<tr><td>8</td><td>13-14</td></tr>
<tr><td>9</td><td rowspan="3">High School</td><td>14-15</td></tr>
<tr><td>10</td><td rowspan="2">Senior High School</td><td>15-16</td></tr>
<tr><td>11</td><td>16-17</td></tr>
<tr><td>12</td><td colspan="3">High school diploma</td><td>17-18</td></tr>
<tr><td rowspan="4"></td><td colspan="3">university freshman year</td><td>18-19</td></tr>
<tr><td colspan="3">sophomore year</td><td>19-20</td></tr>
<tr><td colspan="3">junior year</td><td>20-21</td></tr>
<tr><td colspan="3">senior year and graduation</td><td>21-22</td></tr>
</table>

Shaded area = **compulsory** full-time **schooling**

national	landesweit, national
education system	Bildungssystem
national curriculum	zentraler Lehrplan
operate	betreiben, steuern
government	Regierung
state [steɪt]	Bundesstaat
Department of Education	Bildungsministerium
to set guidelines	Richtlinien erstellen
to allow	erlauben, die Erlaubnis geben
to homeschool sb	jdn. zu Hause unterrichten
to increase	zunehmen, ansteigen
moral	moralisch
religious [rɪˈlɪdʒəs]	religiös
reason	Grund
to prefer	(etw.) vorziehen, lieber tun
non-standard	alternativ, nicht Standard
approach	Ansatz, Methode

---

grade *AE*	Schuljahr, Klassenstufe
nursery school	Kindergarten
kindergarten *US*	Vorschule, Kindergarten in den USA *(etwa ab dem 5. Lebensjahr)*
elementary school *US*	Grundschule
middle school	Sekundarschule
junior high school *US*	*(etwa:)* Unterstufe der weiterführenden Schule
combined	kombiniert
high school *US*	die amerikanische Form der Gesamtschule (nicht „Hochschule")
senior high school	*hier:* Schule für Schüler(innen) der Stufen 10–12
diploma	Diplom
freshman	Student(in) im ersten Jahr
sophomore [ˈsɒfəmɔː]	Student(in) im zweiten Jahr
compulsory schooling	Schulpflicht

rf5sr3u

Talking about education

First day at high school

David and Max are exchange students from Europe and have just arrived at a high school near Seattle that they will be **attending** for the next year.

MEMBER OF STAFF Will all the exchange students who have just arrived please meet in the **entrance hall** for the **principal**'s welcoming **speech**. Thank you.

DAVID Hi, my name's David. I'm from England. Where are you from?

MAX I'm from Germany. My name is Max. I only **arrived** on Saturday and don't know anyone **except** my **host family**.

DAVID Me **neither**. I got here on Friday. Let's listen to what the principal has to say, maybe we will be in the same class. Do lessons start at eight o'clock every morning? In England my first lesson was at nine.

MAX I think it is eight every day, I'm **used to** that though, it is the same in Germany.

DAVID At least we finish around two o'clock though which is cool. In England we have school until four. Do you finish at two in Germany?

MAX Sometimes, but I also have classes until five on some days. That makes a really long day.

PRINCIPAL Welcome to our high school everybody. Our school day will be different to what you have been used to at home, but I hope you will **settle in** fast and be happy here. School starts at eight o'clock every day and finishes at two o'clock. Then there is time for sports activities and other clubs and **societies**. There are a few **rules** at this school that are important for you to know. Here are some of the important ones, you can **check out** all of them on the school **notice board** over here on the right. OK, important **dress code** rules are: skirts and shorts must meet the **fingertip** rule – that is, they must be longer than your fingertips when you **stretch** your arm along your legs; tops with less than two fingers **width** on the shoulder or are **backless** are not allowed; they shouldn't be so short that they show your **midriff**, and please make sure they have no **rude** comments on them; **undergarments** must not be **visible** and **necklines** must be **modest**; please always wear **appropriate footwear** – **flip flops** and **high heels** are not appropriate; hats and **sunglasses** are also not necessary inside the school building. I think those are the **basics** about the dress code. »

to attend [ə'tend]	besuchen
member of staff	Lehrkraft
entrance hall	Aula, Eingangshalle
principal ['prɪnsəpl] *AE*	Schulleiteri(n), Rektor(in)
speech	Rede
to arrive	ankommen
except	außer
host family	Gastfamilie
neither ['naɪðə]	auch nicht
to be used to sth	(an) etw. gewohnt sein
to settle in	einleben, sich zuhause fühlen
society *AE*	Verein, Schul-AG
rule	Regel
to check out	ausprobieren
notice board	Pinnwand, Schwarzes Brett
dress code	Kleiderordnung, Kleidervorschrift
fingertip	Fingerspitze
stretch	ausstrecken
width	Breite
backless	rückenfrei
midriff	Taille, Bauch
rude	unhöflich, beleidigend
undergarment	Unterwäsche
visible	sichtbar
neckline	Ausschnitt
modest	zurückhaltend, sittsam
appropriate [ə'prəʊprɪət]	passend, geeignet
footwear	Schuhe, Schuhwerk
flip flops	Flip-Flops, Badesandalen
high heels	Stöckelschuhe, hochhackige Schuhe
sunglasses *(pl)*	Sonnenbrille
the basics	das Wichtigste, die Grundlagen

rf5sr3u

MAX	That isn't any different than at our school.
DAVID	We had a school **uniform** which **limited** what we could wear.
PRINCIPAL	OK. Just a few more things then you can go to your **individual** classes. **Punctuality** is very important at this school. If you are late, we need a **note** from your parents. If you need to leave the classroom during class, you need to get a **hall pass** from the teacher. Please keep all your **belongings** in your **locker**. I think that was everything for now. I hope you have a great year here at our school.

Later in the canteen

MAX	So what happens now Isaac? **Lessons** are over for the day and we've had lunch, but the school buses don't go until four.
ISAAC	Now there is time for **study** and sport. You can try out for the basketball, baseball, soccer or football team – unless you want to be a cheerleader instead? Only joking, that is for the girls.
DAVID	I play football at home, I'd like to try out for the soccer team.
MAX	I want to try something new, so I think I'll go for the baseball team. What do you think Isaac?
ISAAC	Go for it. All the teams are always looking for new members.
DAVID	I have a question. Is it right that our **timetable** is the same for every day? We really have the same lessons every day of the week for a whole year?
ISAAC	We have the same **classes** every day but not for the whole year. Each subject is part of a course which can be for one or two **semesters**. At the end of a semester we get grades and when we have **passed** all the required courses we can graduate. If you look at your **schedule**, we don't call it timetable here, you can see there are also **electives**. These are subjects like **astronomy** or **journalism** that you choose to take on top of the compulsory subjects like English, Math and Science. You have to choose your electives by the end of the week.
MAX	Thanks Isaac, I wanted to ask about the electives. I think it is a really good idea that we can do other subjects too. We can't do that at my school unless there are enough people for the course. Often there aren't enough for the **unusual** courses.

uniform ['ju:nɪfɔ:m]	Uniform
to limit	einschränken
individual [ˌɪndɪ'vɪdʒuəl]	einzelne, jeweilig
punctuality	Pünktlichkeit
note	schriftliche Entschuldigung
hall pass	ein Pass, mit dem Schüler nachweisen, dass sie das Klassenzimmer mit Erlaubnis der Lehrkraft verlassen haben
belongings	Eigentum
locker	Schließfach, Spind

lessons ['lesəns]	der Unterricht *(an diesem Tag)*
study	Lernen, Hausaufgaben machen
timetable	Stundenplan
class	Unterricht(sstunde), Kurs; Klasse
semester	Halbjahr
to pass	*(eine Prüfung)* bestehen
schedule ['skedʒu:l] *AE*	Stundenplan
elective	Wahlfach
astronomy [ə'strɒnəmi]	Astronomie
journalism ['dʒɜ:nəlɪzm]	Journalistik
unusual [ʌn'ju:ʒl]	ungewöhnlich

rf5sr3u

DAVID	In England we can choose three subjects for A levels, four if you are really **smart** and you have those subjects every day all week. There are a few other subjects we also have to do like **PE**, but not many unusual ones. You have to **pick** your subjects carefully as they **determine** what subjects you can study at university. If you do your A levels in English, German and Music, you can't study sciences.
MAX	Isaac, can you give me a **copy** of the **pledge of allegiance** please? If we have to say it every day, I need to **learn it by heart**.
DAVID	We don't have it either. We do have **assembly** once a week when the **headteacher** talks to the whole school, and we have **registration** with our **tutor group** every morning before first lesson.
ISAAC	The pledge of allegiance is really easy though and you'll quickly learn it. I'll say it and you write it down. I pledge allegiance to the **flag** of the United States of America, and to the **republic** for which it stands, one **nation** under God, **indivisible**, with **liberty** and **justice** for all.
MAX	Can you say it a bit slower, please? I can't write **that fast**.
DAVID	**Hold on** while I get a pen and paper so I can write it down.

smart	schlau, clever, intelligent
PE *BE (Physical Education)*	Sport *(Schulfach)*
to pick	auswählen
to determine [dɪ'tɜ:mɪn]	entscheiden
copy	Kopie, Exemplar
pledge of allegiance [ˌpledʒ əv ə'li:dʒəns]	Treuegelöbnis, Treueschwur *(Fahneneid auf die amerikanische Flagge)*
to learn sth by heart	etw. auswendig lernen
assembly	Schulversammlung
headteacher *BE*	Schulleiter(in), Rektor(in)
registration [ˌredʒɪ'streɪʃn]	tägliche Anmeldung
tutor group *BE*	Schulklasse

flag	Fahne, Flagge
republic	Republik
nation	Nation, Volk
indivisible	untrennbar
liberty	Freiheit *(im Sinne von Bürgerrechten und Grundrechten)*
justice	Gerechtigkeit
that fast	so schnell
to hold on	warten, halten

rf5sr3u

In the evening

DAVID	This **chicken** is great. Can I have **some more**, please?
MOM	Sure, **help yourself**, David. You don't have to ask. I'm glad you like it. How was your first day at school?
DAVID	It was cool. I was **surprised** that we have the same classes every day.
MOM	Did you get into the soccer team?
DAVID	I will **find out** tomorrow. I hope so. They were all really nice guys. On the bus home I met the **boy next door**, Sam.
MOM	Sam had his first day at middle school today. When do you change schools in England?
DAVID	We go to primary school until we are eleven, then we change to secondary school for Year 8. I was talking to Max today. He is an exchange student from Germany. Their system isn't an easy one. They go to primary school until they are ten. Then, depending on their **marks**, they go to a different school until they are either 16 or 18. A lot more people do **apprenticeships** in Germany after school than in England, too. Some people do **vocational qualifications** which are **work-related** and are good for getting both **job-related skills** and **practical skills**.
MOM	Apprenticeships sound good. Here in the US, kids don't usually do them. They either study at university after high school or they **get a job**.
DAVID	It's **strange** how different countries have different school systems, isn't it?
MOM	Enough about school and education, your chicken is getting cold. I'm glad your first day was good. Don't forget the bus **picks** you **up** at 7:30 at the end of the road.
DAVID	Thanks for **reminding** me.

chicken	Hähnchenfleisch
some more	etwas mehr
to help oneself	sich selbst bedienen, sich etwas nehmen
surprised	überrascht
to find out	herausfinden, erfahren
boy next door	Nachbarsjunge
mark *BE*	Note
apprenticeship [ə'prentɪsʃɪp]	Lehre, Ausbildung
vocational qualification [vəʊˌkeɪʃnəl kwɒlɪfɪ'keɪʃn]	berufliche Qualifikation
work-related	arbeitsbezogen, berufsbezogen
job-related skills	berufsspezifische Kenntnisse
practical skills	praktische Fertigkeiten
to get a job	einen Job suchen
strange [streɪndʒ]	seltsam, eigenartig
pick up	abholen
to remind	erinnern

rf5sr3u

3 World of work

While you are still at school, you may want to or even have to increase your **pocket money** with a weekend job, **evening job** or an after school job. This could be **babysitting** for a neighbour's child for some euros **per evening** or **delivering** free newspapers or **flyers** on a **pay per-piece basis** or **stocking shelves** in a **supermarket** after **closing time**. Usually you got this job by asking the people who **hired** you **personally** or making a **phone call**. Often you don't have a **formal interview** either.

At some time during your school life you will usually have to do some **work experience**, and at the latest when you are 16 you may want a **holiday job** or after your **exams** even start an **apprenticeship**. For these jobs a phone call won't be enough. Other people may also want the **position** you are **applying** for and **therefore** the **company** will want your application in **written** form – and not just a short **note**.

When you apply for a job, you need to send a number of **documents** with your application. Whether applying online or **by post**, these documents are the same. You need:

- a **letter of application**
- a **CV** (**curriculum vitae**) (BE)/**résumé** (AE)
- **references** from past jobs or **work placements**/**internships**
- **proof** of your **qualifications** (**certificates** or your last **school report**)

The first two documents you have to prepare really **carefully** as they are the things that **sell** you to a possible future **employer**. The first thing they see is your letter and CV. After reading them they decide if your application will be taken further or not.

pocket money *BE*	Taschengeld
evening job	Job für abends
babysitting	Babysitten
per evening	pro Abend
to deliver	austragen, ausliefern
flyer	Flugblatt, Handzettel, Werbebeilage
pay per-piece basis	Bezahlung nach Stückzahl
to stock shelves	Regale befüllen
supermarket	Supermarkt
closing time	Geschäftsschluss
to hire	einstellen
personally [ˌpɜːsənˈli]	persönlich
phone call	Anruf
formal [ˈfɔːml]	formell, offiziell
interview	Bewerbungsgespräch

work experience	Praktikum; Berufserfahrung
holiday job	Ferienjob
exam	Prüfung, (Abschluss)Klausur
apprenticeship	Ausbildung, Lehre
position [pəˈzɪʃn]	Stelle, Arbeitsplatz
to apply	sich bewerben
▸ application	Bewerbung
therefore	deshalb
company	Firma
written	schriftlich
note	Notiz, Nachricht

document	Dokument, Schriftstück
▸ documents	Unterlagen, Dokumente
by post	per Post
letter of application	Bewerbungsschreiben
curriculum vitae (CV) *BE*	Lebenslauf
résumé [ˈrezjuːmeɪ] *AE*	Lebenslauf
reference [ˈrefrns]	Empfehlung(sschreiben)
work placement *BE*	Praktikum
internship *AE*	Praktikum
proof [pruːf]	Nachweis(e)
qualification [ˌkwɒlɪfɪˈkeɪʃən] *BE*	Bildungsabschluss
certificate [səˈtɪfɪkət]	Zeugnisurkunde
school report *BE*	Schulzeugnis
carefully	sorgfältig
to sell [sel], sold [səʊld], sold [səʊld]	verkaufen
employer	Arbeitgeber(in)

vzmwwbe

Talking about future jobs

Talking to the careers advisor

CAREERS ADVISOR So, Peter. You filled out this **questionnaire** for me last month and now I finally have the **results**. It was quite interesting to see what **suggestions** the careers computer programme **came up with**.

PETE OK. I'm not really **convinced** it will help me but tell me what it said.

CAREERS ADVISOR Well, it **linked** your favourite school subjects, Biology and Design Technology with your love of **the outdoors** and your **interest in** animals and plants. It came up with the following suggestions: **landscape designer**, **zookeeper**, **gardener**, **forester** or a **specialist** in a **garden centre**. As you can see, they are all sort of **connected** with each other. What do you think?

PETE I'm **amazed**. **Apart from** the zookeeper as there isn't a zoo round here, they are all things that had been going through my mind. My biggest **issue** is to find out how to get one of those jobs. What do I have to do? Are there **courses** at **college**?

CAREERS ADVISOR What a **relief** that the programme came up with some **suitable** suggestions. The first step would be trying out one of these jobs. How about doing some work experience? I have some names and addresses here of both gardeners and landscapers who have **places** for students. **Otherwise**, the local garden centre has places, too. You can either write them an email or a letter or you can **give them a call**.

PETE Oh, I think I'll send them an email. I don't feel **comfortable** talking on the phone and I might forget something **important**. Can you check my email before I send it, please?

CAREERS ADVISOR Of course I can. It doesn't have to be long. Don't forget to tell them why you would like to do the work placement, when you would like to do it, and give them a bit of information about yourself – your interests and favourite subjects for example.

PETE Thanks a lot Mr Cage. I'll write it **tonight**. Can I come and see you again tomorrow, please? »»

careers advisor	Berufsberater(in) *(in der Schule)*
questionnaire [ˌkwestʃə'neə]	Fragebogen
result [rɪ'zʌlt]	Ergebnis, Resultat
suggestion [sə'dʒestʃn]	Vorschlag
to come up with	bereitstellen, anzeigen
to convince [kən'vɪns]	überzeugen

to link	verknüpfen, verbinden
the outdoors	die freie Natur
▸ outdoors	draußen, im Freien
interest in sth	Interesse für etw.
landscape designer	Landsdchaftsgestalter(in)
zookeeper	Tierpfleger(in)
gardener	Gärtner(in)
forester	Förster(in)
specialist	Fachkraft
garden centre *BE*	Gartencenter, Gartenmarkt
to connect	verbinden
amazed	erstaunt, verblüfft
apart from	außer, neben; abgesehen von
issue	Thema, Problem
course	Kurs, Lehrgang
college ['kɒlɪdʒ]	Fachschule, Berufsfachschule

relief	Erleichterung
suitable ['su:təbl]	passend, geeignet
place	Arbeitsmöglichkeit, Stelle
otherwise	sonst
to give sb a call	jdn. anrufen
comfortable ['kʌmfətəbl]	wohl, angenehm
important	wichtig
tonight	heute Abend

vzmwwbe

CAREERS ADVISOR	Sure. One other thing. Have a look at this **leaflet** about the courses at the local college and then come and see me next Thursday. It tells you what **GCSEs** you need, how long the courses are and what **opportunites** you have after the courses.
PETE	Thanks again. You have been a real help.

Pete, Sarah and Dave

PETE	Wow, that Mr Cage and his careers computer programme are really good. It came up with **exactly** the jobs I'd been thinking about. He told me to do some work experience and he gave me this leaflet about college courses. He is going to read my email tomorrow that I have to write tonight to these people about a placement.
DAVE	Hey, Pete **slow down**. What jobs did this super programme come up with?
PETE	You know how I love animals and plants and hate **being stuck** inside, whatever the **weather** I'm outside.
DAVE	Yeah, I think you're mad but **never mind me**.
PETE	Well Mr Cage suggested being a gardener, zookeeper, forester or even a landscape gardener. No zoos round here, so that is out of thc question, but the others sound good. I think to **become** a landscape gardener, I would have to go to college and learn a lot.
DAVE	He didn't really help me last week. I have to go again tomorrow to see if he has any more ideas. Hey Sarah, what did Mr Cage say to you?
SARAH	My problem is that I have no idea what I want to do, I haven't really got any favourite subjects and I spend all my free time **working as** a **waitress** in my mum's café. I don't want to work there when I finish school. Mr Cage has suggested that I do a **BTEC course**. I like children and you can do a **childcare** course. After the course I could work in a **nursery**, **train** to be a **nurse** or even **qualify** to **run** a **playschool**. I know it's the **typical** thing for a girl but it's something I could **see myself** doing. ›››

leaflet	Broschüre
GCSE *(General Certificate of Secondary Education)*	Prüfungen, die man in GB mit 16 ablegt *(entspricht dem Mittleren Abschluss)*
opportunity	*(hier: berufliche)* Möglichkeit

exactly	ganz genau
to slow down	langsam machen
to be stuck	festsitzen, feststecken
weather	Wetter
never mind sb	sich nicht um jdn.kümmern, sich nicht stören lassen
to become [bɪˈkʌm], became [bɪˈkeɪm], become [bɪˈkʌm]	(von Beruf) werden

to work as	arbeiten als
waitress	Kellnerin, Serviererin
▸ waiter	Kellner
BTEC course	berufliche Ausbildung, die ein Fachabitur einschließt
childcare	Kinderbetreuung
nursery	Kinderkrippe, Kinderhort
to train	eine Ausbildung machen, sich schulen lassen
nurse	Krankenschwester, Krankenpfleger
to qualify	eine Abschluss machen, sich qualifizieren
to run [rʌn], ran [ræn], run [rʌn]	führen
playschool	Kindergarten
typical	typisch
to see oneself	sich vorstellen

vzmwwbe

In the Easter holidays I'm going to help in the **day nursery** at the college. That way I can see the college and see if it would be a job for me. Have to **dash**, see you guys later.

Dave and Pete

DAVE I don't want to work outside – I hate **fresh air**, **screaming** kids would **drive me mad** and I'm not sure if playing all these computer games will help my future.

PETE Did you tell Mr Cage what you do in your free time? I mean you don't just play the games, you write to the **video game developers** and tell them what you think and make suggestions how they can **improve** them.

DAVE That is just for fun though. You can't do that for a job.

PETE Try talking to Mr Cage about it. He can tell you what qualifications and **marks** you need and where to write to.

DAVE You know Pete, I think it is **worth a try**. At least that way I will know which subjects I have to be better at, which **A levels** I should do and also if I should write to the computer company on the **industrial estate** about a placement. Maybe they do games, too.

Dave and Pete meet again

DAVE Hey Pete, I spoke to Mr Cage and he has given me loads of tips. Thanks for **encouraging me** yesterday. It really helped me to **make up my mind** about these things.

PETE I'm glad I could help. I told my parents what Mr Cage said yesterday, and they helped me write my email. They weren't really **sure** whether I'd like the idea of working in a garden centre because it is more inside but it is an **alternative** if the other things don't **work out**.

DAVE Yeah, I spoke to my granddad about everything, too. He has been **retired** for quite a few years and I wasn't really sure what he did when he worked. All I knew was that he had worked in an **office**. »

day nursery	Kinderhort, Kindertagesstätte
to dash	rennen

fresh air	frische Luft
screaming	schreinend, kreischend
to drive sb mad	jdn. in den Wahnsinn treiben
video game	Videospiel
developer	Entwickler(in)
to improve sth	etw. verbessern
mark	Note
to be worth a try	einen Versuch wert sein
A level *(short for: advanced level)*	höherer Schulabschluss in Großbritannien, *(etwa:)* Abitur
industrial estate	Industriegebiet

to encourage sb to do sth	jdn. ermutigen etw. zu tun
to make up one's mind	sich entscheiden
sure	sicher, überzeugt
alternative	Alternative
to work out	klappen, zum Ziel führen
retired	pensioniert, im Ruhestand
office	Büro

vzmwwbe

PETE Working in an office, how boring. So, what did he do in his office?

DAVE He worked for a big **transport company**. They sent **cargo** all around the world, in **planes**, on **container ships** and even by **rail** and road. He worked in the office and had to **ensure** that the right **container** was in the right place at the right time. If it wasn't, there was big **trouble** and he had to **sort it out**. He is interested in loads of different countries, but never had the money or the time to **travel**. Through his job he was **involved** with lots of countries, although he sat in his office sending things all around the world.

PETE That is also one way of connecting your interests and a job. Has he been able to travel now?

DAVE When he retired, the company gave him a **cruise** as a present. He could take grandma with him on the **journey**, too. They **sailed** from Southampton to Hamburg and then to the Caribbean. From there they flew home, that was their one and only **flight**. Unfortunately, soon after grandma was ill and they couldn't travel anymore. He said it wouldn't be the same to travel without her as there would be **no-one to share everything with**.

PETE I understand that.

Dave and Anna

DAVE Hey Anna, have you spoken to Mr Cage yet?

ANNA I saw him last week. I told him that I had decided that I was going to go to the **sixth form college** and do A levels in French, German and English and then **take a year out**. I want to see some of the world before I **settle down**. After that I want to go to **university** and **study** International Business. He was quite **shocked** that he didn't need to help me and that I knew exactly what I wanted. I have even already **applied to** the sixth form college and got a place as long as my GCSE marks are good enough.

DAVE Very well **organised**. »»

transport company	Transportunternehemen, Spedition
cargo	Fracht, Güter
plane	Flugzeug
container ship	Containerschiff
rail	Bahn
to ensure sth [ɪn'ʃɔː]	etw. sicherstellen; etw. gewährleisten
container	Container
trouble	Ärger, Probleme
to sort sth out	etw. in Ordnung bringen, etw. klären
to travel	verreisen, reisen
to be involved with sth/sb	mit etw./jdm. zu tun haben,

cruise	Kreuzfahrt
journey	Reise
to sail	*(mit dem Schiff)* fahren
flight	Flug
to share sth with sb	etw. teilen mit jdm., etw. mit jdm. gemeinsam tun

sixth form college	Oberstufenschule
to take a year out	ein Jahr aussetzen
to settle down	ein geregeltes Leben beginnen, sich niederlassen
university	Universität, Hochschule
to study	studieren
shocked	völlig überrascht; schockiert
to apply to	sich bewerben bei
to organise	organisieren

vzmwwbe

ANNA I think it is important to have **plans**. My **cousin** had no idea what to do after (comprehensive) school and finished school with hardly any GCSEs, no idea what she wanted to do, and now she is **on the dole**. She isn't even trying to get a job or do a college course or get an **NVQ**. She says she's happy living at home, her mum does her **washing** and feeds her, so why should she change anything? She gets **unemployment benefit**. She doesn't even need to do anything and gets money **regularly**. I completely **disagree** and think she's **lazy**. **On the other hand** she showed me what I don't want to **end up** like.

DAVE Now I understand your **organisation**. I don't blame you, I think I'd be the same if I had a cousin like that. I like the idea of a year **abroad**, too, but I'm not very good at languages. Isn't there a programme called Work and Travel?

ANNA Yes, there is. It's a really good organisation. They find you somewhere to live and a job and also organise flights and stuff, so you know that if something **goes wrong** you have someone to **turn to**. My cousin's friend went to Australia and New Zealand for a year with them. I am planning to go to Canada, the French part, and will try and **book** it with the same company.

WORK & TRAVEL

plan	Plan, Absicht
cousin ['kʌzən]	Cousin(e), Vetter, Base
to be on the dole *BE*	Arbeitslosengeld beziehen
NVQ *(National Vocational Qualification)*	Berufsbildungsabschluss in Großbritannien *(schließt in der höchsten Stufe das Fachabitur ein)*
to do the washing *BE*	Wäsche waschen
unemployment benefit	Arbeitslosenunterstützung
regularly ['regjələli]	regelmäßig
to disagree	anderer Meinung sein, nicht zustimmen
lazy	faul
on the other hand	auf der anderen Seite
to end up	*(in einer Situation)* enden

organisation	strukturiertes Vorgehen, Organisation
abroad	im Ausland
to go wrong	schiefgehen
to turn to sb	sich an jdn. wenden
to book	buchen, reservieren

vzmwwbe

Letter of application

Here is an **example** of a letter of application and a CV. The letter has to be **adapted** to fit the job you are applying for, but it will help you start.

1 John Smith
12 High Street
Taunton
Somerset
TA1 6AZ

2 XYZ Bank
HR (**Human Resources**) **Department**
116 Wigmore Road
Luton
LU3 4ZA

3 20th July 2016

4 Dear **Sir** or **Madam**,

5 Application for an apprenticeship as a **bank clerk**

6 I am writing to apply for an apprenticeship as a bank clerk in your bank as **advertised** on your **website**.

7 I am in my **final** year at Highfield Comprehensive School and will be **taking** my GCSEs in May 2017. In 2015 I completed a one-week work placement with AB Bank which helped me decide which **direction** I would like to take after finishing school. I enjoy group work at school, but I also like projects where I have to show my **individual strengths**.
I **enclose** my CV, a **copy** of my last school report and the reference from AB Bank **concerning** my one-week work placement.

8 I **look forward to** meeting you **personally** for an **interview**.

9 **Yours faithfully**,

10 John Smith

11 **Encs.**: CV
School report Year 9
Reference from AB Bank

letter of application	Bewerbungsschreiben
example	Beispiel
to adapt	anpassen
human resources (HR) [ˌhjuːmən rɪˈzɔːsɪz]	Personal(abteilung)
department	Abteilung
Dear Sir or Madam	Sehr geehrte Damen und Herren
bank clerk [ˈbæŋk ˌklɑːk]	Bankangestellte(r), Bankkaufmann, -kauffrau
to advertise sth	etw. veröffentlichen, etw. bewerben
website	Website, Internetauftritt
final	Abschluss-, letzte(r, s)
to take an exam	eine Prüfung machen, eine Prüfung ablegen
direction [dɪˈrekʃn]	Richtung
individual	persönlich, individuell
strength	Stärke
to enclose	beilegen
copy	Kopie
concerning	hinsichtlich, wegen
to look forward to	sich freuen auf
personally	persönlich
interview	*hier:* Vorstellungsgespräch
Yours faithfully	Mit freundlichen Grüßen
Enc(s). *(Enclosure(s))* [ɪnˈkləʊʒə(z)]	Anlage(n)

vzmwwbe

Tips for your letter of application

1. Write your name, address and other **contact data**, e.g. your telephone number and/or email address. You can write them on the right or left (before the name and address of the company you are writing to) at the top of your letter.
2. Write the name and **full address** of the company the letter is to on the left at the top of your letter.
3. Write the full date.
4. If you don't know the person's name you are writing to, write 'Dear Sir or Madam,' or '**To whom it may concern**,'. If you do know their name, write 'Dear Mrs (last name),/Dear Mr (last name),/Dear Ms (last name),'.
5. Write an **appropriate subject line**. This can either come before or after number 4. It can be in **CAPITAL LETTERS**, **in bold** or <u>underlined</u>.
6. The first word in a letter always has a capital letter.
7. Write the **main part** of your letter including a few **details** about you that are important for the job.
8. The last sentence should bring your letter to a **positive** and **polite close**.
9. End your letter with one of these **phrases**:

   Yours faithfully, (if you started your letter 'Dear Sir or Madam,')

   Yours sincerely, (if you started your letter 'Dear Mrs, Mr or Ms …,')
10. **Type** your name leaving enough space for you to **sign** your letter above your typed name.
11. If you are sending enclosures, e.g. your CV, certificates and references, make a list of what you have **included**. It helps you check you have sent everything and the **recipient** can check they have everything.

contact data	Kontaktdaten
full address	vollständige Anschrift
To whom it may concern	Sehr geehrte Damen und Herren
appropriate	geeignet, passend
subject line	Betreffzeile
capital letter [ˌkæpɪtl ˈletə]	Großbuchstabe
in bold	fett gedruckt
underlined	unterstrichen
main part	Hauptteil
detail	Einzelheit, Detail
positive	positiv
polite close	höflicher Abschluss
phrase	Ausdruck, Floskel
Yours sincerely	Mit freundlichen Grüßen
to type	tippen
to sign [saɪn]	unterschreiben
to include = to enclose	beifügen
recipient	Empfänger(in)

vzmwwbe

Curriculum Vitae (CV) / Résumé

Curriculum Vitae

Name: Your full name
Address: Include your full address and postcode.
Telephone: Include both your home number and mobile number.
Email: Your email address, make sure it isn't with an inappropriate, stupid or rude nickname but can be clearly connected with you.

Personal summary

Use this section to write briefly about your education, work history and aims.

For example:

I am a hard-working, reliable and motivated student with a strong science background. I am currently doing my A levels in Maths, Chemistry and Physics and looking to gain experience working in engineering with the aim of becoming a civil engineer.

Main achievements

Make a bullet point list of the main things you have achieved at school and work. Include dates and company names.

For example:

Two weeks work experience at ABC Ltd - March 2015
Young Enterprise Award - 2014
Captain of the school football team - 2012-2013

Skills

List your personal, technical and specialist skills and add examples. Don't just write 'I have excellent communication skills', tell people why.

For example:

Team work – organised a charity fashion show as part of the school committee
Computing - Intermediate skills in Word and Powerpoint
Communication – Work experience at an office reception, led a school science research project

Work experience

Include the job title, the company name, dates from when until when you were employed and also list what you did and your responsibilities. Remember to include any voluntary work, too!

For example:

Work experience, ABC Ltd, March 2015 - Helped to update the company contacts database, researched and wrote articles for the company website. »»

curriculum vitae (CV)	Lebenslauf
full name	vollständiger Name
to include	einfügen, eintragen
postcode *BE*	Postleitzahl
mobile number	Handynummer, Mobiltelefonnummer
inappropriate	unangemessen
rude [ru:d]	unhöflich, beleidigend
nickname	Spitzname
clearly	eindeutig, klar
to connect	verbinden

personal summary ['pɜ:snl]	kurze persönliche Vorstellung
section	Abschnitt, Teil
briefly	in Kürze
work history	beruflicher Werdegang
aim	Ziel
hard-working	fleißig
reliable	zuverlässig
motivated	motiviert
background	Hintergrund, Kenntnisse
currently	zurzeit, momentan
to gain experience	Erfahrungen sammeln
engineering	Technik und Konstruktion
civil engineer	Bauingenieur(in)

achievement	Erfolg, Leistung
bullet point	Aufzählungszeichen
Young Enterprise Award	Auszeichnung als Jungunternehmer
captain	Kapitän

skill	Fertigkeit, Fähigkeit
technical	technisch
specialist skills	Fachkompetenzen
communication skill	Kommunikationsfähigkeit
charity	Wohltätigkeit
committee	Arbeitsgruppe, Gremium
intermediate [ˌɪntə'mi:diət]	mittlere
office reception	Empfang in einem Büro
research	Forschung

work experience	Berufserfahrung
voluntary work	ehrenamtliche Arbeit
database	Datenbank

vzmwwbe

Education
List your schools or educational establishments and all of your qualifications including GCSEs, A levels, Highers, BTEC and any short courses. Put the highest level qualifications first with the results.

For example:
Beeline Sixth Form College: A levels: Maths - A, Physics - B, Chemistry - B
Highfield Comprehensive School: GCSEs: Chemistry - A, Maths - B, English - B, Physics - B, Geography - C, History - C, Design Technology - C

Interests
Don't talk about your social life and only include hobbies like playing an instrument, sport and personal projects. If you have won an award or certificate, either write it here or under 'Main Achievements'.

References
Make sure you have contact details for one or two people who can provide a reference. This should be someone who has managed you at work or during your work experience. If this is your first job, a teacher or tutor can also provide you with a reference. You don't need to include the details of your reference on your CV, just write 'References available on request' here.

Tips for your CV

Everyone knows how important a CV is. It is what potential employers always want to see, regardless of what you have achieved or whether you are at the beginning of your career. You need to understand what a potential employer is looking for in a candidate when you write your CV. After having read the CVs of all the applicants an employer, or in a bigger company the personnel manager, decides who he will invite for an interview. The CV is your way of advertising yourself to an employer. You can show them what qualifications, skills and motivation you have and also what makes you stand out from other people who are also applying for the same position.

Your first CV is different as it won't contain much work experience. Instead it will list your skills, interests, education and achievements. When you have been working for some time, you can use a chronological CV which lists in order of date the places you have worked and what your responsibilities were. Your skills will be highlighted in the responsibilities you had.

It is important to remember that an English CV or American résumé isn't just a translation of your German one. They don't contain a photo for example. You don't have to include all the points above; if you can't write anything, then leave it out. Also remember that you have to write the truth in your CV, don't make anything up.

educational establishment	Bildungseinrichtung
highers	Abitur in Schottland
short course	außerschulische Fortbildung, Weiterbildung

interest	Interesse, Interessensgebiet, Hobby
social life	sozial Leben, Privatleben
instrument	Instrument
award	Preis, Auszeichnung

reference	Empfehlungsschreiben, Referenz
to manage sb	jdn. leiten, jdn. anleiten
available on request	auf Anfrage erhältlich

potential [pə'tenʃl]	möglich, eventuell
whether	ob
career [kə'rɪə]	berufliche Laufbahn, Karriere
to achieve	erreichen, leisten
candidate	Kandidat(in), Bewerber(in)
applicant	Bewerber(in)
personnel manager [ˌpɜːsən'el]	Leiter(in) der Personalabteilung
to advertise	Werbung machen, (be)werben
motivation	Motivation, Leistungsbereitschaft
to stand out	herausragen, sich abheben (von)
position [pə'zɪʃən]	Position, Stelle

to contain	enthalten
instead	(an)statt, stattdessen
interest	Interesse(nsgebiete)
education [ˌedʒʊ'keɪʃn]	Schulbildung, Ausbildung
achievement	Leistung, Erfolg
chronological	chronologisch, zeitlich geordnet
responsibility	Verantwortlichkeit, Verantwortung
to highlight	hervorheben

translation [trænz'leɪʃən]	Übersetzung
truth	Wahrheit
to make sth up	etw. erfinden

vzmwwbe

4 Food

Food in the UK

Traditions

British food has traditionally been **based on beef**, **lamb**, **pork**, **chicken** and fish, and is usually **served** with potatoes and one other **vegetable**.

The most **common** and **typical** foods eaten in Britain include **sandwiches**, **fish and chips**, **pies** like the Cornish **pasty**, **trifle** and **roast dinners**.

Some of the UK's **main dishes** have strange names like **bubble and squeak** and **toad-in-the-hole**. The **staple foods** in Britain are meat, fish, potatoes, flour, butter and eggs. Many dishes are based on these foods. Traditional English dishes have had some **competition** from other dishes over the years, like **curry** or pizza, but when you visit the UK you will still be served traditional foods.

There are lots of different kinds of restaurants in England including **Indian**, **Chinese**, **Italian**, **Greek** and **naturally** British. But usually when the British people **eat out**, they go to the **pub**. They serve **delicious** traditional food as well as curries, **snacks** and pizza or pasta dishes.

Another eating tradition in England is the **takeaway**. There are fish and chip shops as well as all other **specialist** restaurants offering take-away food. As the name suggests, it is food that you **order** and take with you to either eat at home or somewhere else. Having this food is cheaper than eating at a pub or a restaurant as you don't have to pay the costs that a restaurant has – **serving staff**, **lighting**, **plates** and **cutlery** etc. »

to be based on sth	als Grundzutat haben, auf etw. basieren
beef	Rindfleisch
lamb	Lammfleisch
pork	Schweinefleisch
chicken	Hähnchenfleisch
to serve	servieren, reichen
vegetable	Gemüse
common	normal, üblich
typical	typisch
sandwich ['sænwɪdʒ]	belegtes Brot, Sandwich
fish and chips	Fisch mit Pommes
pie	Pastete *(gedeckter, herzhafter Kuchen)*
pasty	Fleischpastete in einer Teigtasche
trifle ['traɪfl] *BE*	Trifle *(geschichteter Nachtisch)*
roast dinner	Braten *(als Hauptmahlzeit)*
main dish	Hauptgang
bubble and squeak	Pfannengericht aus Gemüse und Kartoffelbrei
toad-in-the-hole	überbackene Würstchen
staple food	Grundnahrungsmittel
competition [ˌkɒmpə'tɪʃn]	Konkurrenz
curry	Curry *(mit Curry gewürztes indisches Gericht)*
Indian	indisch
Chinese	chinesisch
Italian	italienisch
Greek	griechisch
naturally	natürlich, selbstverständlich
eat out	Essen gehen *(außer Haus)*
pub	Kneipe
delicious [dɪ'lɪʃəs]	sehr lecker, köstlich
snack	Imbiss, kleine Mahlzeit
takeaway	Essen zum Mitnehmen
specialist ['speʃlɪst]	spezialisiert
order	bestellen
serving staff	Bedienung *(Personal)*
lighting	Beleuchtung
plate	Teller
cutlery	Besteck

6qe982a

A lot of traditional British dishes are made of leftovers. They originate from before the wars, when people didn't have much money and they had to make the food last. This continued through the war when food was rationed. Although times have changed, for most people these food traditions have carried on, but today the dishes will be cooked with fresh ingredients.

Traditional main courses

Roast dinner

You can choose between roast pork, lamb, beef or chicken roast, which is usually served with roast potatoes and vegetables on a plate. A lot of restaurants and pubs have a Sunday carvery. They put a selection of different joints of meat as well as roast potatoes, Yorkshire pudding, stuffing, a wide selection of vegetables and gravies and sauces on a heated buffet and people can help themselves. You pay a set price and most people fill their plates as full as possible.

Toad-in-the-hole

It is hard to imagine what this is, and to be honest, it doesn't sound very appetising. Actually it tastes good and is easy to cook. Toad-in-the-hole is a whole meal in one. First sausages are cooked in the oven until they are brown. Then the batter for Yorkshire pudding (similar to pancake batter) is poured over the sausages and the pan is put back into the oven to carry on cooking at a high temperature. The batter rises in the heat and goes golden brown. Toad-in-the-hole is often eaten with thick onion gravy.

Fish and chips

Everyone knows about fish and chips. Usually you eat them straight out of the wrapper, although nowadays they aren't allowed to be served 'traditionally' – in newspaper. This was decided after it had been found out that the ink on the newspaper isn't very healthy. The fish is covered in batter and then deep fried until it is golden and crispy. The chips are thick, which means they are a bit healthier than thin chips like French fries as they contain less fat. In fish and chip shops you can also order a variety of pies, sausages or chicken nuggets with your chips. There are also side orders of baked beans, mushy peas, pickled onions or pickled eggs.

leftovers	Reste *(von Mahlzeiten)*
to originate	seinen Ursprung haben
war	Krieg
to last	genügen, ausreichen
to continue [kən'tɪnjuː]	fortsetzen, weitermachen
to ration	rationieren, einteilen
to carry on	weitergehen, weitermachen
ingredient	Zutat

---

carvery	Fleischbuffet *(im Restaurant)*
selection [sɪ'lekʃn]	Auswahl
joint of meat	Fleischstück
Yorkshire pudding *BE*	Yorkshirepudding *(fluffige Eierspeise, die als Beilage serviert wird)*
stuffing	Füllung
gravy ['greɪvɪ]	Bratensoße
heated buffet ['bʊfeɪ]	Warmhaltebuffet *(zur Selbstbedienung)*
to help oneself	sich (selbst) bedienen
set price	Festpreis

to imagine sth [ɪ'mædʒɪn]	sich etw. vorstellen
appetising	appetitlich, appetitanregend
sausage ['sɒsɪdʒ]	Würstchen
oven	Backofen
batter	Bierteig
pancake	Pfannkuchen, Eierkuchen
to pour over [pɔː 'əʊvə]	darübergießen
pan	Backform
temperature	Temperatur
to rise [raɪz], rose [rəʊz], risen ['rɪzən]	aufgehen
thick [θɪk]	dickflüssig

straight [streɪt]	gerade, gleich
wrapper	Verpackung
ink	Druckerschwärze; Tinte
healthy	gesund
to cover in sth	überziehen
deep fried	frittiert
crispy	knusprig
thin	dünn
French fries	Pommes Frites
contain	enthalten
fat	Fett
side order	Beilage
baked beans	Baked Beans *(weiße Bohnen in Tomatensoße)*
mushy peas *(GB)*	Erbsenpüree
pickled	eingelegt

6qe982a

Shepherd's pie or cottage pie

The difference between shepherd's pie and cottage pie is the meat that is used. A shepherd's pie is made of minced lamb, meat a shepherd has available, and a cottage pie is made of minced beef. Both dishes are often served on a Monday making use of the leftover meat from the Sunday roast. The meat is mixed with diced vegetables and gravy (usually also what is left from Sunday) and put in an ovenproof dish. It is topped with mashed potatoes and sometimes cheese and baked in the oven until it is cooked through. It contains everything you need so no other preparation is needed.

Lancashire hotpot

Casseroles are very popular in the UK. They are made of diced meat and vegetables cooked in a sauce in the oven for a long time at a low temperature. A Lancashire hotpot comes from the county of Lancashire, in the north of England, and is a casserole with a sliced potato topping. Casseroles are cooked in a dish with a lid on, and for a Lancashire hotpot the lid is removed at the end of the cooking time so that the potatoes turn golden brown.

Bubble and squeak

When you hear this name, you are more likely to think of two cartoon characters and not a traditional British dish. It is typically made from cold (leftover) cooked vegetables, mainly potatoes and cabbage although carrots, peas, brussels sprouts and other vegetables can be used. The chopped vegetables are fried in a frying pan together with the mashed potato until the mixture is well-cooked and brown on both sides. The dish gets its name from the sound and action it makes while it is cooking.

Full English breakfast

Most people don't exactly know what you are served when you order a full English breakfast, but they know it is a plateful. It is such a big plateful that a lot of pubs offer an all day breakfast, this means you can order English breakfast at whatever time of day you are there. What you usually get is bacon, sausage, baked beans, grilled tomatoes, fried mushrooms, fried potatoes or hash browns, fried bread and as much toast as you can eat. A slice of toast is useful to wipe your plate clean when you have finished.

shepherd ['ʃepəd]	Schäfer(in)
cottage ['kɒtɪdʒ]	Häuschen *(auf dem Land)*, kleines Bauernhaus
minced	gehackt *(durch den Fleischwolf gedreht)*
available	verfügbar, vorrätig
to make use	benutzen, verwenden
diced	gewürfelt
ovenproof dish	Auflaufform
topped	bedeckt
mashed potatoes	Katoffelpüree, Kartoffelbrei
to bake	backen
cooked through	gegart
preparation	Vorbereitung
casserole	Auflauf
county	Grafschaft
sliced [slaɪst]	in Scheiben geschnitten
topping	Belag
lid	Deckel *(für Topf oder Pfanne)*
to remove	entfernen, wegnehmen
cooking time	Kochzeit
cartoon	Karikatur, Cartoon
character ['kærəktə]	Figur, Gestalt
cabbage ['kæbɪdʒ]	Kohl, Kraut
brussels sprout	Rosenkohl
chopped	zerkleinert, geschnitten
frying pan	Bratpfanne
mixture ['mɪkstʃə]	Mischung, Gemisch
plateful	*hier:* ordentliche Portion; Teller (voll)
all day	ganztägig
bacon ['beɪkn]	durchwachsener Speck
grilled	gegrillt
fried	gebraten
fried potatoes	Bratkartoffeln
hash browns	Kartoffelrösti
toast	getoastetes Brot
slice [slaɪs]	Scheibe, Stück
to wipe sth clean [waɪp]	sauber wischen, abwischen

6qe982a

Desserts and Sweets

Trifle

This is a very traditional dessert in the UK. It is made in a glass bowl so you can see how nice it looks when it is finished. First of all there is a layer of cake in the bottom. Then there is a layer of mixed fruit, usually from a tin. Jelly, a flavour that goes with your chosen fruit, is poured over these two layers and it is then left to set. The next layer is custard, cool and firm which is topped with a layer of whipped cream and decoration, which can vary from fruit to roasted nuts. When you are served a portion, make sure you get some of each layer.

Spotted dick and custard

If you are going to order this, make sure you leave enough room in your stomach as it is very filling. Spotted dick is a cake that contains raisins or sultanas and is steamed. It is served hot with custard. There are many variations of this dessert, for example chocolate cake with chocolate sauce or plain cake with golden syrup. The sauce is steamed with the cake and when the cake is tipped out of the pudding bowl, the sauce from the bottom of the bowl covers the cake.

Apple pie and cream

Apples are one of the fruit that are grown a lot in the UK. You will often find meals including apples on menus. Apple pie is made of pastry with a filling of cooked apples that is baked in the oven and served warm with either whipped cream or ice cream.

Cream tea

Don't misunderstand when you see this on a menu in a pub or café. It isn't, as the name sounds, a pot or cup of tea served with cream. That is not how the British drink their tea. Cream Tea is actually a great favourite not only with tourists but also with locals. You get a pot of tea, with milk, and usually two warm scones, a dish of strawberry jam and a dish of clotted cream. This is how you have it: you cut your scone through the middle and spread it with cream and jam.

There have been endless discussions what comes first, the jam or the cream, and how it is done usually differs from region to region in England. The important thing is to put a big spoonful of each on your scone and then enjoy it.

dessert [dɪˈzɜːt]	Nachspeise, Nachtisch
bowl	Schüssel; Schale
layer	Schicht
tin *BE*	Konservendose
jelly [dʒeli]	Gelee; Wackelpudding
flavour [ˈfleɪvə]	Geschmacksrichtung
to go with sth	zu etw. passen
to pour [pɔː]	gießen
to set	fest werden
custard [ˈkʌstəd]	(dicke) Vanillesoße
firm	fest
to top	krönen, bedecken
whipped cream	geschlagene Sahne
decoration	Verzierung
to vary	variieren
roasted nuts	geröstete Nüsse

stomach [ˈstʌmək]	Magen, Bauch
filling	sättigend
to contain	beinhalten
raisin	Rosine
sultana	Sultanine
to steam	dämpfen, im Dampf garen
variation	Abwandlung
plain	einfach, schlicht
golden syrup	Zuckersirup
to tip out	*hier:* stürzen
pudding bowl	Wasserbadform
bottom	unterer Teil, Boden
to cover sth	etw. abdecken

including	mit *(als Zutat)*
pastry [ˈpeɪstri]	Teig
filling	Füllung

menu	Speisekarte
pot	Kanne
tourist	Tourist(in)
local	Einheimischer
scone	brötchenartiges Teegebäck
dish	Schälchen, Schale
strawberry jam	Erdbeerkonfitüre, Erdbeermarmelade
clotted cream	dicke Sahne
to have	machen, essen
to spread [spred], spread [spred], spread [spred]	bestreichen
to differ	sich unterscheiden
spoonful	Löffel

6qe982a

Food in the USA

Traditions

America's history is reflected in its food. It started with the food of the Native Americans that was later influenced when the first Europeans colonised America. The British brought with them ingredients that were unknown, but they also found vegetation and animals that they had never seen before. They either used these items in the same way as their own or they ignored them completely. Even their methods of cooking followed the methods used in Britain. This can be seen in some of the early cookery books.

Later, more Europeans arrived from Germany, Ireland and Italy bringing with them new recipes and ingredients. The slaves that were taken from South Africa, mainly to the southern states of the US, also contributed their part and finally the Asian influence has mixed with all the others. Over the centuries many diverse styles of preparing and cooking food have expanded through the various groups of immigrants that have arrived in America from many different countries, but you will still find native ingredients in many American recipes, even if they are not the main ones anymore.

It is said that American food can be divided into six categories:

Native foods

There are several varieties of vegetables (beans, corn and squash), nuts, meat (bison) and fish which originally come from North America. Typical Native American recipes include corncakes and baked squash.

Hybrid dishes

These are old recipes that are adapted to include new ingredients, e.g. cornbread.

Ethnic blends

These recipes occur when different cultures settle together in a region and mix their food. Chop Suey, for example, was thought to have been invented in America by Chinese Americans.

Regional specialities

These relate back to the idea of the American Melting Pot where different nationalities, cultures and traditions have melted together. This melting pot idea also includes food, e.g. Tex-Mex (a mixture of Texan and Mexican food). »»

to reflect	spiegeln, reflektieren
Native American [ˌneɪtɪv əˈmerɪkən]	Ureinwohner Amerikas
to influence sth [ˈɪnflʊəns]	etw. beeinflussen
the Europeans [ˌjʊərəˈpiːənz]	Europäer(innen)
to colonise	besiedeln, kolonisieren
ingredient	Zutat
unknown	unbekannt
vegetation [ˌvedʒɪˈteɪʃn]	Pflanzen, Vegetation
to ignore	ignorieren, nicht beachten
completely	vollkommen
method [ˈmeθəd]	Methode, Art
cookery book	Kochbuch

recipe [ˈresɪpi]	(Koch)Rezept
slave	Sklave(in)
to contribute	beitragen, beisteuern
influence [ˈɪnflʊəns]	Einfluss
to mix	sich mischen
century [ˈsentʃəri]	Jahrhundert
style	Stil, Art
to expand	ausweiten, sich verbreiten
immigrant	Einwanderer
native	einheimisch

to divide into	aufteilen in
category [ˈkætəgri]	Kategorie, Gruppe
several [ˈsevrl]	einige, manche
variety [vəˈraɪəti]	Sorte
squash	Speisekürbis
bison	Bison *(nordamerikanisches Wildrind)*

hybrid	gemischt, hybrid
to adapt	*(sich)* anpassen

ethnic	ethnisch
blend	Mix, Mischung
culture	Kultur
to settle	sich ansiedeln
to invent	erfinden
Chinese	chinesisch

regional [ˈriːdʒnl]	regional
speciality [ˌspeʃiˈæləti]	Spezialität
to relate to sth	sich auf etw. beziehen
to melt	verschmelzen, schmelzen
▸ melting pot	Schmelztiegel

6qe982a

Traditions and food fads

The history of these foods can be traced back to the Old World and include things like corn dogs and rice crispie treats.

Manufactured foods

These are things which foreigners typically associate with the US and the list is endless. It starts with Campbell's Tomato Soup and stretches as far as Coca Cola and Hershey's bars.

Typically American

Let's take a look at American breakfasts. Breakfast can be a time of the day when the whole family sits down together, on a weekend for example. Fresh pancakes with toppings like maple syrup or fresh fruit, all different kinds of eggs from Eggs Benedict (poached eggs covered with hollandaise sauce and served with smoked salmon) to an omelet (folded over a filling of cheese, bacon and sausage) or even a breakfast Burrito (a tortilla wrapped around an omelet or frittata) or a bowl of cereal are all ways to start the day if you have time.

If you pick something up on your way to work that you are going to eat in the office or at your workplace, your breakfast is more likely to be a bagel topped with sesame seeds or poppy seeds, cut through the middle and spread with cream cheese, a donut which is filled or topped with various flavours, or a breakfast sandwich filled with egg, cheese, bacon and sausage. All this of course, is washed down with coffee.

A favourite American sandwich you often hear mentioned in films is a peanut butter and jelly sandwich. To most non-Americans this doesn't sound very appetising, but it must taste good as it is very popular. Peanut butter can be bought in most European supermarkets, there is both smooth and crunchy peanut butter. The Americans spread this on a slice of bread and then comes a layer of jelly, which is the equivalent of European jam (usually without the pieces of fruit in it). You often see these sandwiches made with grape jelly but you can also use your favourite jam. Then it is topped with another piece of bread. Yummy - at least for most Americans.

food fad	Modeerscheinung bei Lebensmitteln
to trace back	zurückverfolgen
the Old World	die Alte Welt *(Europa, Asien, Afrika)*
corn dog	Würstchen in Maispanade
rice crispie treat	Leckerei aus gepufftem Reis und geschmolzenen Marshmallows
manufactured	(vor)gefertigt
to associate [əˌsəʊʃɪ'eɪt]	verknüpfen, verbinden
Campbell [kæm'bel]	Fimenname
to stretch	sich erstrecken
Hershey's bar [ˌhɜːʃis 'bɑː]	amerikanischer Schokoriegel
pancake	Pfannkuchen, Eierkuchen
maple syrup	Ahornsirup
Eggs Benedict	Eier Benedikt
poached	pochiert *(in Wasser gegart)*
hollandaise sauce [ˌhɒləndeɪz 'sɔːs]	Sauce Hollandaise
smoked salmon [ˌsməʊkt 'sæmən]	Räucherlachs
omelet ['ɒmlət]	Omelett
to fold over	zusammenklappen, falten
burrito	Burrito
tortilla [tɔː'tiːə]	Tortilla *(mexikanisches Fladenbrot)*
to wrap around	einwickeln
frittata [frI'tɑːtə]	Frittata *(italienisches Omelett)*
cereal ['sɪəriəl]	Getreideflocken *(z.B. Cornflakes, Müsli)*
workplace	Arbeitsplatz
bagel	Bagel *(ringförmiges Gebäck)*
sesame seed	Sesamsamen
poppy seed	Mohnsamen
to spread	bestreichen, streichen
cream cheese	Frischkäse
flavour ['fleɪvə]	Geschmacksrichtung
to wash sth down	etw. runterspülen
to mention ['menʃn]	erwähnen
peanut butter	Erdnussbutter
jelly *AE*	Gelee
appetising	appetitlich, appetitanregend
smooth	gleichmäßig
crunchy	knusprig
slice [slaɪs]	Scheibe, Stück
layer	Schicht
equivalent	Entsprechung
jam	Konfitüre, Marmelade
piece of fruit	Fruchtstück
grape	Traube
yummy ['jʌmi]	lecker

6qe982a

Barbecuing is a very popular method of cooking in the US. Meat is cooked for a long time at a low temperature. Usually a wood fire is used and the smoke adds a special flavour to the cooked meat. In the US, burgers, steaks and chicken are barbecued but not usually sausages.

There are four major barbecuing styles, Carolina and Memphis, which usually use pork, and Kansas City and Texas, which mainly use beef as well as some pork. This method of cooking dates back to colonial times. Popular occasions for a barbecue are Independence Day, Memorial Day and Labor Day and, although in winter, the Super Bowl, the championship game of the National Football League.

Seafood is very popular, particularly in the coastal areas in the US. Not only is a lot of fish eaten, but shrimps, lobsters and crabs are also favourites.

When you ask an American what their favourite food is, their answer can be anything including pizza, sushi, pasta, Mexican or Chinese food, ice cream, burgers or even just chocolate. When there is such a variety available, it is hard to choose. Talking about choice and what Americans love, diners need to be mentioned. Wherever you are, you will always find diners offering an awesome choice of cookies, donuts, muffins and ice cream. The toppings and fillings you can choose from will make your decision a hard one when you are asked to order. Allow plenty of time to choose, and maybe try a few different ones even if you have a favourite. Sometimes the strangest sounding flavours are the best.

As we have seen, America covers many tastes and styles as it is such a vast country. Here's a small selection of typical regional foods. »»

barbecuing	Grillen
temperature ['temprətʃə]	Temperatur
wood fire	Holzfeuer
smoke	Rauch, Qualm
steak	Steak
chicken	Hähnchenfleisch
sausage ['sɒsɪdʒ]	Wurst, Würstchen

major	wesentlich, wichtig
Carolina [ˌkærl'aɪnə]	Nord- und Südkarolina
Memphis ['memfɪs]	amerikanische Großstadt in Tennessee
pork	Schweinefleisch
Kansas City [ˌkænzəs 'sɪti]	amerikanische Großstadt in Kansas
Texas ['teksəs]	amerikanischer Bundesstaat
beef	Rindfleisch
colonial [kə'ləʊniəl]	kolonial, Kolonie-
occasion [ə'keɪʒən]	Anlass
Independence Day *(US)*	Unabhängigkeitstag
Memorial Day *(US)*	Volkstrauertag
Labor Day *(US)*	Tag der Arbeit
championship ['tʃæmpiənʃɪp]	Meisterschaft

seafood	Meeresfrüchte
particularly [pə'tɪkjələli]	besonders
coastal area	Küstengebiet
shrimp	Garnele
lobster	Hummer
crab	Krebs, Krabbe

sushi ['su:ʃi]	Sushi
pasta	Nudeln
available	vorhanden
choice	Auswahl, Wahl
diner ['daɪnə] *AE*	Restaurant *(am Straßenrand)*
wherever	wo (auch) immer
awesome ['ɔ:səm]	beeindruckend, fantastisch
cookie *AE*	Keks, Plätzchen
donut	Donut, Krapfen
topping	Belag
decision [dɪ'sɪʒn]	Entscheidung
to order	bestellen
to allow plenty of time [ə'laʊ]	sich viel Zeit nehmen, jdm. viel Zeit lassen
strange [streɪndʒ]	seltsam, eigenartig

taste	Geschmack
vast	gewaltig, riesig
selection [sɪ'lekʃn]	Auswahl

6qe982a

In New England (northeast) it will be no **surprise** to see many dishes that are popular in the UK. These include **baked beans**, fruit pie (apple or **strawberry** and **rhubarb** are popular), **fish cakes** (often made with crab meat) or even **pub grub** (a pie and a **pint** of **beer**).

A traditional Southern meal is **pan-fried** chicken (coming originally from Scotland) served with **mashed potatoes** and **cornbread**, with a **dessert** of **pecan** or **peach** pie. **Coleslaw**, made from **cabbage**, is also popular as a **side dish** or with barbecued meats. Cabbage is the **base** for a lot of meals in the South.

Further south you will find other **influences** in the food. There is the **Creole cuisine**, which uses **hot sauces** made from **peppers** grown in Louisiana as well as seafood such as crabs, **oysters** and shrimps. Rice is often served with meals as well as ham produced in Virginia.

Tex-Mex is another **term** often used to describe American food. This is a **mixture** of American and Mexican dishes. It is most popular in Texas. Its main ingredients include **grated** cheese, meat (especially pork and beef), beans and **spices** as well as tortillas. Chili con Carne is a Tex-Mex **invention** that everyone knows.

Specialities

Since the 19th century when New York **chefs** wanted to serve the **high society** speciality dishes, meals like **Waldorf salad**, Eggs Benedict and the New York Strip Steak were **introduced**. **Similarly**, more and more restaurants and hotels in the big cities want to **make a name** for themselves.

They have been experimenting with steak **in recent years** to find out at what **temperature** and how long it is best to **hang** a piece of meat to get the best **results** when it is later put on the **grill**. Some places have tried to make a name for themselves with the size of the **portions** they **serve** or the size of their burger or hot dog.

surprise	Überraschung
baked beans	Baked Beans *(weiße Bohnen in Tomatensoße)*
strawberry ['strɔːbəri]	Erdbeere
rhubarb ['ruːbɑːb]	Rhabarber
fish cake	Fischfrikadelle
pub grub	Kneipenessen
pint [paɪnt]	Pint, 0,57 Liter *(etwa: eine Halbe)*
beer [bɪə]	Bier

pan-fried	in der Pfanne angebraten
mashed potatoes	Katoffelpüree, Kartoffelbrei
cornbread	Maisbrot
dessert [dɪ'zɜːt]	Nachspeise, Nachtisch
pecan	Pekannuss
peach [piːtʃ]	Pfirsich
coleslaw	Krautsalat
cabbage ['kæbɪdʒ]	Kohl, Kraut
side dish	Beilage
base	Grundlage, Basis

influence	Einfluss
Creole cuisine [ˌkriːəʊl kwɪ'siːn]	kreolische Küche
hot sauce	scharfe Soße
pepper	Paprika; Pepperoni
oyster ['ɔɪstə]	Austern

term	Begriff
mixture	Mischung, Gemisch
grated	gerieben
spice [spaɪs]	Gewürz
invention [ɪn'venʃn]	Erfindung

chef [ʃef]	Chefkoch, Chefköchin
high society	High Society, gehobene Kreise
Waldorf salad	Waldorfsalat *(mit grünem Salat und Walnüsse)*
to introduce [ɪntrə'djuːs]	einführen
similarly ['sɪmɪləli]	auf ähnliche Weise
to make a name	bekannt werden

in recent years ['riːsənt]	in den letzten Jahren
temperature ['temprətʃə]	Temperatur
to hang [hæŋ], hung [hʌŋ], hung [hʌŋ]	hängen
result [rɪ'zʌlt]	Ergebnis
grill	Grill
portion ['pɔːʃn]	Portion
to serve	servieren

6qe982a

This brings us to our next point. A lot of dishes that people think of as being **typically** American actually **originate** from other countries. Hot dogs and hamburgers come from Germany and pizza from Italy. These dishes have been given an American **touch** though, in Chicago the pizzas have a much thicker **crust** than a traditional Italian pizza and hamburgers have different toppings such as bacon, fried onions or coleslaw. The changes to these foods, although **minor**, have now been **passed back** to their originating countries and the people there believe they are eating something American.

To **round off** all these pizzas and burgers, how about a piece of New York **Cheesecake**. This **delicious**, **creamy** dessert is a must. It has a **crispy base** made of **biscuits** mixed with butter, then a layer of cream cheese mixed with quark which is baked in the oven. It often has a **fruity** topping of either strawberry or raspberry **purée**, or can be eaten **plain**.

Eating habits

As can be expected, there are all types of restaurants in the US. What is known worldwide, and has also **spread** worldwide, are the restaurant **chains** selling fast food. Everyone knows their names. But why are they so popular? Not just in the US but all over the world and **to be honest**, with most **age groups**.

No one has any time. Everything has to be done faster. This means **prepared** faster, **ordered** faster, served faster and even eaten faster. There are high standards that all the restaurants in the same chain have to **adhere to** in order to be allowed to use the **brand** name. There is a constant quality that everyone expects, it doesn't matter in which country they order their burger, coffee or chicken.

Fast food is available in such a variety though. There are burgers and fries, obviously, and also pizzas. There are diners that only serve donuts and coffee or others that **specialise in** sandwiches and **baguettes** that are **filled to order** with just what you want. Usually you have to answer so many questions just to get a sandwich though: What sort of bread? **Wholemeal**, white, **rye**, brown …? What fillings? ham, cheese, egg, **tuna**, **pastrami**, … What sauces you want? Do you want a **soda** with it? The list goes on and on.

Another **time saving** factor about fast food is that if you're **in a hurry**, you don't even need to **get out** of your car to order, pay and get your food. The **drive through** idea, that started in America, very quickly **caught on** around the world, and you don't usually see a burger restaurant nowadays without a 'drive thru'. You get your food quickly and can find somewhere quiet to eat it or even eat it while you **continue** your **journey**. Just be careful that what you ordered is what you get in your **paper bag** at the last window, check the **contents** before you **drive away**.

typically	typisch
to originate	abstammen
touch [tʌtʃ]	Note, Hauch
crust	Kruste
minor	weniger wichtig, unbedeutend
to pass back	zurückgeben
to round off	abschließen
cheesecake	Käsekuchen
delicious [dɪˈlɪʃəs]	sehr lecker
creamy	kremig, sahnig
crispy	knusprig
base	Boden
biscuit [ˈbɪskɪt] *BE*	Keks, Plätzchen
fruity	fruchtig
purée [ˈpjʊəreɪ]	Püree, Mus
plain [pleɪn]	schlicht, ohne Belag
to spread	sich ausbreiten
chain	Kette
to be honest [ˈɒnɪst]	um ehrlich zu sein, ehrlich gesagt
age group	Altersgruppe
to prepare [prɪˈpeə]	zubereiten
to order	bestellen
to adhere to	einhalten
brand	Marke
to specialise in	sich spezialisieren auf
baguette [bæˈget]	Baguette, Stangenbrot
to fill to order	auf Bestellung belegen
wholemeal	Vollkorn
rye	Roggen
tuna [ˈtjuːnə]	Thunfisch
pastrami [pæsˈtrɑːmi]	Rauchfleisch
soda *AE*	Limonade, Mineralwasser
time saving	zeitsparend
in a hurry	in Eile
to get out	(aus dem Auto) aussteigen
drive through	Drive-in
to catch on	sich durchsetzen
to continue	fortsetzen, weitermachen
journey	Reise, Fahrt
paper bag	Papiertüte
contents	Inhalt
to drive away	wegfahren

6qe982a

5 The British Isles

Geography

The British Isles are a group of islands in the northwest of Europe. They are the home of different countries and **sovereign states**, and it is very **confusing** to know which **belong to** which. Here is an **overview**.
The British Isles: They **are made up of** two **main islands**, Great Britain and Ireland, and also some well known smaller islands like the Isle of Wight, the Isle of Man, the Channel Islands and the Isles of Scilly. Around the British Isles there are more than 6,000 other smaller islands.
Sovereign states: The British Isles are **divided between** two sovereign states. The Republic of Ireland covers the major part of the island called Ireland, and the United Kingdom of Great Britain and Northern Ireland covers the north-east of Ireland and the whole of Great Britain.
The UK is made up of four countries: England, Wales, Scotland and Northern Ireland.
In 2013 the British Isles had a **population** of **approximately** 69 million people. 54 million of these people were in England, 7 million in Ireland (2 million in Northern Ireland and 5 million in The Republic of Ireland), 5 million in Scotland and 3 million in Wales.
The **coastline** of the British Isles is nearly 32,000 kilometres long. **In comparison**, Germany's coastline is only 2,400 kilometres long. No place in the British Isles is **further** than 125 km (or one and a half hours by car) from the sea.
Dublin is the **capital city** of the Republic of Ireland and is in the east of Ireland. London is the capital city of the UK and is in the south east of England, and the River Thames **flows** through it from west to east.

England

There are 46 **counties** in England, from Kent in the south east to Cumbria in the north west and from Cornwall in the south west to Northumberland in the north east. England has a number of large cities, usually **well-known** for their famous football teams, e.g. Liverpool, Manchester or Newcastle. England has a very mixed **landscape**. Not only is there the very beautiful coast, but also 10 **national parks**. They are **free** to drive through, so you can enjoy the **countryside**. You just have to **beware** of the **wildlife**, like deer, rabbits or even sheep walking **freely** across the roads and also **grazing** on the **verges** next to the roads. The roads are often very **narrow** and sometimes only as **wide** as your car. »»

the British Isles [aɪlz]	die Britischen Inseln
sovereign state ['sɒvrɪn steɪt]	unabhängiger Staat
confusing	verwirrend
to belong to	gehören
overview	Überblick
to be made up of	sich zusammensetzen aus
main island	Hauptinsel
divided between	aufgeteilt zwischen
population [ˌpɒpjə'leɪʃn]	Bevölkerung
approximately [ə'prɒksɪmətli]	annähernd, ungefähr
coastline	Küstenlinie
in comparison	im Vergleich
further	weiter
capital (city)	Hauptstadt
to flow [fləʊ]	fließen

---

county ['kaʊnti]	Grafschaft *BE*; Verwaltungsbezirk *AE*
well-known	bekannt
landscape	Landschaft
national park	Nationalpark, Naturschutzgebiet
free	kostenlos
countryside ['kʌntrisaɪd]	Land, Landschaft
to beware	aufpassen
wildlife	Wildtiere
freely	frei
to graze	grasen, weiden
verge	Seitenstreifen
narrow ['nærəʊ]	eng, schmal
wide	breit

vdx3dwc

This is another reason for driving slowly, you never know when you might meet a car or tractor coming **towards** you.

England, like the rest of the British Isles, is famous for its bad **weather**. Everyone thinks it rains the **whole time**, but this isn't true. The counties in the south west, Cornwall, Devon and Dorset, are known as the English Riviera, and even **palm trees** grow there as the **climate** is so **mild**.

There are many famous **sights worth seeing** in England, just to name a few: Stonehenge is near Salisbury in the south, and no-one really knows why or even how it was built. Hadrian's Wall is in the north and was built by **the Romans** to mark the **border** between the north and the south. Nottingham is where Robin Hood's **adventures** took place, and you can **follow in his footsteps** if you visit Nottingham and Sherwood Forest.

There are **various** ways of getting to England from **abroad**. There are a number of **airports**, Europe's biggest one is Heathrow which is near London. You can also travel by **ferry** from Calais or Dunkirk to Dover or take the train through the Channel Tunnel from Calais.

Scotland

Scotland **is situated in** the north of the British Isles. Its capital is Edinburgh and other big cities are Aberdeen and Glasgow. The highest **mountain** in the British Isles, Ben Nevis (1,345 m high), is in Scotland and also the famous Loch Ness with its **mysterious** monster Nessie. **Lakes** are called **lochs** in Scotland and there are a lot of them in Scotland's **rugged** landscape.

There are a lot of islands **scattered around** the north coast of Scotland. Some of the bigger, more famous ones are the Shetland Islands and the Orkney Islands. Others are smaller and can only be **reached** by **fishing boats** that visit the **islanders regularly** to deliver them their **necessities of life**. Scotland is the coldest part of the British Isles and has the **roughest** weather.

Wales

Wales is to the west of England. It too has a capital, Cardiff, which is in the south of Wales. It has a nice **castle**, an airport and a football **stadium**. All the **Welsh** speak English, but only a few of them also speak Welsh, therefore they have started teaching it at school again. The landscape in Wales is different from England, it is hilly everywhere. In the south there are the Brecon Beacons and in the north Snowdonia where you find the highest Mountain in Wales, Mount Snowdon (1,085 m high). The longest **zip-line** in Europe is in Wales, too.

Anglesey, to the north west of Wales, is an island. It is **connected to** the **mainland** by two bridges across the Menai Strait. From Holyhead, Fishguard or Pembroke in Wales you can **catch** a ferry **across** the Irish Sea to Rosslare in Ireland.

towards	in Richtung, auf … zu
weather	Wetter
the whole time [ˌhəʊl'taɪm]	die ganze Zeit
palm tree [ˌpɑːm 'tri]	Palme
climate ['klaɪmɪt]	Klima
mild [maɪld]	mild
sight [saɪt]	Sehenswürdigkeit
worth seeing	sehenswert
the Romans	die Römer
border	Grenze
adventure	Abenteuer
to follow in sb's footsteps	in jds. Fußstapfen treten
various ['veəriəs]	verschiedene
abroad [ə'brɑːd]	im Ausland
airport ['eəpɔːt]	Flughafen
ferry	Fähre
to be situated in	gelegen
mountain ['maʊntɪn]	Berg
mysterious	geheimnisvoll, rätselhaft
lake	(der) See
loch [lɒk/lɒx] *(Scottish word for 'lake')*	See *(schottisches Wort für „lake")*
rugged ['rʌgɪd]	wild, felsig
scattered around	verstreut sein, verstreut liegen
to be reached	zu erreichen sein, erreichbar sein
fishing boat	Fischerboot
islander ['aɪləndə]	Inselbewohner(in)
regularly ['regjələli]	regelmäßig
necessities of life	täglicher Bedarf, was man zum Leben braucht
rough [rʌf]	rau, stürmisch
castle ['kɑːsəl]	Burg, Schloss
stadium	Stadion
the Welsh	die Waliser
▸ Welsh	walisisch
zip-line	Seilrutsche, Seilbahn
to connect to	verbinden mit
mainland	Festland
to catch	fahren mit, nehmen; fangen
across	über

vdx3dwc

Ireland

Ireland is an island to the left of Great Britain. It is divided into Northern Ireland, which belongs to the United Kingdom, and the Republic of Ireland, which is the only country in the British Isles to use the Euro. The Republic of Ireland is nearly five times bigger than Northern Ireland. The capital of Northern Ireland is Belfast and the capital of the Republic of Ireland is Dublin. Apart from these two big cities, there are mainly towns and villages and lots of countryside in Ireland.

One of the sights worth seeing in Ireland is the Giant's Causeway. It is a series of steps stretching out into the sea in the north of Northern Ireland.

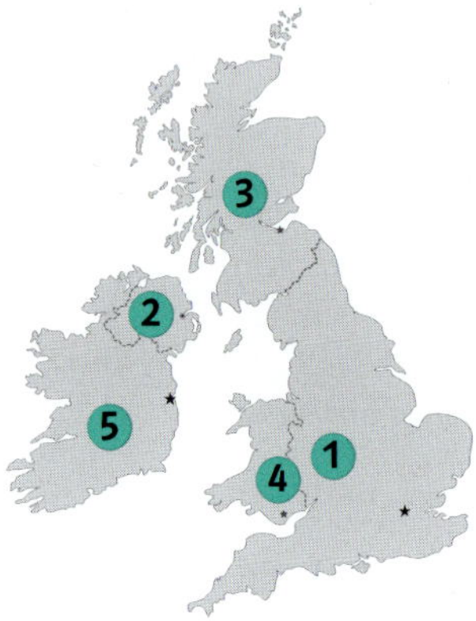

1 England
2 Northern Ireland
3 Scotland
4 Wales
5 Ireland

Government and politics

The UK is a parliamentary democracy and also a constitutional monarchy. The head of the government is the prime minister and the head of state is the monarch (queen or king). The UK doesn't have a single, written constitution.

The UK parliament meets in the Palace of Westminster in London. It has two parts: The House of Commons and the House of Lords. They both have the same responsibilities. They make laws, check the work of the government and they debate current issues.

The House of Commons has 646 members who are elected by the public. The members of the House of Lords are appointed by the monarch unless they are life peers. The prime minister and the Members of Parliament (MPs) meet and debate in the (House of) Commons.

In a general election, people vote for an MP to represent their area, also known as constituency, in the House of Commons. »

to divide into	aufteilen in
euro (€) ['jʊərəʊ]	Euro
times	-mal, Mal(e)
▸ ten times bigger	zehnmal größer
apart from	außer, neben; abgesehen von
mainly	hauptsächlich, vor allem
series	Reihe
to stretch out	*hier:* bis (ins Meer) reichen, hinausstrecken
parliamentary democracy	parlamentarische Demokratie
constitutional monarchy	konstitutionelle Monarchie
head of government	Regierungschef(in)
prime minister [ˌpraɪm'mɪnɪstə]	Premierminister(in), Ministerpräsident(in)
head of state	Staatsoberhaupt
monarch ['mɒnək]	Monarch(in)
single	einzeln
constitution [ˌkɒnstɪ'tju:ʃn]	Verfassung
parliament ['pɑ:ləment]	Parlament
the House of Commons	das Unterhaus
the House of Lords	das Oberhaus
responsibility	Verantwortung
to make a law	ein Gesetz verfassen
to debate [dɪ'beɪt]	debattieren, diskutieren
current	aktuell
issue	Frage, Thema, Problem
member	Mitglied
to elect sb	jdn. wählen
the public	die Öffentlichkeit
to appoint sb (to a post)	jdn. ernennen, jdn. in ein Amt berufen
unless	wenn nicht, falls nicht
life peer	Mitglied des Oberhauses auf Lebenszeit
general election	Parlamentswahlen
to represent [ˌreprɪ'zent]	repräsentieren
constituency	Wahlkreis

vdx3dwc

The candidate with the most votes becomes the MP in that constituency. The political party with the most seats usually forms the government. If no party has an absolute majority, there is a hung parliament. If this happens, one party can try to govern without a majority or two (or more) parties can form a coalition.

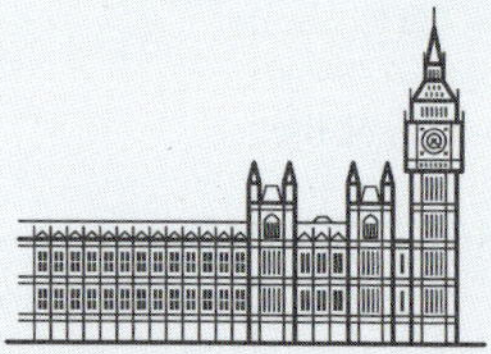

Due to the majority vote system, or first-past-the-post system, there is mainly a two-party system – the Conservative Party and the Labour Party. In the 2015 election, the Scottish National Party was the third largest party. There are other smaller parties, like the Liberal Democrats, the Green Party and the eurosceptical UK Independence Party (UKIP), they don't usually win many seats in an election.

The leader of the winning party becomes the Prime Minister and appoints approximately 20 Cabinet members. These include the Chancellor of the Exchequer, the Foreign Secretary and the Home Secretary. The party with the second largest number of MPs becomes the Opposition with its own leader and Shadow Cabinet. The person in charge of the Commons is the Speaker who is elected by the MPs. She or he acts as chairperson and must remain politically impartial.

The British Empire and the Commonwealth

The British Empire

Until the end of the 19th century the British Empire covered an area of nearly one quarter of the world and included more than one quarter of the population. It was made up of colonies, protectorates and territories. The Queen was the head of these areas and the British government ran them. The colonies supplied Great Britain with important raw materials such as cotton, tea and rubber helping it to become the world's major industrial power.

candidate ['kændɪdət]	Kandidat(in)
vote	Stimme; Abstimmung
absolute majority	absolute Mehrheit
hung parliament	Parlament ohne klare Mehrheitsverhältnisse
to govern ['gʌvən]	regieren
to form a coalition (with)	eine Koalition bilden (mit)
first-past-the-post system	Mehrheitswahlrecht
the Conservative Party [kən'sɜːvətɪv,pɑːti]	die Konservative Partei *(in GB)*
the Labour Party ['leɪbə,pɑːti]	die Labour Party *(sozialdemokratische Arbeiterpartei Großbritanniens)*
the Scottish National Party [,skɒtɪʃ'næʃnl,pɑːti]	*(etwa:)* die Schottische Nationalpartei
the Liberal Democrats [,lɪbrl'deməkræts]	die Liberaldemokraten *(Partei in GB)*
the Green Party	die Grüne Partei *(in GB)*
eurosceptical ['jʊərə,skeptɪkl]	euroskeptisch
UKIP *(UK Independence Party)* ['juːkɪp]	Partei für die Unabhängigkeit Großbritanniens
election [ɪ'lekʃən]	Wahl(en)
leader	Vorsitzende(r)
Cabinet	Kabinett
Chancellor of the Exchequer ['tʃɑːnslə] *BE*	Finanzminister(in)
Foreign Secretary *BE*	Außenminister(in)
Home Secretary *BE*	Innenminister(in)
the Opposition [,ɒpə'zɪʃən]	die Opposition
shadow cabinet [ʃædəʊ'kæbɪnət] *BE*	Schattenkabinett *(potenzielle Regierungsmannschaft der Opposition)*
to be in charge of sth	für etw. verantwortlich sein
speaker	Sprecher(in)
chairperson	Vorsitzende(r)
to remain	bleiben
impartial	unparteiisch
to include	umfassen, einschließen
colony	Kolonie
protectorate [prə'tektərət]	Schutzgebiet, Protektorat
territory ['terɪtəri]	Hoheitsgebiet, Territorium
head	Oberhaupt
to supply sb with sth	jdn. mit etw. versorgen
raw material	Rohstoff, Grundstoff
cotton	Baumwolle
rubber	Gummi
major ['meɪdʒə]	Haupt-, größte/r/s
industrial power	Industriemacht, Wirtschaftsmacht

vdx3dwc

The first overseas settlement was founded on the east coast of America in 1607. Colonies in the Caribbean, India, Australia and Africa were founded in the following centuries. The church sent people to these countries to try and join the people together through Christianity. This often didn't work and the original inhabitants of some of these countries were mistreated.

At the end of the 19th century countries like Canada, Australia and New Zealand started to regain their independence through decolonization. In 1997 Britain gave the last important colony, Hong Kong, back to the the Chinese. Britain still has 14 overseas territories.

The Commonwealth

The Commonwealth was founded in 1931 and is made up of 54 independent sovereign states in a voluntary association. The countries in the Commonwealth are all around the world and are rich and poor and also large and small. The Queen (or King) of Great Britain is the head of the Commonwealth. It is also called a 'family of nations' as so many different nations have been brought together. The population of the Commonwealth is two billion and includes different languages, nationalities, cultures and religions. Human rights, democracy and a good government are important to the Commonwealth nations, and they meet every two years to discuss their aims and needs.

History

The Agricultural Revolution

The Agricultural Revolution took place between the mid-17th century and the late 19th century. The revolution started with some changes farmers made. They had found new methods that improved farming and led to an increased productivity of agriculture.

One method was crop rotation. Instead of leaving fields empty all winter, farmers planted clover that has a positive fertilising effect on the soil. Turnips, that even grow in colder seasons, were planted for food. As a consequence, more food was available and the population started to grow rapidly, and then more food was needed. The Agricultural Revolution led to the Industrial Revolution.

overseas settlement [ˌəʊvəsiːz 'setlmənt]	Siedlung in Übersee
to found	gründen
the Caribbean [ˌkærɪ'biːən]	die Karibik
Christianity [ˌkrɪsti'ænəti]	Christentum
original inhabitant [ə'rɪdʒənəl ˌɪnhæbitnt]	Ureinwohner(in)
to mistreat [mɪs'triːt]	schlecht behandeln

to regain [rɪ'geɪn]	wiederbekommen, wiedererhalten
independence	Unabhängigkeit
decolonisation	Entkolonalisierung, Übergabe der Macht an die ursprünglichen Bewohner einer Kolonie
the Chinese	die Chinesen, der chinesische Staat

sovereign state ['sɒvrɪn ˌsteɪt]	unabhängiger Staat
voluntary association [ˌvɒləntrɪ ə'səʊsieɪʃn]	freiwilliger Zusammenschluss
nation ['neɪʃən]	Nation, Staat, Land
religion [rɪ'lɪdʒən]	Religion
human rights	Menschenrechte
democracy [dɪ'mɒkrəsi]	Demokratie
government ['gʌvənmənt]	Regierung
aim	Ziel
need	Bedürfnis

agricultural revolution [ˌægrɪkʌltʃərəl 'revəluːʃn]	landwirtschaftliche Revolution, Agrarrevolution
mid-17th century	Mitte des 17. Jahrhunderts
late 19th century	dem späten 19. Jahrhundert
method	Methode, Verfahren
to improve	verbessern
farming	Ackerbau und Viehzucht
increased [ɪn'kriːst]	erhöht
productivity	Produktivität, Leistungsfähigkeit
agriculture	Landwirtschaft

crop rotation	Fruchtwechsel
clover	Klee
fertilising effect	düngende Wirkung
soil [sɔɪl]	Erde, Boden
turnip	Herbstrübe
consequence ['kɒnsɪkwəns]	Konsequenz, Folge
available	vorrätig, verfügbar
rapidly ['ræpɪdli]	schnell, rasch
the Industrial Revolution	industrielle Revolution

vdx3dwc

The Industrial Revolution

The Industrial Revolution was the **period** between 1760 and about 1840. One of the most important **inventions triggering** the revolution was James Watt's **steam engine** which was used to make **power**. This power made it possible to change the **manufacturing processes** and increase productivity in **factories**.

In the Yorkshire **cotton mills** new power **looms** were introduced to speed up the production of cloth. The Industrial Revolution was a **major milestone** in British history as it **influenced** every **aspect** of people's lives. It was the first step in improving the **standard of living** of the whole population.

Some Kings and Queens

King Henry VIII became **heir** to the **throne** after his **elder** brother, Prince Arthur, died. He was King from 1509 to 1547. He was famous for his six **wives** as well as **investing** in the **navy** and beginning the English Reformation, which **led** to the **formation** of the Church of England, also known as the Anglican Church. He died in London in 1547 and was followed by his son Edward VI who was only King for six years.

Queen Victoria was the Queen of England from 1837 to 1901. She was 18 when she became Queen and was connected with the Industrial Revolution, **economic progress** in Great Britain and also the British Empire. The British East India Company, which had **ruled** much of India, was **dissolved** after the Indian **Rebellion** of 1857. Britain's protectorates in India were officially included in the British Empire. Queen Victoria didn't like the actions of either side in the conflict and was glad when the power of the company was taken over by the state. Her actions during this time got her the name the **Empress** of India. Her **reign** was the second longest in history when she died on 22nd January on the Isle of Wight after nearly 64 years on the throne.

King George VI was the King of England from 1936 to 1952 and was Queen Elizabeth II's father. After his brother Edward VIII **abdicated**, George became king, a job he hadn't been **prepared** for. In 1939 he became the first British **monarch** to visit the United States of America. He was king **throughout World War II** and worked **closely** with the **Prime Minister**, Winston Churchill. He was a **popular** king and everyone was very sad when he **died in his sleep** in February 1952 after a **lung** operation when he was only 56 years old.

Queen Elizabeth II, the **present** Queen, was 25 when she became Queen after the death of her father in 1952. She is **married to** Prince Philip and they have four children, eight grandchildren and five **great-grandchildren**. »»

period	Zeit
invention [ɪn'venʃən]	Erfindung
to trigger sth	etw. auslösen
steam engine	Dampfmaschine
power	Kraft, Energie; Strom
manufacturing process [ˌmænjə'fæktʃərɪŋ ˌprəʊses]	Herstellungsprozess
factory ['fæktri]	Fabrik
cotton mill	Baumwollfabrik
loom	Webstuhl
major milestone	wichtiger Meilenstein
to influence	beeinflussen
aspect	Aspekt
standard of living	Lebensstandard
heir [eə]	Erbe
throne [θrəʊn]	Thron
elder	ältere*(r, s)*
wife [waɪf] , wives [waɪvz]	(Ehe)Frau
to invest	investieren
navy	Marine, Seestreitkräfte
to lead [li:d], led [led], led [led]	führen
formation [fɔ:'meɪʃn]	Entstehung, Bildung
economic progress	wirtschaftlicher Fortschritt
to rule	herrschen
to dissolve	auflösen
rebellion	Aufstand, Rebellion
empress ['emprəs]	Kaiserin
▸ emperor	Kaiser
reign [reɪn]	Herrschaft
to abdicate	abdanken
to prepare [prɪ'peə]	vorbereiten
monarch ['mɒnək]	Monarch(in), König(in)
throughout [θru:'aʊt]	während
World War II	der zweite Weltkrieg
closely [kləʊsli]	eng zusammen
prime minister [ˌpraɪm'mɪnɪstə]	Premierminister(in)
popular	beliebt
to die in one's sleep	im Schlaf sterben
lung	Lunge
present	gegenwärtig, derzeitig
married to	verheiratet mit
great-grandchild ['greɪtgræn,tʃaɪld], great-grandchildren ['greɪtgræn,tʃɪldrən]	Urenkel(in)

vdx3dwc

The Queen enjoys celebrating her special anniversaries with the public. The diamond jubilee of Elizabeth II in 2012 was celebrated with parades not only in the British Isles but also across the Commonwealth. It was important for the Queen that these countries were included in the celebrations and that members of the royal family visited them in 2012.

Although her accession to the throne on the death of her father was on 6th February 1952, her coronation wasn't until 2nd June 1953. The period of mourning for the King had to be respected. She is now the monarch with the longest reign in Great Britain.

Sport

A lot of sport is played in the British Isles. The British don't excel at winter sports very much. This is no doubt due to the temperature not getting low enough for a lot of snow in winter, and there aren't enough ski slopes or ice rinks to practise on. There are a number of sports which the British are famous for. Here is some information about football and for other typically English sports there are some fact cards with more information.

Football (or soccer as it is known in the US)

- Football is a, if not the, national sport in the British Isles. The rules are the same worldwide. There are a number of successful teams and lots of international players play football for British teams. In London alone there are several famous teams, for example, Arsenal, Chelsea, West Ham and Tottenham Hotspur.

Rugby

- There are two sorts of rugby - Rugby League and Rugby Union. The rules are similar.
- Number of players in a team: 13 rugby league / 15 rugby union
- Size of field: 100 m long x 70 m wide, the H-shaped goal is 5.6 m wide and the crossbar is 3 m high.
- Duration of game: 80 minutes, split into two 40 minute halves. ›››

to celebrate ['seləbreɪt]	feiern
anniversary [ˌænɪ'vɜːsri]	Jubiläum
the public	Öffentlichkeit
diamond jubilee	sechzigjähriges Jubiläum
celebration [ˌselə'breɪʃən]	Feier
royal family	königliche Familie
accession [ək'seʃn]	Beitritt
on the death of	zum Tod von
coronation	Krönung
period of mourning	Trauerzeit
to respect	respektieren
to excel	sich hervortun, mit besonderen Leistungen auffallen
no doubt	ohne Zweifel, zweifellos
due to	wegen, aufgrund von / dessen, dass
temperature ['temprətʃə]	Temperatur
ski slope	Skipiste, Skihang
ice rink	Eisbahn, Schlittschuhbahn
to practise	trainieren
fact card	Steckbrief
soccer	Fußball
national ['næʃənəl]	national
rule	Regel
worldwide	weltweit, auf der ganzen Welt
successful [sək'sesfəl]	erfolgreich
international [ˌɪntə'næʃənəl]	international
several ['sevərəl]	mehrere, einige
wide	breit
crossbar	Querlatte, Querbalken
high	hoch
duration [ˌdjuːr'eɪʃn]	Dauer
to split [splɪt], split [splɪt], split [splɪt]	aufteilen, teilen

vdx3dwc

- Aim: The oval ball has to move forward by players running with it or kicking it, they aren't allowed to throw it forward. Players can be tackled and the game starts with a scrum. Points can be scored in the following ways: A try is scored by putting the ball on the ground in the in-goal area and is worth five points. If it is converted by kicking it over the crossbar of the goal, the team gets another two points. A penalty kick or drop goal each score three points.

Cricket

- Number of players in a team: 11
- Size of field: Not fixed, but the diameter of the field should be between 450 and 500 feet. The pitch in the middle is 20.12 m long x 3.05 m wide.
- Duration of game: three to five days, at least six hours of cricket is played each day, one day matches last at least six hours.
- Aim: To score the most runs using a bat and a ball and put out the opposing batsman. It is played on a grass field with a flat strip in the middle called the pitch. To score a run, you have to run from your end of the pitch to the other end, after hitting the ball, which the bowler throws, before the other team catches it.

Hockey

- Number of players: 11
- Size of pitch: 91.4 m long x 55 m wide, the goal is 3.66 m wide x 1.2 m deep x 2.14 m high.
- Duration of game: 70 minutes, split in two 35 minute halves.
- Aim: Using a hockey stick, a player must control the ball and get it into the other team's goal to score a point. The entire stick has to stay below shoulder level for safety reasons. The stick has a face, a flat side, for hitting the ball and a rounded backside. The ball is not allowed to be hit with the rounded side. »»

aim	Ziel
oval ['əʊvl]	oval, eiförmig
to move forward	(sich) vorwärts bewegen
to throw [θrəʊ], threw [θru:], thrown [θrəʊn]	werfen
to tackle sb	jdn. angreifen
scrum	Gedränge
point [pɔɪnt]	Punkt
to score	(Punkte) erzielen, Tor(e) schießen
try	Versuch
ground	Boden
to be worth	zählen, den Wert haben
to convert	verwandeln
penalty kick	Straftritt
drop goal	Dropgoal *(beim Rugby ein aus dem Spiel getretener Schuss auf das Tor)*

fixed	festgelegt
diameter [ˌdaɪ'æmətə]	Durchmesser
pitch	Pitch, Spielfeld
run	Lauf
bat	Schlagholz, Schläger
to put out	*hier:* den Schlagmann dazu bringen, Fehler zu machen, damit dieser ausscheidet
opposing [ə'pəʊzɪŋ]	gegnerisch, zum Gegener gehörend
batsman	Schlagmann
bowler	Ballwerfer(in)

deep	tief
hockey stick	Hockeyschläger
to control	kontrollieren, beherrschen, unter Kontrolle bringen
entire [ɪn'taɪə]	ganz, komplett
below [bɪ'ləʊ]	unter, unterhalb
shoulder level	Schulterhöhe
safety reason	Sicherheitsgrund
face	flache Seite des Hockeyschlägers
rounded backside	runde/abgerundete Rückseite

vdx3dwc

Netball

- Number of players: 7
- Size of court: 30.5 m long x 15.25 wide, goal rings are 38 cm in diameter on posts that are 3.05 m high.
- Duration of game: 60 minutes, split in two 30 minute halves
- Aim: Each team tries to score goals by passing the ball down the court and shooting it through the goal ring at the opponents end. Players have special positions and have to stay in certain areas of the court. A player can only hold the ball for three seconds before passing it on. It cannot be bounced.

Famous faces

Lots of famous people come from the British Isles. From **authors** and **inventors** to sports people and **actors** and **actresses**. Here is some information about a few of them.

Authors

- Name: Joanne K. Rowling
- Date and place of birth: 31st July 1965 in Yate, Gloucestershire, UK
- Marital status: married, 3 children
- Occupation: novelist
- Famous for: The Harry Potter fantasy series, which is the best-selling book series in history. It has been made into a series of films, too.

- Name: William Shakespeare
- Date and place of birth: 26th April 1564 in Stratford-upon-Avon, UK
- Date and place of death: 23rd April 1616 in Stratford-upon-Avon, UK
- Marital status: married, 3 children
- Occupation: playwright, poet, actor
- Famous for: He wrote mainly tragedies, including Hamlet, Othello and Macbeth. His works are well-known as the finest in the English language.

ring	Ring, Kreis
to pass the ball	den Ball weitergeben, passen
to shoot [ʃuːt], shot [ʃɒt], shot [ʃɒt]	schießen
opponent [əˈpəʊnənt]	Gegner, Gegenspieler
position [pəˈzɪʃən]	Position *(Funktion als Spieler(in))*
certain [ˈsɜːtn]	bestimmt
to bounce [baʊns]	prallen

---

author [ˈɔːθə]	Autor(in), Schriftstellerin(in)
inventor [ɪnˈventə]	Erfinder(in)
▸ to invent	erfinden
actor	Shauspieler
actress [ˈæktrəs]	Schauspielerin

---

marital status [ˌmærɪtəlˈsteɪtəs]	Familienstand
married	verheiratet
▸ get married	heiraten
occupation [ˈɒkjəpeɪʃn]	Beruf
novelist [ˈnɒvəlɪst]	Romanschriftsteller(in)
fantasy series	Fantasy Serie
best-selling	meistverkauft

---

playwright [ˈpleɪraɪt]	Dramatiker(in), Autor(in) von Theaterstücken
poet [ˈpəʊɪt]	Dichter(in)
mainly	hauptsächlich, vor allem
tragedy [ˈtrædʒədɪ]	Tragödie
including	einschließlich
well-known [ˌwelˈnəʊn]	bekannt, berühmt
finest [faɪnɪst]	beste, feinste

vdx3dwc

Actors and actresses

- Name: Hugh Grant
- Date and place of birth: 9th September 1960 in London, UK
- Marital status: single, 4 children
- Occupation: actor, producer
- Famous for: He became famous after his first film Four Weddings and a Funeral in 1994. His films have earned over $ 2.4 billion. He has received a Golden Globe and a BAFTA award. He has always claimed that acting is just a job he happened to be good at.

- Name: Kate Winslet
- Date and place of birth: 5th October 1975 in Reading, Berkshire, UK
- Marital status: married, 3 children
- Occupation: actress, singer
- Famous for: Her best-known role was in the film Titanic. She has won a number of awards including one Oscar, three BAFTA awards and four Golden Globes. At the age of 12 she did her first advert for television which was the start of her acting career.

Musicians

- Name: David Bowie
- Date and place of birth: 8th January 1947 in London, UK
- Date and place of death: 10th January 2016 in New York, USA
- Marital status: married, 2 children
- Occupation: singer, songwriter, actor, producer
- Famous for: He was famous for his pop music over five decades. His final album was released the week before he died. It is estimated that he sold 140 million records worldwide during his lifetime.

- Name: Adele Laurie Blue Adkins
- Date and place of birth: 5th May 1988 in London, UK
- Marital status: single, 1 child
- Occupation: singer, songwriter
- Famous for: Her career started when a friend posted her demo-recording on MySpace. She has a number of entries in the Guiness Book of World Records, and she won an Oscar for the theme song 'Skyfall' that she wrote and recorded for a James Bond film.

single ['sɪŋgəl]	ledig
producer [prə'dju:sə]	Produzent(in)
to earn [ɜ:n]	*hier:* einspielen, verdienen
billion	Milliarde
to claim [kleɪm]	behaupten
singer ['sɪŋə]	Sänger(in)
most-known role	bekannteste Rolle
advert	Werbung, Anzeige
acting career	Schauspielkarriere
musician [mju:'zɪʃn]	Musiker(in)
decade ['dekeɪd]	Jahrzehnt
to release [rɪ'li:s]	veröffentlichen
to estimate ['estɪmət]	abschätzen
record ['rekɔ:d]	Schallplatte
worldwide	weltweit, global
lifetime	Lebenszeit
songwriter	Liedtexter(in), Songwriter(in)
career [kə'rɪə]	berufliche Laufbahn, Karriere
to post	im Internet veröffentlichen
demo recording	Demoaufnahme
entry	Eintrag
theme song	Titelsong, Titelmelodie
record [re'kɔ:d]	aufnehmen

vdx3dwc

Sports people

- Name: Andy Murray
- Date and place of birth: 15th May 1987 in Glasgow, Scotland
- Marital status: married, 1 child
- Occupation: (amazingly cool) tennis player
- Famous for: He started playing tennis when he was 3. He won a gold medal at the 2012 Olympic Games in London. In 2013, he won Wimbledon, becoming the first British man to win the title for 77 years since Fred Perry. In 2016 he won Wimbledon for the second time.

- Name: Jessica Ennis-Hill
- Date and place of birth: 28th January 1986, Sheffield, UK
- Marital status: married, 1 child
- Occupation: track and field athlete
- Famous for: At school she excelled at the high jump and heptathlon events. She has won gold medals at Olympic Games and also other international athletic championships.

Inventors and scientists

- Name: Charles Darwin
- Date and place of birth: 12th February 1809 in Shrewsbury, England
- Date and place of death: 19th April 1882 in Kent, England
- Marital status: married, 10 children
- Occupation: naturalist, geologist
- Famous for: He is known best for his evolution theories. He discovered that all species have descended from common ancestors. His scientific theory is that evolution comes from a process of natural selection and looks at the strongest beings, being the ones to succeed.

- Name: John Logie Baird
- Date and place of birth: 14th August 1888 in Helensburgh, Scotland
- Date and place of death: 14th June 1946, Bexhill, England
- Marital status: married, 2 children
- Occupation: engineer, inventor
- Famous for: Where would we be today without his invention ... the colour television. In 1928 his company achieved the first transatlantic television transmission. His technological successes have made him a very important person in the history of television.

medal	Medaille
the Olympic Games = Olympics	Olympische Spiele
▸ Summer Olympics	Olympische Sommerspiele
▸ Winter Olympics	Olympische Winterspiele
track and field athlete	Leichtathlet(in)
high jump	Hochsprung
heptathlon [hep'tæθlɒn]	Siebenkampf
athletic championships	Leichtathletikmeisterschaften
naturalist	Naturforscher(in)
geologist	Geologe, Geologin
evolution theory [ˌi:və'lu:ʃn θɪəri]	Evolutionstheorie
species ['spi:ʃi:z]	Tier- / Pflanzenart
to descend from	abstammen von
common	gemeinsam
ancestor ['ænsestə]	Vorfahre, Vorfahrin
scientific	(natur)wissenschaftlich
process	Prozess, Vorgang
natural selection	natürliche Auslese/Selektion
being	Wesen, Mensch
to succeed [sək'si:d]	Erfolg haben, gelingen
engineer ['endʒənɪə]	Ingenieur(in)
television ['telɪvɪʒən] = TV	Fernsehen
to achieve [ə'tʃi:v]	erreichen
transatlantic	transatlantisch, über den Altlantik (hinweg)
transmission	Übertragung
technological [ˌteknə'lɒdʒɪkᵊl]	technologisch

vdx3dwc

6 The United States of America

Geography

The United States of America is known by **a number of** other names, these **include** the US, the USA and America. It is **made up** of 50 **states**, the **federal district** of Washington DC and five major **territories**. 48 of the American states form an area in the centre of North America. Alaska is to the west of Canada, on the northwestern **edge** of America, and Hawaii is a group of **islands** in the Pacific Ocean. America's territories are **scattered** around both the Pacific Ocean and the Caribbean Sea.

The United States of America **covers an area of** 9.9 million **square kilometres**. It has the fourth largest **total area** (land and sea) in the world behind Russia, Canada and China. There are an **amazing** nine different **time zones**.

The USA has a **population** of over 320 **million** people, which is also the third largest in the world. It can be **divided into** three main **ethnic groups**: White, Black and Asian. Nearly three-quarters of the population is white. About 82% of Americans live in **urban areas**, about half of those live in cities with populations over 50,000. In the US, nine cities have more than one million **residents**, and four **global cities** have over two million (New York City, Los Angeles, Chicago and Houston). There are 52 **metropolitan areas** with populations greater than one million. Most of the fastest-growing areas in the US are in the West or South.

The United States of America is **ethnically diverse** and **multi-cultural**. This is **a result of immigration** to America from many other countries **throughout** its history. The main **language** spoken by 80% of Americans is English. Spanish is spoken by 12% and there are many other languages spoken by the rest of the American population. Alaska **recognises** twenty native languages. English is **therefore** the national language although there is no **official language** in the US.

Most of the American population is **Christian** and within this group **Protestants** form the **majority**. The state of Utah is the only state where the majority of the population follows the **Mormon faith**. Religion is a very **significant** part of the American culture and **church attendance** is very high.

America has a very **diverse landscape**. The Appalachian Mountains are about 2,400 km long and they divide the Great Lakes from the Midwest. The Mississippi-Missouri River, which is the world's fourth longest river system, runs **mainly** from the north to the south through the heart of America. »»

a number of	einige
to include [ɪn'klu:d]	einschließen, umfassen
to be made up of	bestehen aus
state	Bundesland, Staat
federal district	Bundesdistrikt
territory ['terɪtərɪ]	Territorium, Gebiet
edge [edʒ]	*hier:* Ecke; Rand, Kante
island ['aɪlənd]	Insel
scattered	verstreut

to cover an area	sich über ein Gebiet erstrecken
square kilometre	Quadrat Kilometer
total area [ˌtəʊtl 'eərɪə]	Gesamtfläche
amazing [ə'meɪzɪŋ]	erstaunlich
time zone	Zeitzone

population [ˌpɒpjə'leɪʃn]	Bevölkerung
million ['mɪljən]	Million
to divide into	aufteilen in
ethnic group	ethnische Gruppe
urban area [ˌɜ:bən 'eərɪə]	Stadtgebiet
resident	Einwohner(in)
global city	Weltstadt
metropolitan area [metrəˌpɒlɪtn 'eəriə]	Großraum, Großstadtregion

ethnically diverse [ˌeθnɪkli daɪ'vɜ:s]	vielfältig, ethnisch gemischt
multi-cultural	multikulturell
a result of	eine Folge von
immigration [ˌɪmɪ'greɪʃən]	Einwanderung
throughout	während
language ['læŋgwɪdʒ]	Sprache
to recognise	erkennen
therefore ['ðeəfɔ:]	deshalb; also
official language	Amtssprache

Christian ['krɪstʃən]	christlich
Protestant ['prɒtɪstənt]	protestantisch
majority [mə'dʒɒrəti]	Mehrheit
Mormon faith ['mɔ:mən]	mormonischer Glauben
significant [sɪg'nɪfɪkənt]	bedeutend, wichtig, beachtlich
church attendance [ə'tendəns]	Gottesdienstbesuch

diverse [daɪ'vɜ:s]	abwechslungsreich
▸ diversity	Vielfalt
landscape ['lændskeɪp]	Landschaft
mainly ['meɪnli]	hauptsächlich, vor allem

mavbh8d

The flat, fertile prairie of the Great Plains stretches from the Appalachians in the west. On the western edge of the Great Plains are the Rocky Mountains (Rockies), which are approximately 4,300 m high, in Colorado. Farther west are the Great Basin and the rocky deserts such as the Mojave Desert. The Sierra Nevada and Cascade mountain ranges are close to the Pacific Coast to the west. The highest mountain in the country is Alaska's Denali (Mount McKinley). It is 6,190.5 metres high. Active volcanoes are common in Alaska, and Hawaii consists of volcanic islands. The supervolcano in the Yellowstone National Park in the Rockies is the continent's largest volcano.

Here is one really interesting thing about America's diverse landscape: Its lowest and its highest points (of America without Alaska) are both in the state of California, and unbelievably, they are only about 84 miles (135 km) away from each other.

The climate in the United States varies from tropical in the southern tip of Florida to subarctic or polar in Alaska in the north. Hurricanes and tornadoes are also very common in the US.

There are 58 national parks and hundreds of other parks, forests and wilderness areas. The United States is home to 428 mammal species, 784 bird species, 311 reptile species, and 295 amphibian species. About 91,000 insect species have been described. The bald eagle is both the national bird and the national animal of the United States.

The United States of America has the world's largest economy, which is due to its high natural resources and the high productivity of its workers. It is also the world's leading military and economic power, an important political and cultural force and a leader in scientific research and technological innovations. »»

flat [flæt]	flach, eben
fertile [ɪn'fɜ:taɪl]	fruchtbar
≠ infertile	unfruchtbar
prairie [preəri]	Prairie; Grassteppe
to stretch [stretʃ]	sich erstrecken
approximately [ə'prɒksɪmətli]	annähernd, ungefähr
desert ['dezət]	Wüste
mountain range	Gebirge, Bergkette, Gebirgszug
close to [kləʊs]	in der Nähe von, nahe bei
volcano [vɒl'keɪnəʊ]	Vulkan
common	häufig
to consist of	bestehen aus
volcanic island	Vulkaninsel
continent ['kɒntɪnənt]	Kontinent, Erdteil
away from each other [ə'weɪ]	voneinander entfernt
climate	Klima
to vary	unterschiedlich sein, variieren
tropical ['trɒpɪkl]	tropisch
subarctic	subarktisch
polar ['pəʊlə]	polar
hurricane ['hʌrɪkən]	*(tropischer)* Wirbelsturm, Orkan, Hurrikan
tornado [tɔ:'neɪdəʊ]	Wirbelsturm, Windhose, Tornado
national park	Nationalpark, Naturschutzgebiet
forest ['fɒrɪst]	Wald, Waldgebiet
wilderness area [ˌwɪldənəs 'eəriə]	Naturschutzgebiet, Wildnis; Wildnis
mammal ['mæməl]	Säugetier
species ['spi:ʃi:z]	*(Tier- oder Pflanzen-)* Art
reptile ['reptaɪl]	Reptil *(z.B. Eidechsen)*
amphibian [æm'fɪbiən]	Amphibie *(z. B. Frösche)*
insect ['ɪnsekt]	Insekt
bald eagle	Weißkopfseeadler
economy [ɪ'kɒnəmi]	Wirtschaft; Volkswirtschaft
due to ['djuˌtu:]	wegen, aufgrund von; dank
natural resources [ˌnætʃrəl rɪ'zɔ:sɪz]	Bodenschätze
productivity ['prɒdʌkt]	Produktivität
world's leading	weltweit führend
military power ['mɪlɪtri]	Militärmacht
economic power	Wirtschaftsmacht
political [pə'lɪtɪkl]	politisch
cultural ['kʌltʃrəl]	kulturell
force [fɔ:s]	Macht
scientific research [saɪənˌtɪfɪk rɪ'sɜ:tʃ]	wissenschaftliche Forschung
innovation	Innovation, Erneuerung

mavbh8d

There is an awesome 4 million miles (6.4 million kilometres) of public roads in the US. This makes it clear to see that automobiles are the most popular form of transport. About 40% of Americans don't drive cars as we know them, but vans, SUVs or light trucks. There is a rail network in America too, but due to the low population density, it is mainly used for transporting goods and not people. The three largest airlines in the world, based on the number of passengers they transport, are American. Twelve of the 30 busiest airports in the world are in the United States. This clearly shows how much flying the Americans do to get across their huge country.

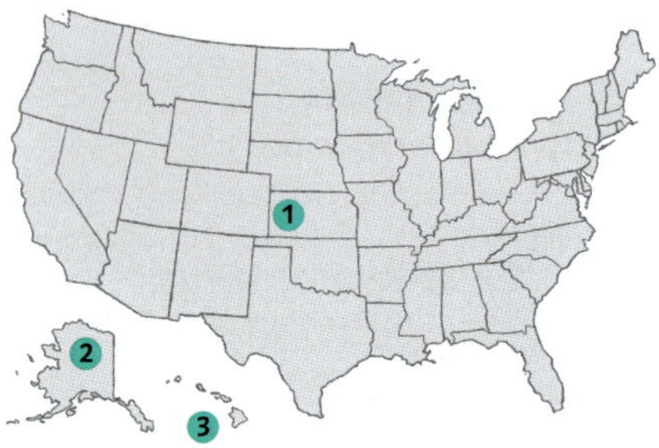

1 Mainland USA
2 Alaska
3 Hawaii

History

The first inhabitants of North America migrated from Siberia via the Bering land bridge and arrived at least 15,000 years ago. They are the ancestors of today's Native Americans.

Colonisation

In the early days of colonisation by the Europeans there were food shortages, lots of people died due to diseases, and there were attacks by Native Americans. Native Americans were also often at war with neighboring tribes. At the same time, many natives and settlers depended on each other.

Settlers traded for food and animal pelts, natives for guns, ammunition and other European goods. Natives taught many settlers where, when and how to cultivate corn, beans and squash. European missionaries thought it was important to civilize the Native Americans and encouraged them to use European agricultural techniques and adopt European lifestyles.

awesome ['ɔ:səm]	beeindruckend, eindrucksvoll
to make it clear to see [klɪə]	etw. deutlich machen; helfen etw. zu verstehen
automobile ['ɔ:təməbi:l]	Auto
form of transport [træns'pɔ:t]	Verkehrsmittel, Transportmittel
van	Lieferwagen
SUV *(sport utility vehicle)* [ˌesju:'vi:]	Geländewagen, SUV
light truck [laɪt]	leichtes Nutzfahrzeug, Kleinlastwagen
rail network	Bahnnetz
population density ['densɪtɪ]	Bevölkerungsdichte
goods	Waren, Güter
airline	Fluggesellschaft, Fluglinie
based on	basierend auf
passenger ['pæsəndʒə]	Passagier(in), Fahrgast
busiest airport	Flughafen mit dem größten Passagieraufkommen

inhabitant [ɪn'hæbɪtənt]	Einwohner(in)
migrate	wandern; zuwandern, abwandern
land bridge	Landbrücke
ancestor ['ænsestə]	Vorfahre, Vorfahrin

colonisation [ˌkɒlənaɪ'zeɪʃn]	Kolonie
food shortage ['ʃɔ:tɪdʒ]	Lebensmittelknappheit
disease [dɪ'zi:z]	Krankheit; Infektionskrankheit
attack	Angriff
▸ to attack	angreifen
neighbouring	benachbart, in der Nähe lebend
tribe [traɪb]	Stamm, kleines Volk
settler	Siedler
to depend on sb [dɪ'pend ɒn]	auf jdn. angewiesen sein

to trade for sth	gegen etw. tauschen
animal pelt	Tierfell
gun	Schusswaffe
ammunition [ˌæmjə'nɪʃn]	Munition
to cultivate	anbauen
corn [kɔ:n]	Mais
bean	Bohne
squash	Kürbis
missionary ['mɪʃənərɪ]	Missionar(in)
to civilize sb ['sɪvəlaɪz]	jdn. zivilisieren, jdm. Kultur beibringen
to encourage sb to do sth [ɪn'kʌrɪdʒ]	jdn. ermuntern etw. zu tun
agricultural technique [ˌægrɪ'kʌltʃərəl]	landwirtschaftliche Methode
to adopt [ə'dɒpt]	annehmen, übernehmen
lifestyle	Lebensstil

mavbh8d

After Spain had sent Christopher Columbus on his first **voyage** to the New World in 1492, other **explorers** followed. The Spanish **set up** small **settlements** in New Mexico and Florida, and France had several small settlements along the Mississippi River. The Virginia **Colony** in 1607 at Jamestown and the Pilgrims' Plymouth Colony in 1620 were the first **successful** English settlements on the eastern coast of North America.

Most settlers in every colony were small **farmers**, but soon other **industries** also **developed**. For example **cash crops** such as **tobacco**, **rice** and **wheat**; **fishing** and **wood** industries developed and **manufacturers** started building ships and **producing rum**.

Slaves were increasingly used to **harvest** crops, and a number of **acts were passed** both **for and against** the use of them. By the end of the 18th **century**, a lot of African slaves were being used for harvesting crops, **especially** in the south.

The American Revolutionary War

The American Revolutionary War was the first successful colonial war of **independence** against a European **power**. Americans **demanded** their **rights** as Englishmen, but the British **insisted on ruling** them and the **conflict resulted in** war.

On 4th July 1776 the United States **signed** the **Declaration of Independence**. One of the things written in the declaration is that **humanity** is **created equal** in their **unalienable rights** and that those rights had not been **protected** by Great Britain. It **finally declared** that the 13 colonies were independent states and had no **allegiance** to the British **crown** in the United States. »»

voyage ['vɔɪɪdʒ]	Seereise
explorer [ɪk'splɔ:rə]	Entdecker(in), Forscher(in)
to set up	errichten, gründen
settlement ['setəlmənt]	Siedlung, Ansiedlung
colony ['kɒləni]	Kolonie
successful	erfolgreich
farmer	Bauer, Bäuerin
industry ['ɪndəstri]	Industrie; Wirtschaftszweig
to develop [dɪ'veləp]	sich entwickeln
cash crop	zum Verkauf angebaute Feldfrucht
tobacco [tə'bækəʊ]	Tabak
rice	Reis
wheat	Weizen
fishing	Fischfang
wood	Holz
manufacturer [ˌmænjə'fæktʃərə]	Fabrikant, Hersteller; Handwerker
to produce [prə'dju:s]	produzieren, herstellen
rum	Rum
slave	Sklave, Sklavin
▸ slavery	Sklaverei
to harvest ['hɑ:vɪst]	ernten
to pass an act	ein Gesetz verabschieden
for and against	dafür und dagegen
century ['sentʃər|i]	Jahrhundert
especially [ɪ'speʃəli]	insbesondere
the American Revolutionary War [wɔ:]	amerikanischer Unabhängigkeitskrieg
independence	Unabhängigkeit
power ['paʊə]	Macht
to demand	(ein)fordern
right	Recht
to insist on [ɪn'sɪstˌɒn]	auf etw. bestehen
to rule [ru:l]	beherrschen
conflict ['kɒnflɪkt]	Konflikt, Auseinandersetzung
to result in sth	zu etw. führen
to sign sth	etw. unterzeichnen
the Declaration of Independence	die Unabhängigkeitserklärung der USA
humanity	Menschheit
created [kri'eɪtɪd]	geschaffen
equal ['i:kwəl]	gleich, gleichberechtigt
unalienable rights [ʌn'eɪliənəbl]	unveräußerliche Rechte
to protect	schützen
finally ['faɪnəli]	schließlich, abschließend
to declare [dɪ'kleə]	erklären
allegiance [ə'li:dʒəns]	Treue
crown [kraʊn]	*hier:* Herrschaft; Krone

mavbh8d

The fourth day of July is celebrated as Independence Day every year. George Washington, who had led the revolutionary army to victory, was the first president elected under the new constitution from 1789 until 1797.

The Trail of Tears is the name given to the Indian removal policy from the 1830s that moved Indians to the west into their own reservations. It was claimed that this was done in order to protect them. The California Gold Rush of 1848–49 increased the number of people who emigrated from the west, from countries like China.

The American Civil War

The American Civil War, from 1860 to 1865, was started due to different opinions between the northern and southern states, particularly about black slavery. Initially this war was for the union of both the thirteen slave states and the free states, but the second aim that developed was to abolish slavery. It was the deadliest war in American history, approximately 618,000 soldiers and many civilians were killed in it. In 1865 the war ended and three amendments to the US Constitution were brought about: The prohibition of slavery, US citizenship to nearly four million African Americans who had been slaves, and also the promise to give them the right to vote.

After the civil war, new railways made relocation easier for settlers. They meant that internal trade expanded, but they also increased conflicts with Native Americans. In 1869, a new Peace Policy was designed to protect Native-Americans from abuse, avoid further war and also to secure their eventual US citizenship.

The world wars

The United States remained neutral from the outbreak of World War I, in 1914, until 1917 when it did join the war after all, helping to beat the Central Powers including Germany, who had started the war. The war ended in 1918 when Germany was finally defeated (and asked for an armistice). In 1920 the women's rights movement won the right for women to vote and also stand for electoral office. »»

to celebrate sth	etw. feiern, begehen
army ['ɑ:mi]	Armee, Truppen
victory ['vɪktəri]	Sieg
to elect [ɪ'lekt]	wählen
constitution [ˌkɒnstɪ'tju:ʃən]	Verfassung, Grundgesetz
removal	Umsiedlung
policy	*(eine bestimmte)* Politik
reservation	Reservat
to claim sth	beanspruchen
in order to	um zu
to increase ['inkri:s]	erhöhen; zunehmen
≠ to decrease	abnehmen, zurück gehen
to emigrate	auswandern
the American Civil War	amerikanischer Bürgerkrieg
opinion [ə'pɪnjən]	Meinung
particularly [pə'tɪkjələli]	besonders
slavery ['sleɪvri]	Sklaverei
initially [ɪ'nɪʃli]	anfangs, ursprünglich
union ['ju:njən]	Vereinigung, Zusammenschluss
to abolish [əb'ɒlɪʃ]	abschaffen
civilian [sɪ'vɪliən]	Zivilist(in)
amendment [ə'mendmənt]	Zusatz(klausel)
prohibition [prə'hɪbɪtʃn]	Verbot
citizenship ['sɪtɪznʃɪp]	Staatsbürgerschaft
right to vote	Wahlrecht
railway ['reɪlweɪ] *BE*	Eisenbahn
relocation	Umzug, Wohnortwechsel
internal trade	Binnenhandel *(innerhalb eines Staates)*
to expand	zunehmen
abuse [ə'bju:s]	Missbrauch
to avoid [ə'vɔɪd]	vermeiden
to secure [sɪ'kjʊə]	sichern
eventual [ɪ'ventʃuəl]	später, letztendlich
world war	Weltkrieg
▸ World War I	der Erste Weltkrieg
▸ World War II	der Zweite Weltkrieg
to remain [rɪ'meɪn]	bleiben
neutral ['nju:trl]	neutral
outbreak	Ausbruch
to beat [bi:t], beat [bi:t], beaten [bi:tən]	schlagen, besiegen
the Central Powers	Mittelmächte
to defeat [dɪ'fi:t]	besiegen, schlagen
armistice ['ɑ:mɪstɪs]	Waffenstillstand
women's rights movement	Frauenrechtsbewegung
to stand for sth	sich um ein Amt bewerben
electoral office	Wahlamt

mavbh8d

The United States was again neutral at the beginning of World War II. While Germany conquered much of continental Europe, the United States began supplying material to the Allies in March 1941. On December 7, 1941, Japan launched a surprise attack on Pearl Harbor, making the United States join the Allies. During the war, the United States helped Great Britain, the Soviet Union and China, and together they planned the postwar world. The United States lost more than 400,000 soldiers, but it was relatively undamaged and had even greater economic and military influence than before.

After World War II the United States and the Soviet Union shared power during what is known as the Cold War. The US experienced both constant economic growth and also a rapid growth of its population. In 1959 Hawaii became the 50th and last state of the USA.

From the civil rights movement up to today

A growing civil rights movement, led by Martin Luther King, used non-violence to abolish segregation and discrimination. The first step in bringing an end to racial discrimination came after a number of court decisions and new laws, which resulted in the Civil Rights Act of 1964.

The internet spread from the military to international academic networks and then on to the public in the 1990s and made a huge impact on the global economy, society and also culture. On September 11th 2001 Al-Qaeda terrorists crashed planes into both towers of the World Trade Center in New York City and also the Pentagon near Washington, D.C., killing nearly 3,000 people. In response, the United States launched the War on Terror, which included the war in Afghanistan and the Iraq War from 2003 until 2011.

Barack Obama, the first African American and multiracial president of the United States of America, was elected in 2008. He served as president for eight years. He couldn't be re-elected after these eight years.

to conquer ['kɒŋkə]	erobern, unterwerfen
continental ['kɒntɪnəntl]	kontinental
to supply sth to sb	jdn. mit etw. versorgen
material [mə'tɪəriəl]	Material; Ausrüstung
the Allies ['ælaɪz]	die alliierten Streitkräfte, die Alliierten
to launch [lɔːnʃ]	starten
surprise attack	Überraschungsangriff
postwar	nach dem Krieg, Nachkriegs-
soldier	Soldat(in)
relatively ['relətɪvli]	verhältnismäßig, relativ
undamaged	unbeschädigt, unversehrt
influence ['ɪnfluəns]	Einfluss

---

to share [ʃeə]	teilen
the Cold War	der Kalte Krieg
to experience sth	etw. erleben, erfahren
constant	stetig, ständig
growth [grəʊθ]	Wachstum

---

civil rights movement	Bürgerrechtsbewegung
non-violence	Gewaltlosigkeit
segregation	*hier:* Rassentrennung
discrimination	Diskriminierung
racial ['reɪʃl]	aufgrund der Rasse
court	Gericht
decision [dɪ'sɪʒən]	Entscheidung
to result in sth	zu etw. führen, zur Folge haben

---

to spread [spred], spread [spred], spread [spred]	sich verbreiten
academic [ˌækə'demɪk]	wissenschaftlich, akademisch
network ['netwɜːk]	Computernetzwerk; Netzwerk
the public	die Öffentlichkeit
impact	Auswirkung
global ['gləʊbl]	weltweit, global
terrorist	Terrorist(in)
the Pentagon ['pentəgɒn]	das Pentagon
in response	als Antwort

African American [ˌə'merɪkən]	Afro-Amerikaner(in)
multiracial	multiethnisch
to elect [ɪ'lekt]	wählen
to serve	dienen
to re-elect	wiederwählen

mavbh8d

Government and politics

The United States is the world's oldest **surviving federation**. It is a **constitutional republic** and **representative democracy**. There are three **levels** of **government**: **federal**, **state** and **local**.

The federal government is made up of the **legislative**, **executive** and **judicial branch**. Their **power** comes from **Congress**, the President and the federal **courts**. Congress is the **House of Representatives** and **the Senate**. The House of Representatives has 435 **voting** members, who each **represent** a **congressional district** for a two-year **term**.

The **seats** in the house are **divided up** every ten years **among** the states **according to** their population. The Senate has 100 members with each state having two senators, elected for six-year terms. The President serves a four-year term and cannot be elected more than twice. The **Supreme Court**, led by the Chief Justice of the United States, has nine members, who serve **for life**.

The **structure** and **responsibilities** of the federal government and its **relationship** with the **individual** states are written in the original text of the Constitution of the United States. It has been **amended** 27 times. All the laws are **subject to judicial review**.

The United States is a federal republic of 50 states, a federal district, five territories and eleven **uninhabited** island **possessions**. The states and territories are the main **administrative districts**. They are divided into counties and independent cities. The District of Columbia is a federal district which **contains** the **capital** of the United States, Washington DC. The representatives of the 50 states and the District of Columbia elect the President of the United States. »»

to survive [sə'vaɪv]	überleben
federation	Staatenbund
constitutional republic [ˌkɒnstɪ'tju:ʃnl]	konstitutionelle Republik *(an eine Verfassung gebunden)*
representative democracy [ˌreprɪ'zentətɪv]	repräsentative Demokratie *(Parlamentsmitglieder vetreten das Volk)*
level	Ebene
government ['gʌvnmənt]	Regierung
federal ['fedərəl]	auf Bundesebene
state	auf Bundeslandebene
local ['ləʊkəl]	auf lokaler Ebene
legislative branch ['ledʒɪslətɪv]	gesetzgebender Zweig, Legislative
executive branch [ɪg'zekjətɪv]	ausführender Zweig, Exekutive
judicial branch [dʒu:'dɪʃl]	rechtsprechender Zweig, Judikative
power	Macht
Congress	*(amerikanischer)* Kongress
court [kɔ:t]	Gericht
the House of Representatives	Abgeordnetenhaus in den USA
the Senate	der Senat
voting	stimmberechtigt
to represent [ˌreprɪ'zent]	politisch vertreten, repräsentieren
congressional district	Bundeswahlkreis
term	*hier:* Legislaturperiode
seat [si:t]	Sitz *(im Parlament)*
to divide up [dɪ'vaɪd]	teilen, aufteilen
among [ə'mʌŋ]	unter, zwischen
according to [ə'kɔ:dɪŋtʊ]	entsprechend, gemäß
the Supreme Court	Oberstes Bundesgericht
for life	auf Lebenszeit, lebenslänglich
structure ['strʌktʃə]	Struktur, Aufbau
responsibility	Verantwortung
relationship [rɪ'leɪʃənʃɪp]	Beziehung, Verhältnis
individual	einzeln
to amend sth	*hier:* etw. ergänzen
subject to	unterliegen
judicial review	richterliche Nachprüfung
uninhabited	unbewohnt
possession [pə'zeʃn]	Besitz, Landbesitz
administrative district	Verwaltungsbezirk
to contain [kən'teɪn]	enthalten
capital ['kæpɪtl]	Hauptstadt

mavbh8d

The state governments are all **structured** in the same way. The **governor** (**chief executive**) of each state is elected directly by the people. Some **state judges** and **cabinet officers** are **appointed** by the governors of the **respective** states, while others are elected by the people.
The local government's **duties** are commonly **split** between **county** and **municipal** governments. If you ever get a **speeding ticket**, you will have to pay the **fine** or **appear** in a **court** which is run by the local government.

Culture

There are many cultures and a wide variety of **ethnic groups**, **traditions** and **values** in the United States. Apart from the Native American, Native Hawaiian and Native Alaskan populations, nearly all Americans and their **ancestors** **immigrated** to America within the past five centuries.

Mainstream American culture is a Western culture largely based on the traditions of European immigrants with **influences** from other **sources**. More **recent** immigration from Asia and Latin America has added to the cultural mix that has been described as both a **melting pot** and a **salad bowl**. Immigrants and their **descendants** keep their own cultural **characteristics** at the same time as taking on cultural characteristics from their American neighbours.

The American Dream, or the idea that Americans enjoy a high **standard of living**, helps to **attract** immigrants. While most people believe that the United States is a **classless society**, others **identify** clear differences between the country's **social classes**, which **affect socialization**, language and values. While Americans try to be **high-achievers**, being **ordinary** or **average** is **generally** seen as a positive thing.

to structure ['strʌktʃə]	aufbauen
governor ['gʌvənə]	Gouverneur(in) *(entspricht Ministerpräsidentenamt)*
chief executive [ˌtʃi:f ɪg'zekjətɪv]	Regierungschef(in)
state judge	Staatsrichter(in)
cabinet officer	Regierungsmitglied
to appoint sb	jdn. ernennen, jdn. in ein Amt berufen
respective	jeweilig

duty ['dju:ti]	Pflicht, Aufgabe
to split [splɪt], split [splɪt], split [splɪt]	aufteilen, teilen
county	Landkreis
municipal [mju:ˌnɪsɪpl]	städtisch, Stadt-
speeding ticket	Strafzettel wegen Geschwindigkeitsüberschreitung
fine	Geldstrafe
to appear [ə'pɪə]	erscheinen
court	Gericht

ethnic group	Bevölkerungsgruppe
tradition [trə'dɪʃn]	Tradition
values	Werte (moralisch)
ancestor ['ænsestə]	Vorfahre, Vorfahrin
to immigrate	einwandern

mainstream	gängig, allgemein akzeptiert
influence ['ɪnflʊəns]	Einfluss
source [sɔ:s]	Quelle, Ursprung
recent	neueste*(r, s)*, jüngste*(r, s)*
melting pot	Schmelztiegel
salad bowl	Salatschüssel
descendant [dɪ'sendənt]	Nachkomme
characteristic [ˌkærəktə'rɪstɪk]	Merkmal, Kennzeichen

standard of living	Lebensstandard
to attract	anziehen, anlocken
classless society	klassenlose Gesellschaft
to identify [aɪ'dentɪfaɪ]	identifizieren, wahrnehmen
social class	gesellschaftliche Schicht
to affect	betreffen
socialization	Sozialisierung
high-achiever	Leistungsträger(in)
ordinary	gewöhnlich, normal
average ['ævrɪdʒ]	im Durchschnitt
generally	allgemein, üblicherweise

mavbh8d

Music

The **rhythmic** and **lyrical** styles of African American music influenced American music. The blues and old-time music were **adopted** and were popular with global **audiences**. Jazz was developed by musicians such as Louis Armstrong and Duke Ellington in the early 20th century, country music developed in the 1920s and rhythm and blues followed in the 1940s.

Elvis Presley and Chuck Berry are the names **connected with** rock and roll in the mid-50s. In the 1960s, Bob Dylan became one of America's most famous **songwriters** and James Brown developed funk music. More recent American music **directions include** hip-hop and house music. American pop stars such as Elvis Presley, Michael Jackson and Madonna have become **celebrities** around the world. The same can be said for Taylor Swift, Katy Perry, Beyoncé as well as hip hop artists Jay Z, Eminem and Kanye West. Rock bands such as Metallica, the Eagles and Aerosmith are **among** the bands who have sold the most **records** in the world.

Cinema

Hollywood, a northern **district** of Los Angeles in California, is one of the leaders of the film (or movie) industry. In 1895 the first **commercial screening** of a **projected** film was in New York and the United States led the **development** of sound in films in the following **decades**. Since the early 20th century, the U.S. film industry has been **based in** and around Hollywood.

America's top filmmaker, David Llewelyn Wark Griffith, was important for the development of people speaking in films during the **silent film period**. Walt Disney lead the way for both **animated films** and movie **merchandising**. The film industry enjoyed its best time during the 'Golden Age of Hollywood', until the early 1960s, with **actors** such as John Wayne and Marilyn Monroe becoming famous. In the 1970s, film **directors** such as Martin Scorsese, Francis Ford Coppola and Robert Altman were the new names in the 'New Hollywood'. Directors such as Steven Spielberg, George Lucas and James Cameron have become famous for their **blockbuster** films which are often **characterized** by high **production costs**, and earning lots of money at the **box office**.

The **Academy Awards**, also known as the Oscars, have been held **annually** by the Academy of Motion Picture Arts and Sciences since 1929, and the **Golden Globe Awards** have been held annually since January 1944.

Sports

American football

American football is the most popular **spectator** sport in the United States. The National Football **League** (NFL) has the highest **average attendance** of spectators of any sports league in the world, and the **Super Bowl** is watched by more than a hundred million people on television.

rhythmic ['rɪðmɪk]	rhythmisch
▸ rhythm [rɪðm]	Rhythmus, Takt
lyrical	lyrisch
to adopt	übernehmen, annehmen
audience ['ɔːdɪəns]	Publikum, (die) Zuschauer
to connect with	verbinden mit
songwriter	Liedtexter(in)
direction	Richtung
to include	einschließen, umfassen
celebrity [sə'lebrəti]	berühmte Persönlichkeit, gefeierter Star
among [ə'mʌŋ]	unter, zwischen
record ['rekɔːd]	Schallplatte
district	Stadtteil
commercial	kommerziell, gewerblich
screening	Filmvorführung
to project	projezieren
development	Entwicklung
decade ['dekeɪd]	Jahrzehnt
to be based in	ansässig sein in
silent film	Stummfilm
period ['pɪəriəd]	Zeitraum
animated film	Zeichentrickfilm
merchandising	Vermarktung
actor, actress	Schauspieler(in)
director	Regisseur(in)
blockbuster	Kino-Kassenschlager
characterized ['kærəktəraɪzd]	geprägt, gekennzeichnet
production costs	Drehkosten, Herstellungskosten
box office	Kinokasse
Academy Award *(Oscar)*	Oscar *(Filmpreis)*
annually ['ænjuəli]	jährlich
Golden Globe Award	Golden Globe *(Film- und Fernsehpreis)*
spectator	Zuschauer(in)
league [liːg]	Liga, Spielklasse
average ['ævərɪdʒ] **attendance** [ə'tendəns]	Durchschnitts-Zuschauerzahl; Teilnahme
Super Bowl	Super Bowl *(Finalspiel der NFL)*

mavbh8d

It is a sport played by two teams of eleven players on a field that is 120 yards long and 53 1/3 yards wide and has goalposts at each end. Goals are scored by getting the oval shaped ball into the other team's end zone for a touchdown (6 points) or by kicking it through the opponent's goalposts for a try after a touchdown (1 point) or a field goal (3 points).

Baseball

Baseball has been thought of as the national sport in America since the late 19th century. Major League Baseball (MLB) is the top league. It is a game played with a bat and a ball by two teams of nine players. Each team takes it in turns to bat the ball and catch the ball in the field. A point is scored when the batting team scores a run by hitting the ball, then running around the three bases and returning to the home plate where the player started. If the ball goes in the wrong direction, is caught in the air or passed to the baseman (player guarding the base) the runner is about to reach, then there is no point and the runner is out. There is no time limit for a game of baseball. It usually finishes after the ninth inning.

Basketball and ice hockey

Basketball and ice hockey are America's next two leading professional team sports. The top leagues are the National Basketball Association (NBA) and the National Hockey League (NHL). These four leading sports are each played in a season at different but overlapping time of the year.

My roundtrip of the USA

New York City (New York)

- Last year my parents and I went on a roundtrip of the USA. We started on the east coast in The Big Apple. We first took a sightseeing bus tour so we could get an overview of the city. We decided it would be the first thing we did in every city on our journey. After touring the main sights and the five boroughs of NYC, it was hard to choose which places to visit, but our time was short. First we went on a ferry to Liberty Island to take a closer look at the Statue of Liberty. She didn't look very big from Manhattan, but up close it was different. With her torch in her right hand and holding a tablet of stone with the date of the Declaration of Independence in her left, Lady Liberty stands 93 metres high from the ground to the top of her torch. ›››

goalpost	Torpfosten
oval ['əʊvl]	oval, eiförmig
end zone	Endzone
touchdown	Touchdown
to kick [kɪk]	schießen
opponent [ə'pəʊnənt]	Gegner(in), Gegenspieler(in)

---

baseball	Baseball
bat	Schläger
point [pɔɪnt]	Punkt
to score	erzielen
base [beɪs]	Base, Laufmal
home plate	Schlagmal
baseman	Spieler an einem Laufmal
to guard [gɑ:d]	bewachen
runner	Läufer(in)
time limit	Zeitlimit, zeitliche Begrenzung
inning	Inning, Durchgang

---

professional [prə'feʃnl]	professionell, Profi-
season	Saison
overlapping	überschneidend

---

roundtrip	Rundreise
sightseeing	Besichtigung von Sehenswürdigkeiten
bus tour	Busreise
overview	Überblick
to decide [dɪ'saɪd]	(sich) entscheiden
journey	Reise
sights [saɪts]	Sehenswürdigkeiten
ferry	Fähre
torch	Fackel
tablet of stone	Steintafel
ground	Boden

mavbh8d

- To the immigrants arriving in New York over 100 years ago, she was the symbol of hope and peace. She was a present from the people of France in 1886, and she is made of copper which has oxidised over the years and turned green. We walked up the steps inside the statue (I lost count how many) and looked out of the tiny windows in her crown at the Manhattan skyline. Unfortunately, you can't go up the torch any more.
- We then took a ferry to Ellis Island to have a look at the Museum of Immigration and look in the passenger lists to see if we could find any of our ancestors. We don't know anyone in America, so (not really) surprisingly we didn't find anyone we knew. Ellis Island was the gateway to America for over 12 million immigrants and the inspection station from 1892 to 1954. Boats landed here from all over the world and the passengers had to go through health checks before they were allowed into America. If they didn't pass these checks, they were sent back on the next boat. The building has been a museum since 1990 and I thought it was really interesting.
- When in New York City, you have to visit the 102 story skyscraper in Midtown Manhattan on Fifth Avenue between 33rd and 34th Street. Of course, I mean the Empire State Building. It is a total of 443 metres high, including the spire on top. We speeded to the top in a lift, or elevator as the Americans say, although there are races up the stairs, we decided we had done enough stair climbing. There was an amazing view from the observation deck at the top and we could pick out some of the sights we had visited on the bus tour.
- Our last stop of the day, now it was dark, was Times Square. It is in the middle of the Broadway Theatre District and it was full of people. It attracts about 50 million visitors a year to see its bright billboards and advertisements. It felt like all those visitors were there the same day as we were.

symbol	Symbol
hope	Hoffnung
peace	Frieden
present	Geschenk
people	das Volk
copper	Kupfer
to oxidise	oxidieren
statue	Statue
tiny ['taɪni]	sehr klein, winzig
crown [kraʊn]	Krone
skyline	Skyline
unfortunately [ʌn'fɔːtʃənətli]	leider, unglücklicherweise

passenger list ['pæsndʒə ˌlɪst]	Passagierliste
ancestor ['ænsestə]	Vorfahre, Vorfahrin
gateway	Eingang, Tor
inspection station	Kontrollstation
to land	landen
health check	Gesundheitscheck
to allow sb into sth	jdm. Einlass zu etw. gewähren
to pass	bestehen

skyscraper [skaɪ'skreɪpə]	Wolkenkratzer
spire	Spitze
to speed	schnell fahren, sausen
observation deck [ˌɒbzə'veɪʃən dek]	Aussichtsplattform
to pick out	ausmachen, entdecken

stop	Halt
to attract	anziehen
visitor	Besucher(in)
bright [braɪt]	leuchtend, hell
billboard	Reklametafel
advertisement [əd'vɜːtɪsmənt]	Anzeige, Werbung

mavbh8d

Philadelphia (Pennsylvania)

- Our next stop on the way down the coast was Philadelphia. This is an important place in American history. Again we took a bus tour, but we already knew we were going to get off the bus at the National Historical Park. We wanted to visit Independence Hall, which was formerly known as the Pennsylvania State House. It is where both the Declaration of Independence and the United States Constitution were debated and adopted. The Liberty Bell, which is now on the other side of the park, originally hung in the steeple of this building.
- We crossed the park on leaving Independence Hall to go to the Liberty Bell Centre. We wanted to see the Liberty Bell which had been made in a foundry in London and cracked the first time it was rung. We got close enough to see the words that were cast in it: "Proclaim LIBERTY throughout all the land unto all the inhabitants thereof." The bell was used to call lawyers to legislative sessions and other citizens to public meetings in the Pennsylvania State House.

Washington DC

- You can't visit the east coast of the US without making a stop at Washington. There were so many historical things to see there. We went past the Jefferson Memorial on our tour bus. We could see the statue of Thomas Jefferson, the third president of America (from 1801 to 1809), standing in the middle of the memorial. It was erected in his honour as he was one of the Founding Fathers of America and the drafter and writer of the Declaration of Independence. We then saw the memorial of the 16th president of the United States (from 1861 until his assassination in 1865), Abraham Lincoln. He was sitting on a huge stone chair.
- This memorial was where Martin Luther King made his very famous 'I have a dream' speech in August 1963 at the end of the 'March on Washington for Jobs and Freedom'. We got off the bus here to walk through the park to get to the Washington Monument. This is an awesome tower that looks like a needle. It has no windows, apart from a few at the very top. After taking the lift, we had a view in all directions across Washington. »»

coast [kəʊst]	Küste
formerly	ehemals
to debate	verhandeln, diskutieren
to adopt	verabschieden
Liberty Bell	Freiheitsglocke
to hang [hæŋ], hung [hʌŋ], hung [hʌŋ]	hängen
steeple [sti:pl]	Turm
to cross	überqueren
foundry [faʊndri]	Gießerei
to crack	eine Sprung bekommen
to proclaim	ausrufen, verkünden
lawyer	Rechtsanwalt, Rechtsanwältin
legislative session	gesetzgebende Sitzung
citizen	Bürger(in), Staatsbürger(in)
public meeting	öffentliche Versammlung
historical	geschichtlich, historisch, Geschichts-
memorial	Denkmal, Gedenkstätte
to erect	errichten
in sb's honour	jdm. zu Ehren
the Founding Fathers	Gründungsväter
drafter	Verfasser(in)
writer	Schreiber(in)
assassination [əˌsæsɪ'neɪʃn]	Attentat
stone	Stein
speech	Rede
march	Marsch, Demonstration
freedom	Freiheit
monument ['mɒnjəmənt]	Denkmal, Monument
needle	Nadel
direction	Richtung

mavbh8d

- We had tickets for a tour of the White House which we had booked before we arrived in Washington. We had to be at the gates at 3 o'clock otherwise we couldn't go in. We just made it. We went on a self-guided tour and were lucky enough to see the Oval Office, that we only knew from TV, as well as the banqueting hall and other important rooms. The President wasn't home but there were still lots of security guards.
- As we had learnt so much about the history of America and the sun was shining, we went to the Smithsonian National Zoological Park on our last day in Washington. We saw giant pandas, Asian elephants, gorillas, tigers and cheetahs and had a lovely picnic. What amazed me most, we visited all these different places and we didn't have to pay a single dollar in admission, I couldn't believe it.
- To save some time, although I would have been happy to carry on driving, we handed in our rental car at the airport and took an internal flight to Orlando in Florida.

Orlando (Florida)

- The next days were relaxation pure. We went to see Mickey Mouse and all his friends in Walt Disney World, we looked at Cape Canaveral from where America sent its space shuttles into space. They didn't land here though. It was in the middle of nowhere next to the ocean, which I suppose makes sense as they didn't want anyone living close, in case anything went wrong. We then drove past Fort Lauderdale, where we saw lots of huge cruise ships waiting to sail to the Caribbean. Before we took the Overseas Highway that runs through the Florida Keys from Key Largo to Key West, we went on an airboat tour of the Everglades. This is a huge region of tropical wetlands where there are lots of rare species. We saw too many crocodiles for my liking.

ticket	Eintrittskarte; Fahrkarte
to book	buchen
gate	Tor
otherwise	sonst, andernfalls
self-guided	ohne Führung, auf eigene Faust
banqueting hall ['bæŋkwɪtɪŋ ˌhɔːl]	Festhalle
security guard	Sicherheitsdienst

panda	Panda
gorilla	Gorilla
cheetah	Gepard
dollar ($)	Dollar
admission	Eintritt

rental car	Mietauto, Leihwagen
internal flight	Inlandsflug

relaxation [ˌriːlæk'seɪʃən]	Entspannung
space shuttle	Raumfähre
space	Weltraum
nowhere	nirgendwo, nirgends
ocean ['əʊʃən]	Ozean, Weltmeer
to make sense	Sinn machen, sinnvoll sein
in case	falls
cruise ship	Kreuzfahrtschiff
Overseas Highway	Straße in Florida, die teilweise über das Meer führt
airboat	*(propellergetriebenes)* Sumpfboot
region ['riːdʒən]	Region, Gebiet
tropical wetland	tropisches Sumpfgebiet
crocodile ['krɒkədaɪl]	Krokodil
for one's liking	für jds. Geschmack

mavbh8d

New Orleans (Louisiana)

- Our next stop was New Orleans, that took a bit of driving from Florida, and the landscape we saw from the highway wasn't very exciting either. We had been told the place to go to was the French Quarter. It is the oldest neighbourhood in New Orleans with buildings that date from before 1803. Since the 1920s the buildings there have been protected and therefore must not be demolished. Everything was so colourful, the buildings were painted in pastel colours and the ironwork balconies were, too. The historic park in the French Quarter is Jackson Square. It is the place where in 1803, Louisiana was made US territory. Next to Jackson Square we were drawn to St. Louis Cathedral. It is one of the oldest cathedrals in the United States. It is a very powerful looking white building with black tiles on its towers. There were a lot of nice things to just look at and absorb in New Orleans.
- Next, our itinerary took us to the west coast. We decided we would start at the top of the map again and work our way down. We took a red-eye flight to Seattle from New Orleans so we could all sleep in the plane and start sightseeing on arrival.

Seattle (Washington)

- As we flew over Seattle, while coming into land, we saw its most famous sight, The Space Needle. We were fit for sightseeing after our sleep on the plane and hopped on a bus tour of Seattle. Then we headed to the observation tower of the Space Needle to see Seattle from above. It is 184 metres high and only took us 41 seconds in the lift; it has an observation deck and a rotating restaurant. We headed for the restaurant and enjoyed the views of the Seattle skyline, Elliot Bay and the surrounding islands, Mount Rainer and the Cascade Mountains while eating our lunch.
- Our next stop in Seattle was Pike Place Market. It is a public market overlooking Elliot Bay and was opened in 1907. It is one of the oldest farmers' markets in the US and is also where the first Starbucks opened its doors to the public. It is Seattle's most popular tourist destination, and apart from the market it includes family owned restaurants and shops. I found a very good comic book shop.

landscape	Landschaft
neighbourhood ['neɪbəhʊd]	Nachbarschaft
to protect	schützen, beschützen
to demolish	zerstören; beschädigen
colourful	bunt, farbig
to paint	(an)streichen
pastel colour	Pastellfarbe
ironwork ['aɪənwɜːk]	schmiedeeiserner Gegenstand
balcony	Balkon
historic	historisch
cathedral	Kathedrale, Dom
tile [taɪl]	Fliese
tower	Turm
to absorb	aufnehmen

itinerary [aɪ'tɪnərərɪ]	Reiseplan
red-eye flight = night flight	Nachtflug
arrival	Ankunft

---

coming into land	im Landeflug
to head	gehen
observation tower	Aussichtsturm
from above	von oben
to rotate	rotieren, sich drehen
surrounding	umliegend

overlooking	mit Blick auf
farmers' market	Bauernmarkt
destination [ˌdestɪ'neɪʃn]	Reiseziel

mavbh8d

San Francisco (California)

- I was most excited about our next destination. There were so many things I wanted to see in San Francisco. I didn't know what to choose first and if we would have time for everything. I wanted to drive over the world-famous Golden Gate Bridge linking San Francisco with Marin County. It is a 1,200-metre-long suspension bridge, and I had read that it is painted orange (no, it isn't rusty) so that pilots can see it when they are flying into San Francisco. There is a team of painters who are employed permanently to make sure it stays orange. They can't be scared of heights for this painting job, as they do it up to 220 feet above the sea. They always have to be harnessed to the bridge while working.
- One of the other things I knew about San Francisco is the cable cars. They are fantastic. We took one to Fisherman's Wharf. This is one of the busiest and well-known tourist attractions in San Francisco. It gets its name from the mid to late 1800s when Italian immigrant fishermen came to the city to take advantage of the increased population due to the gold rush. There are restaurants here, museums (including a waxwork museum) and also the San Francisco Maritime National Historical Park, so we were kept very busy.
- The next day we took a ferry from Pier 33, near Fisherman's Wharf, to Alcatraz Island. Most people know it from the film 'Escape from Alcatraz', which tells you that on this island there used to be a prison. There is also the oldest operating lighthouse on the island as well as lots of rock pools and a massive seabird colony. After spending the day outside, we decided that a visit to Chinatown for dinner was a good idea. It is the oldest Chinatown in North America and the largest Chinese community outside of Asia. There aren't just restaurants there but places of worship, hospitals, parks, and also you can really feel the Chinese culture and hear the language spoken all around you.
- We wanted to see if we could make our fortune so the next place on our trip was Las Vegas. To get there, we drove through Yosemite National Park, please check out how to say this before visiting otherwise it could be embarrassing. After travelling through Yosemite, in the Sierra Nevada Mountains with its ancient sequoias (trees) and granite cliffs, we headed for Death Valley. This is the lowest, driest and hottest area in North America. Its lowest point is 86 metres below sea-level and it holds the record for the highest recorded air temperature – 56,7 °C on 10th July, 1913. We had plenty to drink with us and fortunately our car made it through the desert without breaking down.

world-famous	weltberühmt
to link [lɪŋk]	verbinden
suspension bridge	Hängebrücke
rusty	rostig
pilot	Pilot(in)
employed [ɪm'plɔɪd]	beschäftigt, angestellt
permanently	dauerhaft, fest
to be scared of sth	vor etw. Angst haben
height	Höhe
to harness	befestigen

cable car	*hier:* seilgetriebene Straßenbahn
fisherman	Fischer
advantage	Vorteil
due to ['djuˌtuː]	wegen, aufgrund von
gold rush	Goldrausch
museum	Museum
waxwork	Wachsfigur
maritime	See-, Meeres-

prison	Gefängnis
to operate	in Betrieb sein
lighthouse	Leuchtturm
rock pool	Felsenbecken, Tümpel
massive	riesengroß
seabird	Meeresvogel
colony	Kolonie
community	Gemeinschaft, Gemeinde
outside	außerhalb
worship	Gottesdienst

to make a fortune	ein Vermögen machen
Yosemite [ˌjə'seməti]	Yosemite
embarrassing	peinlich, unangenehm
ancient ['eɪntʃənt]	sehr alt, uralt
sequoia [sɪ'kwɔɪə]	Mammutbaum
granite	Granit
cliff	Felsen
below	unter
sea-level	Meeresspiegel
record ['rekɔːd]	Rekord
▸ to record [rɪ'kɔːd]	aufzeichnen, aunehmen
air temperature	Lufttemperatur
plenty	viel, eine große Menge
to break down, broke down [ˌbrəʊk 'daʊn], broken down [ˌbrəʊkn 'daʊn]	eine Panne haben

mavbh8d

Las Vegas (Nevada)

- What I found strange about Las Vegas is that it is a city in the middle of the Mojave Desert. Whoever thought of building a city here, where there is little water, no electricity or other necessities, had a good imagination. I quickly forgot these thoughts as we drove past the hotels and casinos of the Las Vegas Strip. We heard that there are also museums and Arts Centres in Las Vegas, but we just wanted to experience a show and watch people lose their money in the casinos.
- We wanted to see the Grand Canyon too, so we went on a helicopter trip from Las Vegas and flew over the Grand Canyon. I think this is the best way to see it just to get a feeling of its size. We saw the glass-bottomed horseshoe-shaped observation platform built on Native American land, and we were made speechless by the breathtaking views and the red of the stone cliffs. We all took lots of amazing photos.

Los Angeles (California)

- The last city on the west coast of our tour was of course, Los Angeles. We saw the huge white letters spelling the word Hollywood set in the Hollywood hills. I had seen it in so many films, but it was amazing to actually see it in real life. We walked down the Hollywood Walk of Fame, finding the pink stars of our heroes and heroines from both film and music. We looked in the shop windows on Rodeo Drive, even though we knew we couldn't afford anything, but it was great fun. We then went to Universal Studios, the big movie-themed amusement park. We visited the wizarding world of Harry Potter, we went behind the scenes at a real working movie studio and we went on some incredible rides.

strange [streɪndʒ]	seltsam, eigenartig
electricity [ˌelɪk'trɪsəti]	Elektrizität, Strom
necessities	das Lebensnotwendige, das (zum Leben) Allernotwendigste
imagination [ɪˌmædʒɪ'neɪʃən]	Vorstellungskraft, Fantasie
casino	Kasino, Spielbank
strip *AE*	Geschäftsstraße
to experience [ɪk'spɪəriəns]	erfahren, erleben
show	Show, Aufführung

helicopter	Hubschrauber
feeling	Gefühl
size	Größe
glass-bottomed	mit Glasboden
horseshoe-shaped	hufeisenförmig
speechless	sprachlos
breathtaking ['breθˌteɪkɪŋ]	atemberaubend
view	Aussicht, Blick

---

spelling	Buchstabieren; Rechtschreibung
real life	das wirkliche Leben
hero ['hɪərəʊ]	Held
heroine ['herəʊɪn]	Heldin
to afford [ə'fɔ:d]	sich leisten
movie-themed	mit Filmthemen
amusement park	Vergnügungspark, Freizeitpark
wizarding world	Zauberwelt
behind the scenes	hinter den Kulissen
real	echt
working	arbeitend
incredible [ɪn'kredɪbl]	unglaublich, sagenhaft
ride	Fahrgeschäft

mavbh8d

Route 66

- All that was left to do after Los Angeles was to get to Chicago for our flight home. Naturally we chose to use Route 66. We started in Los Angeles in California and travelled through Flagstaff in Arizona, Albuquerque and Santé Fe in New Mexico, Amarillo in Texas, Oklahoma City and Tulsa in Oklahoma; we sneaked through Kansas on our way to St. Louis in Missouri and finally Springfield and Chicago in Illinois. Nowadays Route 66 is just a picturesque highway taking you past these cities and the many towns along it. Before it was almost entirely replaced by a modern highway system, it used to guide lots of tourists through these places providing them with lots of people who spent their money there. True fans still stop off at these places to see them and get a true Route 66 feeling.
- In Chicago we only had time for the sightseeing bus tour and then it was time to leave the US and take with us all the memories and knowledge we had gathered over the weeks of our roundtrip. It was definitely the holiday of a lifetime that none of us will ever forget.

Canada

Geography

Canada is a **sovereign state** in the northern part of North America. It **stretches** from the Atlantic Ocean in the east to the Pacific Ocean in the west, and the Arctic Ocean **lies to the north**. On a map you can see Canada's ten **provinces** in a line in the south and its three territories in a line above the provinces in the north. Canada is the second largest country in the world (after Russia). Canada's **border** with the United States is the world's longest land border.

The capital of Canada is Ottawa, the largest city is Toronto, which is further south. English and French are the official languages of Canada. The **currency** is the Canadian dollar. The inhabitants of Canada are a good **mix of nations**. People from England, France, Scotland, Ireland and Germany make up 75% of the **population**.

Canada has a population of over 36 million, about 80% of it live near the southern border. Canada is **sparsely populated** as most of the country is **covered with** forest, **tundra** and the Rocky Mountains. The south is warmer in the summer months, but **on the whole** Canada has a cold or very cold climate.

The best-known symbol of Canada is the **maple leaf**, which can be seen on the **national flag**. Another symbol of Canada is the **beaver**, which is on the five cent **coin**, the '**nickel**'.

to sneak	schleichen
nowadays	heutzutage
picturesque	malerisch
highway *AE*	Autobahn, Schnellstraße
entirely [ɪn'taɪəli]	ganz und gar, völlig
to replace sth	etw. ersetzen
to guide	führen
to provide sth for sb	jdn. mit etw. versorgen
to stop off	anhalten, Pause machen
memory	Erinnerung
to gather	sammeln
definitely ['defɪnətli]	bestimmt, sicher
lifetime	Leben
none	keine
sovereign state ['sɒvrɪn ˌsteɪt]	unabhängiger Staat
to stretch	sich erstecken, reichen
to lie to the north *(east/south/west)*	im Norden liegen *(Osten/Süden/ Westen)*
province	Provinz
border	Staatsgrenze
currency ['kʌrənsi]	Währung
mix of nations	Mischung verschiedener Nationalitäten
population	Bevölkerung
sparsely	dünn, spärlich
populated	besiedelt, bewohnt
to cover with	bedecken
tundra	Tundra, Kältesteppe
on the whole	insgesamt, im Großen und Ganzen
maple leaf	Ahornblatt
national flag	Nationalflagge
beaver	Bieber
coin [kɔɪn]	Münze, Geldstück
nickel	Nickel *(5-Cent-Stück)*

mavbh8d

History

Canada has been inhabited by various native peoples over the centuries. At the beginning of the 16th century, British and French colonies were **founded** on the Atlantic coast. By the end of the 18th century Canada, **geographically** as it **exists** today, was **in the hands of** the British. In 1931, Canada was given its independence from the United Kingdom, and it **received full sovereignty** in 1982 when the last **remaining ties** of **legal dependence** on the British parliament were **removed**. Canada is a federal **parliamentary** democracy and also a **constitutional monarchy**. Queen Elizabeth II is the **head of state**.

Sport

Ice hockey and **lacrosse** are Canada's official national sports. Most of the larger **metropolitan areas** have **franchises** in the National Hockey League (NHL). Other teams play in American leagues, too. Canada is a very sporting nation, and has **participated in** every Olympic Games since 1900. **Popular** spectator sports in Canada include **curling** and Canadian football, which **is similar to** American football.

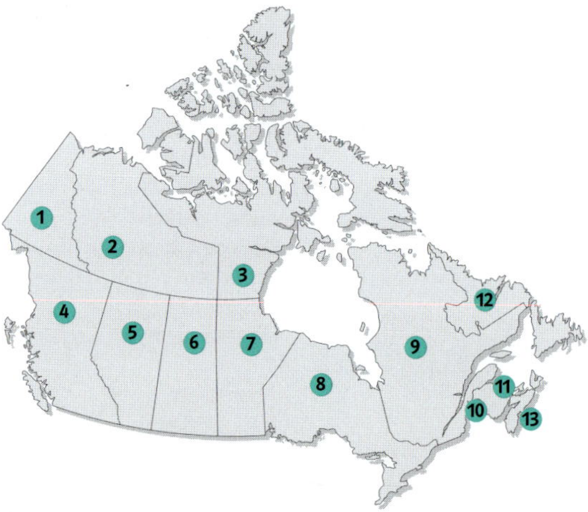

1. Yukon
2. Northwest Territories
3. Nunavut
4. British Columbia
5. Alberta
6. Saskatchewan
7. Manitoba
8. Ontario
9. Quebec
10. New Brunswick
11. Prince Edward Island
12. Newfoundland and Labrador
13. Nova Scotia

to found	gründen
geographically	geographisch
to exist [ɪg'zɪst]	existieren
in the hands of	unter der Herrschaft von, in den Händen von
to receive [rɪ'siːv]	bekommen, erhalten
full sovereignty ['sɒvrəntɪ]	vollständige Souveränität *(eigene Staatshoheit)*
remaining	übrig geblieben, restlich
tie	Verbindung, Bindung
legal	rechtlich, juristisch
dependence	Abhängigkeit
to remove	entfernen, lösen
parliamentary	parlamentarisch
constitutional monarchy	konstitutionelle Monarchie
head of state	Staatsoberhaupt

---

lacrosse	Lacrosse
metropolitan area [metrəˌpɒlɪtn 'eəriə]	Großraum, Großstadtregion
franchise ['frænʃaɪz]	Lizenznehmer *(Mannschaft und Lizenz einer Liga werden gemeinsam gekauft, Auf- und Abstieg gibt es daher nicht.)*
to participate in sth	an etw. teilnehmen
popular	beliebt
curling	Curling, Eisstockschießen
to be similar to sth	etw. ähnlich sein

mavbh8d

7 Australia

Geography

Geographical structure

Australia is on the other side of the **globe**, that's why it's also known as **down under**. The people who live there, the **Australians**, are also known as **Aussies**. Australia is the hottest and driest **continent** in the world. It is also the world's smallest continent, and at the same time it is the world's largest island with a **population** of 18 million people. That is only about two people **per square kilometre**.

Australia is **divided** into six states and two **mainland territories**. The six states are Western Australia to the west, Queensland in the north east, New South Wales and Victoria in the south east, South Australia in the centre (in the south) and the island of Tasmania which is below the state of Victoria. The Northern Territory **covers** the centre (in the north) and in New South Wales you can find the very small Australian Capital Territory which **surrounds** Canberra.

Australian cities

Canberra is Australia's **capital city**, although it is one of Australia's smaller cities. All of Australia's big cities **are situated** on the coast and not in the **desert** area in the middle of Australia. Sydney is the biggest city in Australia with about four million **inhabitants**. It is famous for the Opera House, which has a **roof** that looks like the **sails** of a ship, and the Harbour Bridge, which is used for amazing **fireworks** on New Years Eve. Other famous Australian cities are Perth, Melbourne, Brisbane and Adelaide.

The Outback

The Outback is the biggest part of Australia. There are no big cities, just towns, villages and **single stations,** that is why not many people live there. The red **dust**, the **heat**, the wide **horizons** and the **kangaroos** are all **symbols** of the Outback. Many people who live in the Outback work on the **huge** sheep and **cattle stations**. These are in places where there is enough **rainfall** so that the animals **survive**. Australia is the home of about 150 million sheep – there are **approximately** eight times as many sheep as people in Australia. It is easy to understand why Australia **exports** more wool than any other country in the world.))))

geographical [ˌdʒiːəˈgræfɪkl]	geographisch
structure [ˈstrʌktʃə]	Struktur, Aufbau
Australia	Australien
globe	Erdkugel, Globus
down under [ˌdaʊn ˈʌndə]	*(ugs.)* Australien
Australian	Australier(in)
Aussie	*(ugs.)* Australier(in)
continent	Kontinent, Erdteil
population [ˌpɒpjəˈleɪʃn]	Bevölkerung
per square kilometre	pro Quadratkilometer

to divide [dɪˈvaɪd]	teilen, ein-/unterteilen
▸ divided into	aufgeteilt in
mainland	Festland
territory [ˈterɪtərɪ]	Gebiet, Territorium
to cover an area [ˈeərɪə]	sich über ein Gebiet erstrecken
to surround	umgeben

capital (city)	Hauptstadt
to be situated	liegen, sich befinden
desert [ˈdezət]	Wüste
inhabitant	Einwohner(in)
roof	Dach
sail	Segel
fireworks [ˈfaɪəwɜːks]	Feuerwerk

the Outback	Outback *(australisches Hinterland)*
single station [ˈsɪŋgl ˌsteɪʃn] *AusE*	ein einzelner (Bauern)Hof im Outback
dust	Staub
heat	Hitze
horizon [həˈraɪzn]	Horizont
kangaroo	Känguru
symbol	Symbol, Wahrzeichen
▸ a symbol of	ein Wahrzeichen für
huge [hjuːdʒ]	riesig
cattle station [ˈkætl ˌsteɪʃn] *AusE*	riesige Rinderzucht im Outback
rainfall	Niederschlag
to survive	überleben
approximately	etwa, annähernd
to export	exportieren

rqfe8gx

The Outback is very hot and arid and most of it is empty. The loneliest, uninhabited parts of the Outback are known as Never-Never land. This refers to the way people think about the Outback life as well as an actual geographical location. Australia also has the longest fence in the world. It is the dingo fence and it is over 5,000 kilometres long and about 100 years old. It was built by bushmen to stop the dingoes, wild dogs that live in the Outback, from killing the sheep and cattle on the stations.

The Great Barrier Reef

Australia is also well-known for the Great Barrier Reef which is off the Queensland coast in the northeast of Australia. It is famous for its coral and also the colourful, rare fish that can be found there. To preserve this wonderful place, the Great Barrier Reef Marine Park was opened in 1975.

The Great Ocean Road

The Great Ocean Road is a stretch of road that is 243 kilometres (151 miles) long and runs along the south-eastern coast of Australia. It was built between 1919 and 1932 by soldiers who returned from World War I. It was dedicated to the soldiers that were killed during World War I (from 1914 to 1918) and it is the world's largest war memorial. The road winds its way through varying terrain along the coast and is an important tourist attraction in the region. A section of the Great Ocean Road is annually used for The Great Ocean Road Marathon which started in 2005.

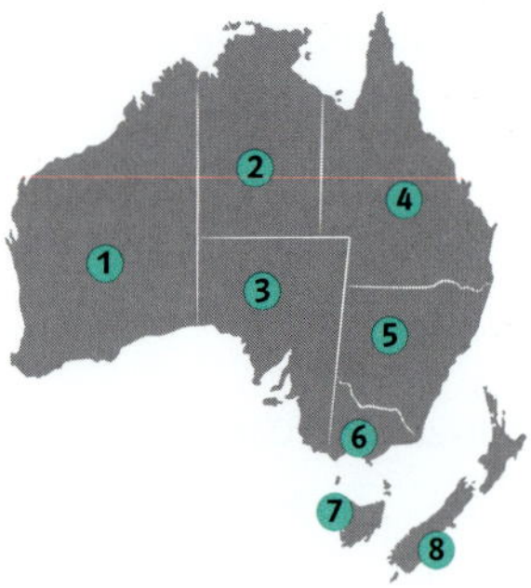

1 West Australia
2 Northern Territory
3 South Australia
4 Queensland
5 New South Wales
6 Victoria
7 Tasmania
8 New Zealand

History

The first settlers

Australia had been uninhabited for a very long time. The first settlers in Australia were the Aborigines, now known as Native Australians. They came to Australia from the north on boats and rafts about 60,000 years ago. Only about 10% of today's Australians are Aborigines.

arid	trocken, dürr
uninhabited	unbewohnt
≠ inhabited	bewohnt
Never-Never	einsame Landstriche im Zentrum Australiens
to refer to sth/sb	sich beziehen auf etw./jdn.; verweisen auf etw./jdn.
actual ['æktʃʊəl]	tatsächlich, wirklich
location [ləʊ'keɪʃn]	Ort, Gegend
fence [fens]	Zaun
dingo	Dingo *(australischer Wildhund)*
bushman	Buschbewohner(in) *(des Outbacks)*
to kill	töten, umbringen

reef	Riff
well-known [wel'nəʊn]	bekannt
coral	Koralle
rare	selten, rar
to preserve [prɪ'zɜ:v]	erhalten
to open	eröffnen

ocean ['əʊʃn]	Ozean, Weltmeer
stretch of road	Abschnitt einer Straße, Streckenabschnitt
to run along sth	etw. entlang verlaufen
to return from	zurückkehren von
to be dedicated to sb	jdm. gewidmet sein
soldier ['səʊldʒə]	Soldat(in)
World War I	der Erste Weltkrieg
memorial	Denkmal
to wind [waɪnd]	sich schlängeln
varying	unterschiedlich; abwechslungsreich
terrain	Gelände, Terrain; Landschaft
tourist attraction	Sehenswürdigkeit
region ['ri:dʒn]	Region, Gebiet
section ['sekʃn]	Abschnitt
annually	jährlich

settler	Siedler(in)
▸ to settle	sich ansiedeln
▸ settlement	Besiedlung, Ansiedlung
Aborigine [,æbə'rɪdʒəni]	Ureinwohner(in) Australiens
Native Australian	australische(r) Ureinwohner(in)
raft	Floß

rqfe8gx

The Europeans arrive

In the 17th century Dutch explorers went to Australia and landed on the north and west coasts. They didn't settle but left Australia again. However, they gave the Australian continent the name New Holland. In 1770 Captain Cook landed on the east coast of Australia and he claimed it for England. The first European settlement in Australia was for convicts and their families.

The prisons in Great Britain were so crowded that the government didn't know what to do with all the convicts. Convicts were given the option of leaving Great Britain and moving to Australia, allowing them to take their families with them. Some of them hadn't even committed serious crimes. People were also sent to Australia for just stealing rabbits. The British government sent eleven ships carrying over 700 convicts to start a new colony in Australia. The journey took eight months as it was 12,000 miles by sea. Many of the convicts fell ill on the journey and died. The first boats arrived in January 1788 at the place that is now called Sydney. The convicts were made to build everything new, like houses, roads, etc. in the new colony.

The 19th and 20th century

Around 1850 gold was discovered in Australia and lots of people went there to get rich.

In 1908 the Australians decided to build a new capital city to the south of Sydney and they called it Canberra.

Australia was part of Britain until before World War II which started in 1939. Sometime after 1931, it isn't clear when, Australia as a nation became independent. The states were still part of the British Commonwealth and Australia chose not to exercise its rights. It wasn't until 1986 that the Australian states gained their independence from Great Britain.

The Australians and the Aborigines

The British and the Aborigines didn't live well together. The British shot many animals and destroyed lots of native plants. This upset the Aborigines and they fought with the British. During the battles lots of Aborigines died.

At the beginning of the 20th century, the Australians thought it would be a good idea to protect the Aborigines. They started by taking away their children and making them work for white people. The children weren't allowed to speak their own language or see their parents. This went on until the late 1960s and only in 2008 did the Australian government apologise to the Aborigines, and now they live better lives.

century ['sentʃəri]	Jahrhundert
Dutch	holländisch, niederländisch
explorer	Entdecker(in); Forscher(in)
▸ to explore	entdecken, erforschen
to land	landen, an Land gehen
to claim sth	auf etw. Anspruch erheben, etw. in Besitz nehmen
convict	Sträfling
prison	Gefängnis
crowded	überfüllt
option ['ɒpʃn]	Wahl, Möglichkeit
to commit	begehen, verüben
serious crime	schwere Starftat, schlimmes Verbrechen
to steal [sti:l], stole [stəʊl], stolen ['stəʊln]	stehlen
to carry	transportieren; tragen
colony	Kolonie
journey ['dʒɜ:ni]	Reise
to fall ill	krank werden
to be made to	gezwungen werden
gold	Gold
rich	reich
World War II	der Zweite Weltkrieg
nation ['neɪʃn]	Nation, Volk
independent	(politisch) unabhängig, selbständig
▸ independence	Unabhängkeit, Selbstständigkeit
to exercise one's rights	von seinem Recht Gebrauch machen
to gain	bekommen
to shoot [ʃu:t], shot [ʃɒt], shot [ʃɒt]	schießen
to destroy	zerstören
native	einheimisch
battle	Schlacht
to protect	schützen
to take away	wegnehmen
white people	Weiße
language ['læŋgwɪdʒ]	Sprache
to apologise [ə'pɒlədʒaɪz]	entschuldigen

rqfe8gx

Life in Australia

Australian animals

For millions of years, Australia **had been isolated** from the rest of the world. This meant that its plants and animals **developed differently**.

There are some very **cute** looking animals such as **koala bears** and kangaroos, but there are also some very nasty ones living in Australia too, like **sharks** and **saltwater crocodiles** (salties).

Koala bears look very cute, but they aren't always cute, and can bite and hurt people. Usually they aren't very **busy** animals as they spend 16 to 18 hours a day asleep in trees, however, they can run as fast as rabbits. They smell like **eucalyptus** because they only eat eucalyptus leaves, and they aren't bears at all - they are **marsupials** like kangaroos.

Kangaroos are also animals that are **linked** with Australia. They carry their babies, called **joeys**, in their **pouches**. They eat grass and can go without water for a long time. They sleep during the day and are very **lazy** when it's hot. They **kick** with their strong back legs or box with their 'arms' when they fight.

Among the not so nice animals of Australia is the **sea wasp,** a **box jellyfish**. Sea wasps live in the warm waters to the north and **sting** anything they **touch**, and people can die within five minutes of being stung. Another very **poisonous** sea animal is the blue ring **octopus**. Its **venom** can kill in minutes if it bites you. All Australians know how to use **mouth-to-mouth** and **heart massage** in case you are bitten, as there is no antivenom. Blue ring octopuses are **shy creatures**, but you should stay away from them.

Snakes, spiders and crocodiles are also animals linked with Australia. There are many poisonous snakes and spiders and the saltwater crocodiles, or salties, are **dangerous**, too. They usually lie very **still** and wait to **attack** their **prey**, but they can run as fast as **humans**. They can weigh between 900 and 3,000 pounds and are most **active** at night. You should never **provoke** them. In the areas where they live, you shouldn't walk near rivers or the sea as they can **jump out** of the water very quickly.

The Flying Doctor Service

Sometimes the people who live on cattle stations in the Australian Outback live more than a thousand miles from the nearest **public buildings**. This can be a problem when they are ill, because they can't just drive to a doctor or a **hospital**. They can call the Flying Doctor Service though. The **service** has about sixty **planes** which fly about 73,500 kilometres every year. »

to be isolated	isoliert sein
to develop	sich entwickeln, entfalten
differently	unterschiedlich

cute [kju:t]	süß
koala bear	Koalabär
shark	Hai(fisch)
saltwater crocodile	Salzwasserkrokodil

busy	tätig
eucalyptus [ju:kəl'ɪptəs]	Eukalyptus
marsupial	Beuteltier

to link	verbinden
joey	junges Känguru
pouch	Beutel
lazy	faul
to kick	treten

sea wasp	Seewespe
box jellyfish	Würfelqualle
sting	Stich
to touch	berühren
poisonous ['pɔɪznəs]	giftig
▸ to poison sb	jdn. vergiften
octopus	Tintenfisch, Krake
venom	Gift
≠ antivenom	Gegengift
mouth-to-mouth (resuscitation) [rɪˌsʌsɪ'teɪʃn]	Mund-zu-Mund Beatmung
heart massage	Herzmassage
shy	scheu, schüchtern
creature ['kri:tʃə]	Lebewesen, Kreatur

dangerous ['deɪndʒrəs]	gefährlich
still	ruhig, still
to attack [ə'tæk]	angreifen, attackieren
▸ attack	Angriff
prey	Beute
human ['hju:mən]	Mensch
active	tätig
to provoke	provozieren, herausfordern
to jump out	herausspringen

public building	öffentliches Gebäude
hospital	Krankenhaus
service ['sɜ:vɪs]	Service, Dienstleistung
plane	Flugzeug

rqfe8gx

It is one of the most comprehensive aeromedical organisations in the world. The service first started as a one year test in 1928.

It is a non-profit making organisation and relies on donations to continue its hard work. The doctors not only come in an emergency, they also have regular clinics, for example for pregnant women or for people with dental problems or mental health problems.

The School of the Air

The School of the Air started in 1951. It is for kids who live in the Outback and who would have to travel thousands of miles every day just to get to school.
With the School of the Air, students just switch on their computers and school starts. Boarding schools are too expensive so they have this computer school instead.
When it first started in Alice Springs, two-way radio was used, but now students use the modern broadband system. The teachers use a video, webcam and whiteboard and the students can see the teachers and not just hear them. Even better, the students can hear their classmates and take part in discussions with them.
The students have half-hour lessons with teachers in all subjects every week, fitted into a timetable like at a normal school. Any extra things they need, for science experiments for example, are sent by post. The students have to use their own stationery and they must do their homework. They regularly have to send it to their teachers, who check it, mark it and send it back. The teachers visit the students annually and they write progress reports for the parents twice a year. The students can contact a support teacher if they have problems and need help.
The School of the Air in Alice Springs has over 145 enrolled students who live in an area of more than 521,000 square miles. That is like having one school for students who live in an area three and a half times the size of Germany. For adults the school also offers courses in higher education. There are often summer camps or special activities so that the students can meet up once a year.

comprehensive	umfassend, umfangreich
aeromedical	aeromedizinisch
test	Versuch
non-profit making organisation	gemeinnützige Organisation
to rely on sb/sth [rɪ'laɪ ɒn]	auf jdn./etw. angewiesen sein
donation [ˌdəʊ'neɪʃn]	Spende
to continue [kən'tɪnjuː]	fortsetzen, weitermachen
emergency [ɪ'mɜːdʒənsi]	Notfall
clinic	Beratungsstelle, Sprechstunde
pregnant	schwanger
dental problem	Zahnprobleme
mental health problem ['mentl]	psychisches Problem
to travel	verreisen, reisen
to switch on [ˌswɪtʃ 'ɒn]	an-/einschalten
≠ to switch off	ausschalten
boarding school ['bɔːdɪŋ ˌskuːl]	Internat
instead	anstatt, stattdessen
two-way radio	Funksprechgerät
broadband ['brɔːdbænd]	Breitband
video ['vɪdiəʊ]	Video
webcam	Webcam, Internetkamera
whiteboard	weiße Wandtafel; Whiteboard
discussion [dɪ'skʌʃn]	Diskussion, Besprechung
half-hour	halbstündig
to fit into	hineinpassen
experiment [ɪk'sperɪmənt]	Experiment, Versuch
stationery	Schreibzeug; Briefpapier
regularly ['regjələli]	regelmäßig
to mark	benoten, korrigieren
progress report	Zeugnis, (Halb)Jahresinformation
twice	zweimal
to contact	kontaktieren, Verbindung aufnehmen
support teacher	Betreuungslehrer(in)
to enrol ['enrəʊl]	anmelden
square mile	Quadrat Meile
area	Gebiet; Gegend
size	Größe
to offer	anbieten
▸ offer	Angebot
higher education	Hochschul(aus)bildung
summer camp	Sommerferienlager
once a year	einmal im Jahr

rqfe8gx

The Australian climate

Australians are known for the **comfortable, relaxed way of life**. They love their beach **barbecues**, usually **celebrating** Christmas on the beach with friends. "What?" I hear you cry. Of course the **seasons** are the **other way round** in Australia. When it is hot in Europe in June and July, it is not so hot (I wouldn't say cold) in Australia. When we **unpack** our **scarves**, winter coats and **skis**, the Australians unpack their bikinis and **swimming trunks**.

The sun is very strong in Australia and may cause **skin cancer**. Therefore the schools must **provide education programmes** for sun **safety** and also **shade** in the **school grounds** where the students do sport. Teachers have to **ensure** students wear **protective** clothing, for example **sunglasses** and hats with **broad brims,** when they are in the sun. On areas of the skin that aren't covered by clothing, **sunscreen** should be used.

Sport in Australia

Surfing is the most popular sport in Australia as most people live near the coast. Kids learn how to surf very early, and the waves that the surfies ride can be ten to twenty feet high.

If you want to do another water sport, scuba diving on the Great Barrier Reef is also very popular. You should start with a course if you have never done it before. You can do courses in the classroom and the pool before venturing out to the reef. You should be able to swim 200 metres and also tread water. Before you start a course, you have to take a medical. A good teacher can really make you feel confident and have fun. If you talk to some experienced divers they will tell you the pros and cons and what to look out for on the reef.

The Australians love both rugby and cricket which originates from the time when Australia belonged to the British Empire. Amazingly, you can also do winter sports in the Australian Alps which are in North South Wales.

climate	Klima
comfortable ['kʌmfətəbl]	bequem
relaxed	entspannt
way of life	Lebensstil, Lebensart
barbecue ['bɑːbɪkjuː]	Grillen im Freien
to celebrate ['seləbreɪt]	feiern
season	Jahreszeit
the other way round	andersherum
to unpack	auspacken
scarf [skɑːf]	Schal, Tuch
ski [skiː]	Ski
swimming trunks	Schwimmhosen
skin cancer	Hautkrebs
to provide [prəˈvaɪd]	zur Verfügung stellen, anbieten
education programme	Bildungsprogramm
safety ['seɪfti]	Sicherheit
shade	Schatten
▸ in the shade	im Schatten
school grounds	Schulgelände
to ensure [ɪnˈʃɔː]	sicherstellen, gewährleisten
protective	Schutz-
sunglasses	Sonnenbrille
broad brim	breite Krempe
sunscreen	Sonnencreme
surfing	Wellenreiten
popular	beliebt
surfie	Surfer(in)
to ride [raɪd], rode [rəʊd], ridden ['rɪdn]	reiten
foot, feet	Fuß *(Maßeinheit)*
scuba diving [ˌskuːbə 'daɪvɪŋ]	Gerätetauchen, Sporttauchen
course	Kurs
to venture out [ˌventʃə 'aʊt]	sich heraustrauen
to tread water	Wasser treten
medical	ärztliche Untersuchung
confident	zuversichtlich, überzeugt
experienced [ɪk'spɪərɪənst]	erfahren
diver	Taucher(in)
pros and cons	Vor- und Nachteile
rugby	Rugby
cricket	Kricket
to originate	seinen Ursprung haben
to belong to sth	zu etw. gehören
the British Empire [ˌbrɪtɪʃ 'empaɪə]	das britische Weltreich

rqfe8gx

Australian Food

Australian food is a good **mixture** of British, **Asian** and American **influences** as these are the **nationalities** that make up the **majority** of the population of Australia.

Some of the food the Aborigines eat can take a bit of getting used to. For example, green **ants** or **witchetty grubs**. Witchetty grubs are the **larvae** of a **moth** that can be found in the desert. Another favourite food is kangaroo meat, usually grilled on a barbecue or an open fire in the Outback.

Australian music

A favourite Australian **wind instrument** is the **didgeridoo** which was **developed** by the Aborigines in the last 1,500 years. Lots of people can now play the didgeridoo, not just Aborigines. There are even pop groups who use the instrument in their bands.

New Zealand

Geography

New Zealand is situated to the southeast of Australia in the Pacific Ocean. Two main **islands**, the North and the South Island, and a number of smaller ones **make up the island state**. Wellington, the capital of New Zealand, is on the North Island, so is Auckland which is the largest city in New Zealand. The islands have a **mixed landscape including** both **volcanoes** and **glaciers**. Most people will **recognise** New Zealand if they have seen the Lord of the Rings films that were **filmed** there.

History

New Zealand was first discovered in 1642 by a dutch explorer, and in 1840 **representatives** of Great Britain **signed** a **treaty** with the **Maori** making New Zealand a British colony. Three-quarters of the 4.5 million population are of European **origin** followed by 15% being Maori, who were the first settlers in New Zealand in around 1300.

Animals in New Zealand

One **emblem** of New Zealand is the **kiwi**, a **flightless** bird found in the **forests** in New Zealand. There are more **penguin species** found in New Zealand than in any other country. Different **reptiles** such as **frogs** and **geckos** are also often seen in New Zealand. However, there are no snakes in New Zealand, poisonous or **otherwise**.

mixture ['mɪkstʃə]	Mischung, Gemisch
▸ a mixture of	eine Mischung aus
Asian ['eɪʒn]	asiatisch
influence ['ɪnflʊəns]	Einfluss
▸ influence on	Einfluss auf
nationality	Nationalität
majority	Mehrheit
≠ minority	Minderheit
ant	Ameise
witchetty grub	Witchetty-Made
larvae ['lɑːvə]	Larven
moth	Motte
wind instrument	Blasinstrument
didgeridoo [ˌdɪdʒəri'duː]	Didgeridoo *(Musikinstrument der Aborigines)*
to be developed by	entwickelt sein von
island ['aɪlənd]	Insel
to make up an island state	einen Inselstaat bilden
mixed [mikst]	gemischt
landscape	Landschaft
to include	enthalten, beinhalten
volcano [vɒl'keɪnəʊ]	Vulkan
glacier ['glæsɪə]	Gletscher
to recognise	erkennen
to film	(einen Film) drehen
representative	Vertreter(in)
to sign [saɪn]	unterschreiben
treaty	Vertrag, Abkommen
Maori ['maʊri]	Ureinwohner(in) Neuseelands
origin ['ɒrɪdʒɪn]	Ursprung, Herkunft
emblem	Zeichen, Symbol
kiwi ['kiːwiː]	Kiwi
flightless	flugunfähig
forest	Waldgebiet
penguin ['peŋgwɪn]	Pinguin
species ['spiːʃiːz]	Spezies, Tierart(en), Pflanzenart(en)
reptile ['reptaɪl]	Reptil *(z.B. Eidechsen)*
frog	Frosch
gecko	Gecko
otherwise	anders

rqfe8gx

8 Other English speaking countries

India

Geography

India, in South Asia, is officially called the Republic of India. It is the seventh largest country by area and the second most populated country in the world. India has a total area of 3,287,263 square kilometres and a population of over 1.2 billion people. That makes a population density of 387 people per square kilometre.

India shares land borders with Pakistan, China, Nepal, Bhutan, Myanmar and Bangladesh. The rest of India has a coastline measuring over 7,500 kilometres. In the south is the Indian Ocean, on the southwest is the Arabian Sea and the Bay of Bengal is on the southeast. The beaches of India are sandy, rocky, have cliffs, mudflats or even marshy shores. The main river in India is the Ganges which flows into the sea at the Bay of Bengal.

India is a federal parliamentary republic with a president and a prime minister. India's capital city is New Delhi and the largest city is Mumbai. India consists of 29 states and 7 union territories. All the states and two of the union territories (Puducherry and the National Capital Territory of India) have elected parliaments and governments; the other five territories have appointed administrators. The states and territories are divided into districts.

India is a multilingual and multi-ethnic society. Hindi followed by English are the official languages in India. There are many recognised regional languages.

Asia ['eɪʒə]	Asien
officially [ə'fɪʃli]	offiziell
area ['eəriə]	Fläche, Gebiet
populated	bevölkert, bewohnt
square kilometre	Quadratkilometer
population [ˌpɒpjə'leɪʃn]	Einwohnerzahl, Bevölkerung
billion ['bɪliən]	Milliarde
density ['densɪti]	Dichte

share [ʃeə]	teilen
land border	Landgrenze
coastline	Küstenlinie
to measure ['meʒə]	*hier:* ein Länge haben von; abmessen
rocky	felsig, steinig
cliff	Felsen, Klippe
mudflat	Watt; Wattenmeer
marshy	sumpfig
shore [ʃɔː]	Küste, Ufer
flow [fləʊ]	fließen

federal	bundesstaatlich, Bundes-
▸ federal republic	Bundesrepublik
parliamentary	parlamentarische
prime minister	Premierminister(in)
capital city	Hauptstadt
New Delhi [ˌnjuː 'deli]	Neu-Delhi
Mumbai [ˌmʌm'baɪ]	Mumbai *(früher: Bombay)*
to consist of	bestehen aus
state	Bundesstaat
union territory	Unionsterritorium *(direkt der Bundesebene unterstellt)*
Puducherry [ˌpuːduː'tʃɛrɪ]	Puducherry *(ein Territorium in Indien)*
to elect	wählen
parliament	Parlament
government	Regierung
to appoint sb (to a post)	jdn. ernennen; jdn. in ein Amt berufen
administrator [əd'mɪnɪstreɪtə]	Verwalter(in)
district	Bezirk

multilingual [ˌmʌltɪ'lɪŋgwəl]	mehrsprachig
multi-ethnic	vielvölker-, multiethnisch
society	Gesellschaft
Hindi ['hɪndi]	Hindi
official language	Amtssprache
recognised ['rekəgnaɪzd]	anerkannt

bwn2u4q

The main **religion** in India is **Hinduism** with 80% of the Indian population being **Hindu**. The next biggest religion is **Islam** that 14% **follow**. 5% of the population follow other religions, such as **Christianity**, **Sikhism** and **Buddhism**. Hinduism, Buddhism and Sikhism all **originated** in India.

The Indian **climate** is **influenced** by both the Himalayas (**mountain range**) and also the Thar Desert. The Himalayas **protect** the cold winds blowing from the north and help India keep its warm climate. The **majority** of India's **rainfall** is between June and October which comes through the summer **monsoons**.

About 20% of India is covered by **forests**, 10% of them are **dense** forests. **Due to** its **diverse landscapes**, India is home to a wide variety of **wildlife** and **plant species** that can't be found anywhere else in the world. India has also a number of national parks which offer **tiger spotting** safaris.

India has many national symbols. These include the tiger, the **river dolphin**, the **lotus flower** and the mango.

History

From the early 18th **century**, India was under the **administration** of the British East India Company. Great Britain **established** a number of **coastal outposts** in India. At this time, India had stopped **exporting manufactured goods** and was **instead supplying** the British Empire **with raw materials**.

After the Indian Rebellion in 1857 India was **administered** directly by the UK. After **struggling** for **independence**, India became an independent nation in 1947. India's struggle for independence was led by Mahatma Gandhi and was **marked** as being **non-violent**. You still see the **influence** the UK had on India, for example, the cars drive on the left in India the same as in the UK.

religion [rɪ'lɪdʒn]	Religion
Hinduism ['hɪndu:ɪzəm]	Hinduismus
Hindu	hinduistisch
Islam ['ɪzlɑ:m]	Islam
to follow	angehören; folgen
Christianity [ˌkrɪsti'ænɪti]	Christentum
Sikhism ['si:kɪzm]	Sikhismus
Buddhism ['bʊdɪzm]	Buddhismus
to originate	entstehen
climate	Klima
to influence ['ɪnflʊəns]	beeinflussen
mountain range	Gebirgskette
to protect	schützen
majority	der meiste (Niederschlag)
rainfall	Niederschlag
monsoon [mɒn'su:n]	Monsun, Regenzeit
forest ['fɒrɪst]	Wald, Waldgebiet
dense	dicht
due to ['djuˌtu:]	wegen, aufgrund von
diverse [daɪ'vɜ:s]	vielfältig; abwechslungsreich
landscape	Landschaft
wildlife	Tierwelt
plant species ['spi:ʃi:z]	Pflanzenart
tiger ['taɪgə]	Tiger
to spot	sichten, entdecken
river dolphin	Flußdelphin
lotus flower	Lotusblume
century ['sentʃəri]	Jahrhundert
administration [ədˌmɪnɪ'streɪʃən]	Verwaltung
to establish sth	etw. gründen
coastal ['kəʊstl]	an der Küste gelegen
outpost	Siedlung, Außenstelle
to export ['ekspɔ:t]	exportieren
manufactured goods	fertige Erzeugnisse
instead	(an)statt, stattdessen
to supply sb with sth	jdn. mit etw. versorgen
raw material	Rohstoff
to administer	regieren; verwalten
to struggle ['strʌgəl]	kämpfen, ringen
independence	Unabhängigkeit
▸ independent	unabhängig
to mark	kennzeichnen, bezeichnen
non-violent	gewaltlos
influence ['ɪnflʊəns]	Einfluss

bwn2u4q

Since the 1990s a large **urban middle class** has developed and India has been **transformed** into one of the world's fastest-growing **economies**.

Despite increased economic growth in the last few decades, India **faces** many problems. It has the largest **concentration** of people who are living **below** the World Bank's international **poverty line**. The **proportion** has **dropped** from 60% in 1981 to 25% in 2011. A third of India's children under five are **underweight**, and 15% of its population is **undernourished**.

Reports **support** the **rumours** of **corruption** in India. Today India still has the highest number of people living in **conditions** of **slavery** and the largest number of **child labourers** under the age of 14. It is estimated that over 12 million children (under 14) are **employed** to do **hazardous** jobs.

Bollywood

- The name Bollywood comes from the name Bombay (Mumbai's old name) combined with the name Hollywood. More films are made in the film studios in Mumbai than in Hollywood. It produces the world's most-watched films. The language of most Bollywood films is Hindi, with some English. The films are usually very long, as Indian film fans like value for money. The films are usually love stories with a mixture of corrupt politicians, kidnappings and families who have lived separate from each other. The success of Bollywood has also had an influence on Hollywood films. Nowadays film directors in Hollywood use songs and dances in their films more than they used to.

Sport

- Popular sports in India include tennis, martial arts, field hockey and cricket. Chess, thought to have originated in India, is also played very often. India has hosted a number of important international sporting events including the Asian Games, the Cricket World Cup, the Hockey World Cup and also the Commonwealth Games.

urban ['ɜ:bən]	städtisch
middle class	Mittelschicht
to transform sth	etw. verwandeln, etw. verändern
economy	Wirtschaft
despite	trotz, ungeachtet
increased	erhöht, gewachsen
economic growth	Wirtschaftswachstum
to face	begegnen, konfrontiert sein mit
concentration ['kɒnsən,treɪʃən]	Konzentration, Dichte
below	unter
poverty line	Armutsgrenze
proportion [prə'pɔ:ʃn]	Anteil, Rate
to drop	fallen
underweight	untergewichtig
undernourished [,ʌndə'nʌrɪʃt]	unterernährt
to support	unterstützen
rumour ['ru:mə]	Gerücht
corruption	Korruption, Bestechung
condition [kən'dɪʃən]	Bedingung
slavery ['sleɪvri]	Sklaverei
child labourer	Kinderarbeiter(in)
employed [ɪm'plɔɪd]	beschäftigt, angestellt
hazardous ['hæzədəs]	gefährlich
Bollywood	Bollywood
to combine	verbinden
to produce [prə'dju:s]	produzieren, herstellen
value for money	Preis-Leistungs-Verhältnis
mixture ['mɪkstʃə]	Mischung, Gemisch
▸ a mixture of	eine Mischung aus
corrupt	korrupt, bestechlich
politician [,pɒlɪ'tɪʃən]	Politiker(in)
separate ['seprət]	getrennt
success [sək'ses]	Erfolg
nowadays	heutzutage
director	Regisseur(in)
martial arts [,mɑ:ʃl 'ɑ:ts]	Kampfsport, Kampfkünste
chess	Schach*(spiel)*
sth is thought to	man denkt, dass etw.
Asian Games	Asiatische Spiele *(Sportwettbewerb alle vier Jahren mit Athleten aus Asien)*

bwn2u4q

Mahatma Gandhi

- Mohandas Karamchand Gandhi was born in October 1869 and became known as Mahatma Gandhi. He was the famous leader of the Indian independence movement in India when it was ruled by Britain. He led India to independence and inspired civil rights movements and freedom movements across the world.
- Ghandi studied law in England and qualified as a lawyer before returning to India in 1891. He was a civil rights activist in South Africa from 1893 until 1914. The rest of his life, he spent in India struggling to get Indian independence. He was assassinated on 30th January 1948 at the age of 78 when walking to a prayer meeting with his nieces. His assassin strongly opposed achieving things through non-violent actions.

Sights

- The Taj Mahal, near the city of Agra on the bank of the Yamuna River, is one of India's most famous buildings. It blends ancient local traditions and imported western styles of architecture. It attracts millions of tourists every year. It is built of white marble but looks a beautiful pink in the evening sun. It was built by 20,000 workers and took 22 years (from 1632 to 1653) to build.
- Shah Jahan, Great Mogul of India, had the Taj Mahal built in memory of his wife and as a token of his love, and it is the final resting place of both the Shah and his wife. It is now a UNESCO World Heritage Site and one of the New Seven Wonders of the World.

leader	Anführer(in)
movement	Bewegung
to rule	beherrschen
to inspire	inspirieren
civil rights	Bürgerrechte
freedom	Freiheit
to study	studieren
law [lɔː]	Jura
to qualify ['kwɒlɪfaɪ]	ein Studium abschließen, eine Ausbildung abschließen
lawyer ['lɔɪə]	Rechtsanwalt/Rechtsanwältin
activist	Aktivist(in) *(politisch)*
assassinate [ə'sæsɪneɪt]	ermorden
prayer meeting [preə]	Gebetsstunde, Andacht
niece	Nichte
to oppose sth [ə'pəʊz]	etw. ablehnen, gegen etw. sein
to achieve sth	etw. erreichen
Taj Mahal [ˌtɑːʒmə'hɑːl]	Taj Mahal
bank	*hier:* Ufer
to blend	verbinden, vermischen
ancient ['eɪnʃnt]	alt, historisch
imported	eingeführt, importiert
architecture ['ɑːkɪtektʃə]	Architektur
to attract	anziehen
tourist ['tʊərɪst]	Tourist(in)
marble	Marmor
Great Mogul ['məʊgl]	Großmogul
in memory of	zur Erinnerung an
token of love	Liebesbeweis, Liebeszeichen
resting place	Ruhestätte
the World Heritage Site	Weltkulturerbe
New Seven Wonders of the World	die neuen 7 Weltwunder

bwn2u4q

South Africa

Geography

South Africa's **official** name is the **Republic** of South Africa. It is the most southern **sovereign state** in Africa. It has a total land area of 1,221,037 square kilometres and a population of **approximately** 53 million people. That is a population density of 42 people per square kilometre. The population is **divided into** four **ethnic groups**: 80% are black (of African **origin**), 8% white (of European origin), 3% are Asian and the **remaining** 9% are called coloured and are of mixed origins.

South Africa has a coastline in the south which **stretches along** the South Atlantic and the Indian Ocean and is 2,798 kilometres long. Its **neighbouring** countries **to the north** are Namibia, Botswana and Zimbabwe, and to the east are Mozambique and Swaziland. South Africa also **surrounds** the **kingdom** of **Lesotho** in the east. The highest **peak** in South Africa at 3,450 metres is Mafadi in the Drakensberg. South Africa has three capitals, Pretoria is the **executive** capital, Bloemfontein is the **judicial** capital and Cape Town is the **legislative** capital. However, the largest city in South Africa is Johannesburg.

South Africa is a **multi-ethnic society** with an interesting **combination** of cultures, languages and religions. There are 11 **official languages** in South Africa, from Afrikaans and English to Zulu. This is among the highest number of official languages of any country in the world. The **currency** in South Africa is the South African **rand**. There are approximately 17 rand to one euro. South Africa is two hours ahead of European time.

South Africa's area **consists of** a **vast**, almost flat **plateau** which is **surrounded by** the Great Escapement known as the Drakensberg. To the north of the country is the Kalahari **Desert**. The climate in South Africa goes from the extreme desert heat in the north to the **subtropical** climate in the east. In the southwest, where **wine** is produced, South Africa has an almost **Mediterranean** climate. South Africa's winter is from June to August.

South Africa's **wildlife** is something that everyone **recognises**. **Lions**, **cheetahs**, **leopards**, **rhinos**, **hyenas**, **hippos** and **giraffes** can all be found. There are **national parks** and **reserves** where these species can be seen.

official [ə'fɪʃl]	offiziell
republic ['rɪ'pʌblɪk]	Republik
sovereign state ['sɒvrɪn steɪt]	unabhängiger Staat
approximately	etwa, annähernd
to divide into	aufteilen in
ethnic group	ethnische Gruppe
origin ['ɒrɪdʒɪn]	Abstammung
remaining	übrig geblieben, restlich

to stretch along	sich entlang erstrecken
neighbouring	benachbart, in der Nähe lebend
to the north	nördlich
to surround	umgrenzen, umschließen
kingdom	Königreich
Lesotho [lə'su:tu:]	Lesotho *(Königreich mitten in Sürafrika)*
peak	Gipfel
executive [ɪg'zekjətɪv]	Exekutive *(Regierung und Verwaltung)*
judicial [dʒu:'dɪʃl]	Judikative *(Rechtsprechung)*
legislative ['ledʒɪslətɪv]	Legislative *(Parlamente, die Gesetze beschließen)*

multi-ethnic	multiethnisch
society	Gesellschaft
combination [ˌkɒmbɪ'neɪʃn]	Kombination, Mischung
official language	Amtssprache
currency ['kʌrənsi]	Währung
rand	Rand *(Währungseinheit in Südafrika)*

to consist of	bestehen aus
vast	gewaltig, riesig
plateau	Hochebene, Plateau
surrounded by	umgeben von
desert ['dezət]	Wüste
subtropical	subtropisch
wine	Wein
Mediterranean [ˌmedɪtə'reɪnɪən]	mediterran, Mittelmeer-

wildlife	Tier- und Pflanzenwelt
to recognise	erkennen
lion ['laɪən]	Löwe
cheetah	Gepard
leopard ['lepəd]	Leopard
rhino	Nashorn
hyena [haɪ'i:nə]	Hyäne
hippo	Nilpferd
giraffe [dʒɪ'rɑ:f]	Giraffe
national park	Nationalpark, Naturschutzgebiet
reserve	Reservat

bwn2u4q

History

Settlements of the Bantu-speaking peoples have been dated back to the 4th or 5th century. They weren't the first inhabitants of South Africa, but the ones whose existence has been found. They were the dominant ethnic group at the time of first European contact with South Africa, although the two major historic groups are the Xhosa and the Zulu peoples. A Portuguese explorer was the first known European to land in South Africa in 1487.

Other Europeans, including the British and the Dutch, landed in South Africa over the centuries in order to trade there. The Xhosa people and the Zulus had conflicts with each other and with the Europeans, as they all claimed more land.

In 1867 diamonds were discovered in South Africa followed by gold in 1884. This started the Mineral Revolution that lead to increased economic growth and immigration, but this also caused conflicts between the Boers (Dutch, Flemish, German and French settlers), the British, other Europeans and the original population of South Africa.

Racial segregation has caused much unrest in South Africa over the centuries. Sometimes it was informal, yet at the same time blacks weren't allowed to own land and they weren't allowed to use certain buildings. In 1948, the National Party was elected to power and divided the people of South Africa into three races (black, coloured and white) and developed rights and limitations for each of them.

The white minority controlled the more than four times larger black majority. This legal segregation became known as apartheid. The white people had the highest standard of living while the black majority had the lowest income, education, housing and life expectancy.

settlement	Siedlung
Bantu-speaking	Bantu sprechend
to date to	datieren auf
inhabitant	Einwohner(in)
existence [ɪg'zɪstns]	Existenz, Vorhandensein
dominant	Mehrheits-, Haupt-
major ['meɪdʒə]	wichtig, bedeutend
Xhosa ['kɔ:sə]	Xhosa *(ehemals als Kaffern bezeichnet)*
Zulu ['zu:lu:]	Zulu
Portuguese [ˌpɔ:tʃə'gi:z]	portugiesisch
explorer [ɪk'splɔ:rə]	Entdecker(in)

including	einschließlich
the Dutch	die Holländer, die Niederländer
to trade	(Tausch)Handel betreiben
conflict ['kɒnflɪkt]	Konflikt, Auseinandersetzung
to claim sth	auf etw. Anspruch erheben

diamond ['daɪəmənd]	Diamant
to discover	entdecken
Mineral Revolution	Mineralrevolution *(starke Veränderung eine Landes durch Mineralfunde)*
increased [ɪn'kri:st]	erhöht
economic growth	Wirtschaftswachstum
immigration	Einwanderung
the Boers ['bəʊəz]	die Buren
original [ə'rɪdʒənəl]	ursprünglich, original

racial segregation	Rassentrennung
to cause [kɔ:z]	verursachen
unrest	Unruhen
informal [ɪn'fɔ:ml]	informell, locker *(die Rassentrennung wurde nicht strikt eingehalten)*
elected to power	an die Macht gewählt
race	Rasse
right [raɪt]	Recht
limitation	Einschränkung

minority [maɪ'nɒrəti]	Minderheit
control	unter Kontrolle halten, kontrollieren
majority	Mehrheit
apartheid [ə'pɑ:teɪt]	Apartheid, Rassentrennung
standard of living	Lebensstandard
income	Einkommen
life expectancy	Lebenserwartung

bwn2u4q

In 1990 the government took its first steps to stopping **discrimination**. It **released** Nelson Mandela who had been in **prison** for 27 years for **sabotage**. In 1994 the African National Congress (ANC, a political party opposing discrimination) won the election and has been in power **ever since**. The first black **president** of South Africa, from 1994 to 1999, was Nelson Mandela. Since this time, South Africa has **struggled** with many changes. Many blacks have risen to the middle and upper classes and **poverty** among the whites has increased, while **unemployment** has risen **on the whole**.

Until the end of 2015, the World Bank **classified** South Africa as an upper-middle-**income economy**. Today it is **considered** a developed country and also a newly **industrialized** one. Its economy is the second largest in Africa. However, there is still a lot of poverty and **inequality** in South Africa, and about 25% of the population are unemployed and live below the World Bank's international **poverty line**. South Africa is still **recognised** as a middle power in **international affairs** and has a **significant regional** influence.

Nelson Mandela

- Nelson Mandela was born in July 1918. He was a South African anti-apartheid revolutionary, a politician and the first black president of South Africa. He studied law and joined different groups who fought against racial segregation. In 1961 he led a sabotage campaign against the government, and in 1962 he was arrested and convicted of conspiracy to overthrow the state and was put in prison to serve a life sentence.
- He served 27 years of his sentence before he was released in 1990. In 1994 he led the ANC to victory and became South Africa's first black president. His government focused on trying to stop racism and getting the different ethnic groups of South Africa back together as one nation. He received the Nobel Peace Prize in 1993 as well as many other honours. Nelson Mandela died at the age of 95 in December 2013.

discrimination	Diskriminierung
to release	entlassen
prison	Gefängnis
sabotage	*hier:* Unruhestiftung; Sabotage
ever since	seitdem
president	Präsident(in)
to struggle	kämpfen, ringen
poverty ['pɒvətɪ]	Armut
unemployment [ˌʌnɪm'plɔɪmənt]	Arbeitslosigkeit
on the whole	im Ganzen

classified	klassifiziert
income	Einkommen
economy	Wirtschaftssystem
to consider	in Betracht ziehen
industrialized	industrialisiert
inequality	Ungerechtigkeit
poverty line	Armutsgrenze
to recognise	erkennen
international affairs	internationale Angelegenheiten
significant	bedeutend, wichtig, beachtlich
regional ['ri:dʒənəl]	regional

anti-apartheid [ˌæntɪə'pɑ:rthaɪt]	gegen die Apartheid
revolutionary	Aufrührer(in), Kämpfer(in)
politician [ˌpɒlɪ'tɪʃn]	Politiker(in)
campaign [kæm'peɪn]	Aktion
to arrest	verhaften
to convict	verurteilen
conspiracy [kən'spɪrəsi]	Verschwörung
to overthrow	absetzen, stürzen
to serve [sɜ:v]	verbüßen, absitzen
life sentence	lebenslängliche Freiheitsstrafe

to release [rɪ'li:s]	freilassen
victory	Sieg
to focus on sth	sich auf etw. konzentrieren
Nobel Peace Prize	Friedensnobelpreis
honour	Auszeichnung, Ehrung

bwn2u4q

Sport

- The most popular sports in South Africa are football, cricket and rugby. South Africa hosted the 2010 Football World Cup and the 2003 Cricket World Cup. It also hosted and won the 1995 Rugby World Cup and won the Cup again in 2007 in France. Top athletes for sports, such as swimming, boxing, golf, tennis and formula one, have also come from South Africa.

Sights

- Table Mountain is a flat-topped mountain which is a prominent landmark overlooking the city of Cape Town. Many visitors take the cableway or even hike to its top. It forms part of the Table Mountain National Park. The level plateau is approximately three kilometres wide and has impressive cliffs on its edges. The Table Mountain Cableway takes 65 passengers in each car to the top of the mountain. From the upper cableway station there are views across Cape Town, Table Bay, Robben Island and the Atlantic. As well as sightseeing, rock climbing, caving, hiking and mountain biking are all very popular activities on Table Mountain.

The Caribbean

Geography

The Caribbean is a region southeast of the North American **mainland**, east of Central America and north of South America. It **consists of** the Caribbean Sea, more than 700 islands and also the **surrounding** coasts. The Caribbean islands are organised into 30 territories which include 13 sovereign states, **overseas departments** and also 17 **dependent territories**. The Caribbean **covers an area** of 2,754,000 square kilometres, although its land area is only about 240,000 square kilometres. There is a population of just over 39 million people.

The Caribbean is not a sovereign state, and **therefore** it has no capital city but **several** large cities including Santo Domingo, Havana, Port-au-Prince and Kingston. It is **spread over** two **time zones** that are either four or five hours behind Europe. There are many ethnic groups in the Caribbean which means many different languages are spoken there including English, Spanish, French and Dutch. The main religion in the Caribbean is Christianity. »

to host	ausrichten
athlete ['æθliːt]	Athlet(in)
formula one	Formel 1

flat-topped	mit flachem Gipfel
prominent ['prɒmɪnənt]	auffällig, hervorstehend
landmark	Wahrzeichen
overlooking	mit Blick auf
cableway	Seilbahn
to hike ['haɪk]	wandern
level	eben, flach
impressive	beeindruckend
edge [edʒ]	Rand; Kante
passenger ['pæsndʒə]	Passagier, Fahrgast
rock climbing	Klettern
caving	Höhlenwandern

mainland	das Festland
to consist of	bestehen aus
surrounding	umliegend
overseas department	Überseedépartement *(zu Frankreich gehörend und den Festlandsdépartements gleichgestellt)*
dependent territory	abhängiges Territorium *(politisch zu Großbritannien gehörendes, ansonsten jedoch eigenständiges Gebiet)*
to cover an area ['eərɪə]	sich über ein Gebiet erstrecken

therefore ['ðeəfɔː]	deshalb
several	verschiedene, einige
to spread over [spred], spread [spred], spread [spred]	verteilen über
time zone	Zeitzone

bwn2u4q

As to be expected with so many islands, the landscape and climate in the Caribbean varies. Some islands have flat terrain, for example Barbados, the Cayman Islands and the Bahamas, and others possess huge mountain ranges, like Cuba, Grenada and Trinidad & Tobago. The climate is tropical to subtropical and the region has sunshine all the year round. The year is not divided into the four seasons spring, summer, autumn and winter but only into a dry and a wet season. It is wetter from July to December than from January to June. The region is also often hit by hurricanes, especially from June to November.

The water around the Caribbean contains schools of fish, which migrate there, turtles and also coral reef formations. The deepest point of the Atlantic Ocean, the Puerto Rico trench, is just north of the island of Puerto Rico. Tobacco was an important crop during the colonial era, but nowadays sugarcane to export to Europe has taken over.

History

Before European contact to the Caribbean, it is estimated that the population was approximately 750,000. This dropped after the first European contact as they brought epidemic diseases like measles with them. Between 1500 and 1800 the population increased as slaves arrived from South Africa and military prisoners from Ireland. Immigrants from many European countries also arrived, but many of them died due to diseases. During the 19th century immigrants from India and China also arrived in the Caribbean. The majority of the Caribbean population is African, and there are minorities of mixed-race and European origin.

Food

Caribbean food is a mixture of worldwide tastes, including African, European, Amerindian, East Indian, Arab and Chinese. The immigrants from these different countries brought their traditions with them, and they created their own unique styles for the region. The most common ingredients in Caribbean dishes are rice, beans, peppers, plantains, tomatoes, sweet potatoes, chickpeas and coconut.

Sport

Sport is just as popular in the Caribbean as it is worldwide. Baseball is played in the Dominican Republic, compared with football, cricket and rugby that are played in the British islands, Anguilla, the British Virgin Islands, the Cayman Islands and Montserrat. Trinidad & Tobago even had a team qualify for the 2006 Football World Cup in Germany. Visitors to the Caribbean who want to watch some sport while on holiday will surely find something that appeals to them.

as to be expected	wie erwartet
to vary	sich unterscheiden, variieren
terrain	Gelände, Terrain; Landschaft
tropical	Tropen-, tropisch
sunshine	Sonnenschein
season ['si:zən]	Jahreszeit; Saison
hurricane ['hʌrɪkən]	Hurrikan, Wirbelsturm
especially [ɪ'speʃli]	besonders

to contain	enthalten
school of fish	Fischschwarm
to migrate	wandern
turtle	Wasserschildkröte
coral reef	Korallenriff
trench	Graben
tobacco [tə'bækəʊ]	Tabak
colonial [kə'ləʊniəl]	kolonial, Kolonie-
sugarcane	Zuckerrohr

contact	Kontakt, Berührung
to estimate	schätzen
to drop	fallen, sinken
epidemic disease	ansteckende Krankheit
measles ['mi:zlz]	Masern
slave	Sklave, Sklavin
military ['mɪlɪtri]	militärisch, Militär-
prisoner	Strafgefangene(r), Häftling
mixed-race	gemischter (Herkunft)
origin ['ɒrɪdʒɪn]	Ursprung, Herkunft

worldwide	weltweit, global
taste	Geschmack
Amerindian	indianisch
unique [ju:'ni:k]	einzigartig
ingredient	Zutat
dish	Gericht, Speise
pepper	Paprika; Pfeffer
plantain ['plæntɪn]	Kochbanane
sweet potato	Süßkartoffel
chickpea	Kichererbse
coconut	Kokosnuss

popular	beliebt
baseball	Baseball
compared with	gegenüber, während
to qualify ['kwɒlɪfaɪ]	sich qualifizieren
to appeal	anreizen

bwn2u4q

9 Global world

Fair trade

STEVE Good morning and welcome. This morning I have a **visitor** on my show that is going to talk to me about **fair trade**. I must admit, I see the fair trade **logo** on more and more products in my local supermarket, but I don't really know much about its **background**. I once tried fair trade chocolate and really didn't like it, but I have been **assured** that things have changed. May I **introduce** Daniel Richards from Fairtrade International.

DANIEL Good morning Steve. Thanks for **inviting** me onto your show. I have brought with me a few fair trade products so that you can **taste** for yourself if things have **improved**.

STEVE Thanks Daniel, presents already. So, firstly can you tell me what fair trade is, please? A lot of people think it has something to do with **organic products**, but I'm not sure.

DANIEL Well it hasn't got anything to do with organic products, **apart from** the fact, a lot of the products are healthier as the farms can't **afford** to buy expensive **pesticides** to **spray** their **crops**. This **in turn** means that they are grown **naturally**, but if a product has a fair trade logo on it, it doesn't mean it is organic.

STEVE Oh right, that **makes sense**. So what does it mean?

DANIEL The **goal** of fair trade is to help **producers** of **goods** in **developing countries** get better **trading conditions** and to **promote sustainability**. It **focuses on** products that are **typically exported** from developing countries to **developed countries** but are also **consumed** in **domestic markets**. »»

visitor	Besucher(in)
fair trade	fairer Handel
logo	Logo
background	Hintergrund
to assure	versichern, zusichern
to introduce [ɪntrə'dju:s]	vorstellen
to invite	einladen
to taste	schmecken
to improve	sich verbessern

organic	biologisch, Bio-
product ['prɒdʌkt]	Produkt, Erzeugnis
apart from	außer, neben; abgesehen von
to afford	sich leisten
pesticide ['pestɪsaɪd]	Schädlingsbekämpfungsmittel, Pestizid
to spray	spritzen; (be)sprühen
crop	Feldfrucht, Nutzpflanze
in turn	wiederum
naturally	natürlich

to make sense	Sinn machen, sinnvoll sein
goal	Ziel
producer	Hersteller(in)
goods	Waren, Güter
developing country	Entwicklungsland
trading conditions	Handelsbedingungen
to promote sth	födern
sustainability [səˌsteɪnə'bɪlətɪ]	(dauerhafte) Erhaltung
to focus on sth	sich auf etw. konzentrieren
typically	typischerweise, normalerweise
to export	exportieren
developed country	Industrieland, entwickeltes Land
to consume	verbrauchen, konsumieren
▸ consumer	Verbraucher, Konsument
domestic market	Heimatmarkt, Binnenmarkt

avsx5zq

STEVE So, what are these goods?

DANIEL They include coffee, **cocoa**, fruit and flowers **amongst** other things. The producers are **offered** better trading conditions and get **guaranteed** prices. The **beliefs** of fair trade are that the producers are **enabled** to meet **consumer needs**, there should be a more **equal distribution** of **wealth** among all **nations**, and it is better to buy products from producers in developing countries at a fair price than give them **charity** and **aid**.

STEVE Now I see where the name comes from but what does the logo **symbolize**? It is a very **distinctive** logo.

DANIEL It symbolizes the **relationship** between consumers and **campaigners**, **companies** and **traders**, and **farmers** and **workers** in a **joint endeavour** to **improve** lives and **well-being** through everyday shopping. The circle **incorporates** a blue sky for **optimism**, green for **growth**, and a **raised** arm for **empowerment**. Together they **represent** the **vision** and **values** of fair trade as a modern **movement**.

STEVE That makes me see the logo through different eyes. I had never actually seen the person on the logo. I'd always thought of it as more of **yin and yang**.

DANIEL I've heard that before. Fair trade isn't just a movement that people talk about. There are ten **standards** of fair trade the organisations must follow; they are **monitored** to **ensure** they are keeping to them. They include **reducing poverty** so that the producers, often **family businesses** or **co-operatives**, move from **income insecurity** to **self-sufficiency** and even **ownership**. »»

cocoa ['kəʊkəʊ]	Kakao
amongst	unter, neben
to offer	anbieten
guaranteed	garantiert
belief	Überzeugung; Glaube
to enable	ermöglichen
consumer need	Kundenbedürfnis
equal	gleichmäßig, ausgewogen
distribution	Verteilung
wealth	Reichtum, Wohlstand
nation ['neɪʃn]	Volk, Land, Nation
charity	Spenden, Almosen
aid	Hilfe, Hilfsleistung

to symbolize	symbolisieren
distinctive	auffällig, markant
relationship	Beziehung, Verhältnis
campaigner	Aktivist(in)
company	Firma
trader	Händler(in)
farmer	Landwirt(in), Bauer, Bäuerin
worker	Arbeiter(in)
joint endeavour	gemeinsame Bestrebung
to improve sth	etw. verbessern
well-being	Wohl(ergehen)
to incorporate sth	etw. enthalten
optimism	Optimismus, Lebensmut
growth	Wachstum
raised	erhoben
empowerment	Vollmacht; Selbstbestimmung
to represent	darstellen, repräsentieren
vision ['vɪʒn]	Vision, Vorstellung
values	Werte, Wertvorstellungen
movement	Bewegung

yin and yang	Yin und Yang
standard	Richtlinie
to monitor	überwachen, überprüfen
to ensure sth [ɪn'ʃɔː]	etw. sicherstellen; etw. gewährleisten
to reduce	verringern, senken
poverty	Armut
family business	Familienunternehmen
co-operative	Genossenschaft
income	Einkommen
insecurity	Unsicherheit
self-sufficiency [sə'fɪʃənsi]	wirtschaftliche Unabhängigkeit
ownership	Besitz

avsx5zq

If orders are cancelled or rejected and it wasn't the fault of the producer, they get compensation for the work they have done.

STEVE Ok, I see.

DANIEL The relationships are long term and based on trust, solidarity and respect on both sides. A fair price is agreed on by both sides which guarantees the producers can pay their employees and that the seller covers his costs. The standards also ensure that there is no forced labour or child labour.

STEVE And what about discrimination?

DANIEL There is also no discrimination based on race, religion, disability, gender, health or age for example. A safe and healthy working environment must be provided for employees, and working hours and conditions must comply with national or local laws.

STEVE Now I'm starting to understand what it is all about. There are lots of long words and complicated terminology for our listeners. Have you got an example to make it clearer?

DANIEL Sure. Let's take coffee growers in a country like Costa Rica. They used to have no guaranteed buyers for their beans; the beans were of low quality because they couldn't afford pesticides, and all the work was done by family members to save money. Now they get a guaranteed price, they can pay people to help them, and the quality has improved as they can look after their crops, which in return means they can grow more and earn more money.

STEVE Now that has made it a lot clearer, thanks. Can we taste some of this fair trade coffee and chocolate while my listeners relax to the newest song from my favourite singer?

order	Bestellung
to cancel sth	stornieren, absagen
to reject	ablehnen, zurückweisen
fault	Fehler, Schuld
compensation	Entschädigung
I see.	Aha!, Ich verstehe.
long term	langfristig, Langzeit-
based on	basierend auf
trust	Vertrauen
solidarity	Zusammenhalt
to agree on sth	etw. vereinbaren
employee	Angestellte(r)
seller	Verkäufer(in)
to cover	decken
cost	Kosten
forced labour	Zwangsarbeit
child labour	Kinderarbeit
discrimination	Diskriminierung
▸ to discriminate against sb	jdn. diskriminieren
race	Rennen
disability	Behinderung
gender	Geschlecht
health	Gesundheit
safe	sicher
working environment	Arbeitsumgebung, Arbeitsplatz
working hours	Arbeitszeit
condition	Bedingungen
to comply with	etw. entsprechen, mit etw. überein-stimmen
law	Gesetz
terminology	Begriffe
coffee grower	Kaffeebauer, Kaffeebäuerin
buyer	Käufer(in)
bean	Bohne
to be of low quality	schlechte Qualität haben
to relax	sich entspannen

avsx5zq

Environment

The main topic for many years, that is the same all around the world, is our environment and how we can save it from pollution. Our lives have changed over the last centuries, but it seems the consequences for the environment have not been taken into consideration when moving forward with technology or changing our lifestyle.

Pollution isn't just caused by rubbish being dumped in the ocean or vehicles running on the wrong fuel. It can also be caused by windmills being erected too close to houses or an airport allowing more planes to land and take off – noise is a form of pollution too. Some towns and cities have too much lighting which pollutes the sky and effects what we see at night.

Global warming and climate change are names given to the rise in the Earth's average temperature and what effects it has. There is a lot of talk about greenhouse gas in the atmosphere, a mixture of water vapour, carbon dioxide and methane.

Since the Industrial Revolution (around 1750) human activities have increased the concentration of carbon dioxide in the air. The effects are different around the world, but they will include rising sea levels, more rain, deserts growing and glaciers melting quicker. Overall the weather will have more extremes, from heat waves and droughts to heavy rainfall and floods, and even heavier snowfall in winter.

These changes of the ecosystem lead to humans, animals and plants changing the way they live to adapt to the new situation. A lot of scientists disagree that nature should adapt, and they feel that we should change the way we live to stop these changes happening in the first place. ⟫

environment [ɪn'vaɪrənmənt]	Umwelt
topic	Thema, Gesprächsgegenstand
pollution [pə'lu:ʃn]	Verschmutzung
century ['sentʃəri]	Jahrhundert
consequence ['kɒnsɪkwəns]	Konsequenz, Folge
to take into consideration [kənˌsɪdr'eɪʃn]	berücksichtigen
lifestyle	Lebensstil
to cause [kɔ:z]	verursachen
rubbish *BE*	Müll, Abfall
to dump sth	etw. (ab)kippen, etw. abladen
ocean ['əʊʃn]	Ozean, Meer
vehicle ['vɪəkəl]	Fahrzeug
to run on	betreiben
fuel ['fju:əl]	Brennstoff
windmill	Windrad
to erect	bauen, aufstellen
noise	Lärm
lighting	Beleuchtung
global warming [ˌgləʊbl'wɔ:mɪŋ]	Erderwärmung, globale Erwärmung
climate change	Klimaveränderung
average ['ævrɪdʒ]	durchschnittlich, Durchschnitts-
temperature ['temprətʃə]	Temperatur
greenhouse gas	Treibhausgas
atmosphere ['ætməˌsfɪə]	Atmosphäre
mixture ['mɪkstʃə]	Mischung, Gemisch
water vapour ['veɪpə]	Wasserdampf
carbon dioxide [ˌkɑ:bn daɪ'ɒksaɪd]	Kohlendioxid
methane ['mi:θeɪn]	Methan
the Industrial Revolution	industrielle Revolution
human	menschlich, Menschen-
rising sea level	steigender Meeresspiegel
desert ['dezət]	Wüste
glacier ['glæsɪə]	Gletscher
to melt	schmelzen
overall	insgesamt
extreme [ɪk'stri:m]	Extrem
heat wave	Hitzewelle, Hitzeperiode
drought [draʊt]	Dürreperiode
rainfall	Niederschlag
flood	Überschwemmung, Flut
ecosystem ['i:kəʊˌsɪstəm]	Ökosystem
to adapt to sth	sich an etw. anpassen
scientist	Naturwissenschaftler(in)
to disagree	anderer Meinung sein
nature ['neɪtʃə]	(die) Natur

avsx5zq

A lot of people try and do something to be more **environmentally friendly**, but is it enough? It is normal nowadays for people to sort their rubbish and **recycle** what they can; others are turning to **alternative sources** for their **energy**, and people think twice before they get in their cars and drive to the next shop or pick their children up from school. Some countries have made **laws** to **encourage** companies to think more about the environment. For example, when you buy something in a shop, you don't get **plastic bags** for free anymore. This is supposed to stop the dumping of plastic rubbish in our oceans. If you have to pay for a bag, you will think about using it twice, or **every now and then** a **shopping basket**.

In some areas rubbish is **burned** and not sent to **rubbish dumps** so the people aren't **contributing** to the rubbish **piling up** in the ocean. There are **advantages** and **disadvantages** to lots of ideas, but there is nothing stopping us trying what we can to make our lives environmentally friendly.

Culture

You can do it, too!

When I moved to America, I had great **expectations** of what my new life would be like. I knew the **pavements** weren't going to be **paved with gold**, but you hear all about **the American Dream** and don't know how much of it is true. My dad moved to the US from Mexico and **left me** and my sister and my mom **behind** while he tried to find a job and somewhere for us to live. It seemed like a long time, but it actually only took him two years before he sent us enough money so we could go to him. It had been a hard time for us all, but my father had been **unemployed** for so long, we needed something better.

As my parents hadn't learned English at school, they **struggled** with the language, but there is a strong Mexican **community** where we live and everyone helps each other. There are shops where you can buy Mexican **products**, but also where you can get **advice**. I **was homesick** at the beginning, but I soon made friends at my new school and I **picked up** the language really quickly.

I loved the **skyscrapers** and **freedom** in America, but what I loved even more was American sports. I tried out American football and baseball, even basketball, although I knew I was too small. I **found out** that I was a **natural** at baseball. I was so **keen** and **lived and breathed** baseball.

Being a **member** of the baseball team made me feel I had been **accepted** in the US. I was the star of my high school baseball team and everyone loved me. That was the start of my **career**. ⟫⟫

environmentally friendly	umweltfreundlich
to recycle [ˌriː'saɪkl]	wiederverwerten
alternative	alternativ, Alternativ-
source	Quelle
energy ['enədʒi]	Energie
law	Gesetz
to encourage [ɪn'kʌrɪdʒ]	anregen, ermutigen
plastic bag	Plastiktüte
every now and then	hin und wieder, ab und zu
shopping basket	Einkaufskorb
to burn [bɜːn], burnt/burned [bɜːnt/bɜːnd], burnt/burned [bɜːnt/bɜːnd]	brennen, verbrennen
rubbish dump	Müllkippe
to contribute to sth	zu etw. beitragen
to pile up	sich anhäufen, auftürmen
advantage [əd'vɑːntɪdʒ]	Vorteil
≠ disadvantage	Nachteil
expectation	Erwartung
pavement ['peɪvmənt] *BE*	Gehweg, Bürgersteig
paved with gold	mit Gold gepflastert
the American Dream	der amerikanische Traum
to leave sb behind [liːv], left [left], left [left]	jdn. verlassen, jdn. zurücklassen
unemployed	arbeitslos
to struggle with	kämpfen mit
community	Gemeinde
product	Produkt, Erzeugnis
advice	Rat(schlag)
to be homesick	Heimweh haben
to pick up	aufschnappen, nebenbei lernen
skyscraper	Wolkenkratzer, Hochhaus
freedom	Freiheit
to find out [ˌfaɪnd 'aʊt], found out [ˌfaʊnd 'aʊt], found out [ˌfaʊnd 'aʊt]	herausfinden, entdecken
natural	Naturtalent
keen	begeistert; eifrig
to live and breathe sth	nur für etw. leben
member	Mitglied
to accept	akzeptieren, annehmen
career [kə'rɪə]	Karriere

avsx5zq

I was granted American citizenship and travelled all over America playing baseball. I haven't forgotten my roots or my culture; I'm always reminded of them when I go to visit my parents, but I truly feel that I am American. I think that when you go to a new country, you have to accept their traditions, laws and ways of doing things. You have chosen to live in that country, so why start complaining and trying to change things. I also now understand the meaning of the phrases melting pot and salad bowl. I certainly fit into the melting pot: I have accepted the American way of life, I speak the language, play one of the national sports and feel American. I think my parents are more like salad bowls; they live in America and they speak enough of the language to get by, but their Mexican background, traditions and culture is very important to them.

Work

It seems that as long as you can speak English, you can get a job anywhere in the world. After school, students often work abroad for a year or travel abroad to get a taste of what life is like in another country. Companies have become more international with branches in different countries which makes it easier to move to another country and still keep your job. Some companies encourage their employees to work in a different country for a fixed period of time in order to gain experience and have better chances of getting a higher position.

There are also international projects and organisations that bring together people from all over the world to work together in order to achieve aims that have effects on people worldwide. An example of this is the European research organisation that operates the largest particle physics laboratory in the world called CERN (European Organisation for Nuclear Research).

21 countries work together in a northwest suburb of Geneva, Switzerland, to provide the facilities for physics research and experiments. CERN is also where the World Wide Web was first used in a large computer facility. Experiment results had to be made available to researchers elsewhere, and therefore it became an international network hub in the world.

Unfortunately there are many war zones around the world. International organisations like the United Nations bring together soldiers from all around the world to jointly try and make the world a better place.

to grant	bewilligen, geben
citizenship	Staatsangehörigkeit
root	Wurzel
to remind sb	jdn. erinnern
truly	wirklich
tradition [trəˈdɪʃən]	Tradition
to complain	sich beschweren, sich beklagen
phrase	Ausdruck, Bezeichnung; Phrase
melting pot	Schmelztiegel
salad bowl	Salatschüssel
certainly [ˈsɜːtnli]	sicher, bestimmt
to get by	durchkommen, zurechtkommen
background	Herkunft
abroad	im Ausland
taste	Eindruck, Vorgeschmack
company	Firma
branch	Filiale, Zweigstelle
still	noch
to encourage [ɪnˈkʌrɪdʒ]	ermutigen, zureden
employee	Angestellte(r)
fixed period of time	festgelegte Zeitspanne
to gain experience	Erfahrungen sammeln
higher position	höhere Position, bessere Stelle
to achieve an aim	ein Ziel erreichen
European [ˌjʊərəˈpiːən]	europäisch, Europa-
research	Forschung
▸ nuclear research [ˈnjuːkliə]	Kernforschung
▸ researcher	Forscher
to operate	betreiben
particle physics physics	Teilchenphysik
laboratory [ləˈbɒrətri]	Labor, Anlage
suburb [ˈsʌbɜːb]	Vorort
facility [fəˈsɪləti]	Anlage, Einrichtung
experiment [ɪkˈsperɪmənt]	Experiment, Versuch
result	Ergebnis, Resultat
to make available	zur Verfügung stellen
network hub	Netzwerkknoten
war zone	Kriegsgebiet
the United Nations	die Vereinten Nationen
soldier [ˈsəʊldʒə]	Soldat(in)
jointly [dʒɔɪntli]	gemeinsam, zusammen

avsx5zq

It doesn't matter from where they come from, they come together to work as a team and overcome any discrimination there may be. They have a job to do, and if their neighbour is from England, America, India or Ghana, it doesn't matter. They know what to do and language is no barrier.

Transport

What a whopper!

In 2015 the largest container ship in the world, the MSC Oscar, visited Felixstowe in England. It can carry 124 more containers than the CSCL Globe which used to be the largest ship, although it is shorter in length. It is 396 metres long and 59 metres wide. It can carry 19,224 standard containers which are 12 metres long, 2.6 metres high and 2.4 metres wide. Although the ship wasn't carrying a full load, many people stood on the beach or the public viewing platform to welcome the ship on its first visit to Great Britain.

The MSC Oscar was built in South Korea in 2014 and cost £93 million ($140 million). Oscar is an unusual name for a ship and is the name of the son of the president and chief executive owner of MSC. The deck of the ship is the size of four football pitches, and the distance between the bottom of the hull and the boat's waterline is 16 metres. If its cargo was only washing machines, it could carry 1.15 million. Believe it or not, it only has a crew of 35 on board.

The MSC Oscar travels all around the world from England to Germany to China via Spain and the Suez Canal. It collects containers here, delivers them there and then collects some more. Not all containers contain products, like washing machines, electronic equipment or toys, a lot of them carry waste (from Europe) to be disposed of in China. Where this waste goes Europeans don't seem to worry, as long as it doesn't stay in Europe.

The turn round time of a container ship, it doesn't matter how big it is, is very tight. They have to plan their arrival and departure to fit in with tide times at most ports. The longer a ship stays in a harbour, the more money it costs. While a ship is not moving, it has to pay berthing costs, to be loaded and unloaded, and it is not on its way to the next port where it can unload and make money.

to overcome sth	etw. überwinden
discrimination	Diskriminierung
▸ to disciminate against sb	jdn. diskiminieren
neighbour	Nebenmann, Nebenfrau; Nachbar(in)
barrier ['beriə]	Hindernis
whopper	Riese, Riesending
container ship	Containerschiff
to carry	tragen, laden
container	Container
length [leŋθ]	Länge
standard	Standard
wide	breit
to carry a full load	voll beladen sein
public viewing platform	öffentliche Aussichtsplatform
unusual	ungewöhnlich
president	Präsident(in)
chief executive [ˌtʃi:f ɪgˌzekjətɪv]	Vorstandsvorsitzender
owner	Eigentümer(in)
deck	(Schiffs)deck
football pitch	Fußballfeld
distance	Entfernung
bottom	Unterseite
hull	Schiffsrumpf
waterline	Wasserlinie
cargo	Schiffsladung, Fracht
washing machine	Waschmaschine
crew [kru:]	Schiffsmannschaft
on board	an Bord
Suez Canal [ˌsu:ɪz cə'næl]	Suezkanal
to collect	abholen
to deliver	(ab)liefern
electronic equipment	elektronisches Gerät
waste	Abfall, Müll
to dispose of sth	etw. entsorgen
turn around time	Zeit, die man zum Ent- und Beladen eines Schiffes benötigt
tight [taɪt]	eng, knapp geplant
departure [dɪ'pɑ:tʃə]	Auslaufen, Abfahrt
tide times	Zeiten von Ebbe und Flut
port = harbour ['hɑ:bə]	Hafen
berthing cost	Anlegekosten
to load	(be)laden
to unload	entladen

avsx5zq

Container ships like the MSC Oscar are used for **transporting** goods all around the world, after the containers have been unloaded, they still have to be **forwarded** to their final **destination**, either by train or lorry. The **wagons** or **trailers** are specially **designed** so that a container **fits** exactly when placed there by one of the port's **cranes**. This **enables** the containers to be collected and delivered directly to where they are needed.

Energy

The amount of energy we need to **power** all the **electrical equipment** we have is **huge**. There are many **sources** that we can get it from, and they can be **divided into renewable** and non-renewable sources. The most popular source is a non-renewable source: **fossil fuels** which are **coal**, **oil** and **natural gas**.

Fossil fuels were **formed** when plants and animals died hundreds of millions of years ago. Their **remains decayed** and mixed with the sand and **mud** and were then **buried** deep in the earth. **Pressure** from above and **heat** from below over thousands of years turned them into fossil fuels.

Electrical energy is one form of energy that is needed, but also **mechanical** and heat energy is needed. Oil and gas for example are **pumped** from **wells** deep under the ocean. They are then sent through **pipelines** to be **refined** or cleaned. Coal is **mined** underground near the earth's **surface** and is **burned** to **produce** heat. »»

to transport	transportieren, befördern
to forward	weiterschicken, weiter befördern
destination [ˌdestɪˈneɪʃn]	Ziel, Bestimmungsort
wagon [ˈwægən] *BE*	Eisenbahnwaggon
trailer	Anhänger
designed	konstruiert
to fit	passen
crane	Kran
to enable	ermöglichen

energy [ˈenədʒi]	Energie
to power [ˈpaʊə]	mit Energie/Strom versorgen
electrical equipment	Elektrogeräte
huge [hjuːdʒ]	riesig
source [sɔːs]	Quelle
to divide into	aufteilen in
renewable	erneuerbar
fossil fuel	fossiler Brennstoff
coal	Kohle
oil	Öl
natural gas	Erdgas

to form	bilden
remains	Überreste
to decay	zerfallen
mud	Schlamm, Morast
to bury	begraben
pressure [ˈpreʃə]	Druck
heat	Hitze

mechanical [mɪˈkænɪkl]	mechanisch
to pump	pumpen
well	Bohrloch; Lagerstätte
pipeline	Rohrleitung, Pipeline
to refine sth	etw. raffinieren, etw. veredeln
to mine	abbauen
surface [ˈsɜːfɪs]	Oberfläche
to burn [bɜːn], burnt / burned [bɜːnt / bɜːnd], burnt / burned [bɜːnt / bɜːnd]	verbrennen; brennen
to produce	erzeugen, produzieren

avsx5zq

Nuclear power is also used to make electrical energy. Atoms from a fuel called uranium are split (nuclear fission) inside a reactor. This energy is released as heat which makes water boil and change into steam, that is then used to drive turbine generators.

Unfortunately none of these sources are renewable, which means they can't naturally be restored in a short period of time. At some time in the future, the supply of non-renewable power resources will run out. Because of this, other sources needed to be found to produce more of the earth's electricity. Renewable energy is a source that cannot run out or be exhausted.

It can be obtained from the sun (solar energy), water (hydropower), the wind (windmills), hot water springs (geothermal) and also from biomass like firewood, animal manure, crop residues and other organic waste.

Solar power is provided by the light of the sun. It is free, everlasting and non-polluting. When the sun shines on solar cells, they absorb the energy which causes a chemical reaction that generates electricity. Solar systems can be used to pump water, heat water and, more often nowadays, to provide electricity in homes. Lots of houses have solar panels on their roofs, and in the countryside you can see that farmers now have fields of solar panels.

Hydropower can produce mechanical and electrical energy. To stop rivers, so they form lakes, dams are built. When the water flows down through pipes in the dam, it is guided to a turbine. The force of the water turns the turbine which turns a generator to produce electricity. Hydropower isn't something new, it has been used for hundreds of years to create mechanical energy for grinding, pumping and running machines.

nuclear power ['nju:kliə]	Kernkraft, Atomkraft
atom ['ætəm]	Atom
uranium [jʊ'reɪniəm]	Uran
to split [splɪt], split [splɪt], split [splɪt]	spalten
nuclear fission [ˌnju:kliə 'fɪʃn]	Kernspaltung, Atomspaltung
to release [rɪ'li:s]	freisetzen
to boil	kochen, sieden
steam	Wassserdampf
to drive [draɪv), drove [drəʊv], driven ['drɪvn]	antreiben
turbine [ˌtɜ:baɪn]	Turbine
generator ['dʒenreɪtə]	Generator, Stromerzeuger

naturally ['nætʃrli]	auf natürliche Weise
to restore	wiederherstellen
supply	Vorrat
to run out	ausgehen
exhausted [ɪg'zɔ:stɪd]	aufgebraucht, erschöpft

to obtain sth	gewinnen, erzeugen
solar energy [ˌsəʊlər'enədʒi]	Solarenergie, Sonnenenergie
hydropower	Wasserkraft
windmill	Windrad
spring	Quelle
geothermal [ˌdʒi:əʊ'θɜ:.ml]	geothermisch, mit Erdwärme
biomass	Biomasse
firewood	(Brenn)Holz
animal manure [mə'njʊə]	Gülle, Mist *(aus der Landwirtschaft)*
crop residue ['krɒp ˌrezɪdju:]	Pflanzenreste, Pflanzenabfälle
organic waste	Bioabfall

to provide	bereitstellen
everlasting	dauerhaft
non-polluting	umweltfreundlich
solar cell	Solarzelle
chemical reaction	chemische Reaktion
to generate	erzeugen
solar panel	Sonnenkollektor, Solarmodul
roof	Dach

dam	(Stau)Damm
pipe	Rohr
to guide	leiten
force	Druck, Kraft
to create [kri'eɪt]	erzeugen
to grind	mahlen
to run [rʌn], ran [ræn], run [rʌn]	laufen, betreiben

avsx5zq

Wind power is a power source that has **developed** a lot in the past years. The energy is produced directly from the wind by driving a wind turbine. This resource is free and renewable, and it also **emits** no **harmful greenhouse gases**. There are many windmills next to **motorways** or on hills and mountains, but there are also lots of **wind farms** in the sea, **off the coast**. There is more wind there and the noise of the windmills doesn't **disturb** anyone.

Geothermal power stations use the heat energy from deep in the earth, some by pumping water through special pipes buried underground, others **collect** hot steam to turn turbine generators. People in many areas use **pumps** which **circulate** water that is cooled and heated by the mild earth temperature several feet below the earth's surface. With the help of **heat exchangers**, they can both cool and heat their homes or other buildings and provide them with hot water.

Biomass can either be used directly, via **combustion** to produce thermal energy, or indirectly after **converting** it into various forms of **biofuel**. The conversion of biomass into biofuel can be **achieved** by a number of **biochemical** methods.

English is a global language

The main reason why English is spoken in so many countries around the world lies in the history of Great Britain. It used to be a huge **empire**, with **colonies in the four corners of the world**. English became the **main language** in the countries where English-speaking people **settled**, in Australia and North America for example. It became an **official language** in countries that were part of the Empire, like India, where the British lived but never **permanently** settled.

As the world becomes more global and in a way smaller, English is the common language used for **communicating** in **business**, **politics** and also on the internet. If you have a **meeting** with people from many different countries, the language that everyone will **understand**, some way or another, is English.

When you are on holiday, it doesn't really matter where, you will meet people **from all over the world** and you will want to talk to them. Claudia from Germany, André from France, Francesco from Italy, Sarah from England and Juan from Spain can all sit in a **snack bar** in **Majorca** and **have a conversation**.

The language they all **share**, some will be able to speak it better than others, is English. It is taught at school. Nearly everything on the internet **appears** in English first; the first language things are **translated** into is English, and if you want to keep reading a new **series of books**, it is better to read them in English as they will be **published** earlier. English is also a language people aren't scared of speaking. "**So what?**" if you make **mistakes**. What **counts** is that you try and the other person understands what you mean.

to develop	sich entwickeln
to emit [ɪ'mɪt]	ausstoßen, emittieren
harmful	schädlich
greenhouse gas	Treibhausgas
motorway *BE*	Autobahn
wind farm	Windpark
off the coast	vor der Küste
to disturb [dɪ'stɜ:b]	stören

to collect	sammeln
pump	Pumpe
to circulate	umwälzen
heat exchanger	Wärmetauscher

combustion	Verbrennung
to convert	umwandeln
▸ conversion	Umwandlung
biofuel	Biokraftstoff
to achieve	erreichen
biochemical	biochemische

---

empire ['empaɪə]	Weltreich, Imperium
colony ['kɒlənɪ]	Kolonie
in the four corners of the world	auf der ganzen Welt verteilt
main language	Hauptsprache
to settle [setl]	sich ansiedeln
official language	Amtssprache
permanently	dauerhaft, fest

to communicate	kommunizieren
business	Wirtschaft
politics	Politik
meeting	Treffen, Besprechung, Sitzung
to understand [ˌʌndə'stænd], understood [ˌʌndə'stʊd], understood [ˌʌndə'stʊd]	verstehen, begreifen

from all over the world	aus aller Welt
snack bar	Imbissstube
Majorca [mə'jɔ:kə]	Mallorca
to have a conversation [ˌkɒnvə'seɪʃn]	sich unterhalten, ein Gespräch führen

to share [ʃeə]	teilen, gemeinsam benutzen
to appear [ə'pɪə]	angezeigt werden, erscheinen
to translate	übersetzen, übertragen
series of books	Buchreihe
to publish	veröffentlichen
So what?	Was soll's?, Na und?
mistake	Fehler
to count	zählen

avsx5zq

10 Special days

List of special days

Date	Special day	What you can say
1st January	**New Year's Day**	**Happy New Year!**
14th February	**Valentine's Day**	Happy Valentine!
March/April	**Easter**	**Happy Easter!**
4th Sunday in **Lent** (UK) 2nd Sunday in May (US/AUS)	Mother's Day	Happy Mother's Day!
3rd Sunday in June (UK/USA) 1st Sunday in September (AUS)	Father's Day	Happy Father's Day!
4th July (USA)	**Independence** Day	Happy 4th of July!
1st Monday in September (USA)	**Labor** Day	
31st October	**Halloween**	**Trick or treat!**
5th November (UK)	**Bonfire** Night	Remember, remember the fifth of November. **Gunpowder**, **treason** and **plot**.
4th Thursday in November (USA)	**Thanksgiving**	Happy Thanksgiving!
25th December	**Christmas** Day	**Merry Christmas!** **Season's Greetings!**
Every day	**Birthday**	**Happy Birthday!**

There are lots of special days **throughout the world**. Some are **celebrated** in lots of countries on the same day and others are celebrated in different countries on different days. Some are **religious** and others are **commercial** or **traditional**. All of them bring family and friends together, sometimes presents or flowers are given, at other times cards or just a **greeting** are **passed on**. For some people the days are special, for others they can be a very normal **working day**. Travel with me on my **journey** through the year of these special days. »»

New Year's Day	Neujahr, Neujahrstag
Happy New Year!	Gutes neues Jahr!
Valentine's Day	Valentinstag
Easter	Ostern
Happy Easter!	Frohe Ostern!
Lent	Fastenzeit
independence	Unabhängigkeit
▸ independent	unabhängig
labor *AE* = labour *BE*	Arbeit
Halloween	Halloween
Trick or treat!	Süßes, oder es gibt Saures!
bonfire	Lagerfeuer, Freudenfeuer
gunpowder	Schießpulver
treason	(Landes)Verrat
plot	Verschwörung
Thanksgiving	Erntedankfest
Christmas	Weihnachten
Merry Christmas!	Frohe/Fröhliche Weihnachten!
Season's Greetings!	Fröhliche Weihnachten und ein gutes neues Jahr!
birthday	Geburtstag
Happy Birthday!	Alles Gute zum Geburtstag!

throughout the world	auf der ganzen Welt
to celebrate ['seləbreɪt]	feiern
religious [rɪ'lɪdʒəs]	religiös
▸ religion	Religion
commercial [kə'mɜːʃl]	kommerziell, geschäftlich
traditional [trə'dɪʃənl]	herkömmlich, traditionell
greeting	Grüße, gute Wünsche
to pass on	weitergeben
working day	Arbeitstag
journey ['dʒɜːni]	Reise

cd5bca2

New Year's Eve / New Year's Day

(31st December / 1st January)

The new year starts, rather **obviously**, on New Year's Day, the 1st January. The **celebrations** actually begin on 31st December when friends **gather** to welcome in the new year as the clock **strikes midnight**.

For a lot of people it is a day of rest following a very late night of **partying** with friends. Some people, **naturally**, have to work on New Year's Day, e.g. **nurses**, doctors, **train drivers**, **bus drivers** and **police officers**, to name just a few.

It can be a day of new **beginnings** and also **life changing plans** or **decisions**. People make **New Year's Resolutions**. They decide what they are going to (try and) change or do differently in their lives in the new year. This can be a new job, a **diet** or working harder at something, for example.

The first countries to welcome the new year are Somoa and the Christmas Islands; then, slowly moving west, country after country says "Happy New Year". **Unbelievably**, some 14 hours later the last **outlying** islands of the USA can also start the new year.

New Year celebrations in different countries

Let's take a look at some new year **traditions** around the world. As I know this country best, let's start with the UK.

In England the **custom** for welcoming in the new year is with **hospitality** and **warmth**. The first person, hopefully **male**, through the **front door** should bring with them the following items:

- bread for the kitchen,
- a drink for the **head of the family** and
- **coal** for the fire.

If they are **empty-handed**, they aren't allowed into the house. It is **believed** that these things bring the family good luck throughout the year. This custom is called 'first footing'.

Now staying in Great Britain, let's move to the west.

In Wales, on the first **stroke of the bell** at midnight, the **back door** is opened and **immediately** closed again to let out the old year and any bad luck that is left in it. On the final stroke the door is **re-opened** to let in the **goodness**, luck and **prosperity** of the new year.

Staying in Europe, but moving south, let's visit Spain. »»

New Year's Eve	Silvesterabend
obviously ['ɒbvɪəsli]	offensichtlich; anscheinend
celebration [ˌseləˈbreɪʃn]	Feier
▸ to celebrate	feiern
to gather	sich versammeln, zusammenkommen
to strike [straɪk], struck [strʌk], struck [strʌk]	schlagen
midnight	Mitternacht

to party	feiern
naturally ['nætʃərəli]	natürlich, selbstverständlich
nurse	Krankenpfleger, Krankenschwester
train driver	Lokführer(in)
bus driver	Busfahrer(in)
police officer [pəˈliːsˌɒfɪsə]	Polizeibeamter, Polizeibeamtin

beginning	Beginn, Anfang
life changing plan	lebensverändernder Plan
decision [dɪˈsɪʒn]	Entscheidung
▸ to decide	entscheiden
resolution [ˌrezlˈuːʃn]	Vorsatz
▸ New Year's resolution	*(guter Vorsatz fürs neue Jahr)*
diet ['daɪət]	Ernährung; Diät

unbelievably	unglaublich; unglaubwürdig
outlying	abgelegen

tradition [trəˈdɪʃn]	Tradition, Sitte, Brauch
custom	Brauch, Sitte
hospitality	Gastfreundschaft
warmth	Herzlichkeit; Wärme
male	männlich, Männer-
≠ female	weiblich, Frauen-
front door	Haustür
head of the family	Familienoberhaupt
coal	Kohle
empty-handed	mit leeren Händen
to believe	glauben

stroke of the bell	Glockenschlag
back door	Hintertür
immediately [ɪˈmiːdiətli]	sofort
to re-open	wieder aufmachen
goodness	Herzensgüte, Gütigkeit
≠ badness	Schlechtheit
prosperity	Reichtum, Wohlstand

cd5bca2

In Spain they eat one **grape** each time the bell **tolls** at midnight. This is also for luck and **happiness** in the next twelve months of the new year.

Now let's leave Europe and **head** further west across the Atlantic Ocean.

In the USA they believe that kissing, as midnight **approaches**, is lucky as it cleans everything that is **evil**.

Now our journey takes us south to South America.

In Brazil people believe that **lentils** are a symbol of **wealth** and prosperity. They **serve** food made of lentils at their New Year celebrations. In Rio de Janeiro a boat filled with jewellery, candles and flowers is pushed off the beach into the **ocean**. This brings **health**, wealth and happiness to the Brazilians.

Now we have to jump on a plane to take a look at China.

In the Chinese **lunisolar calendar** a new year begins on the full moon between 21st January and 20th February. This means the Chinese New Year is on a different day each year. The New Year celebrations are also known as the **Spring Festival** and last 15 days. Before the festival many people clean their homes and hang red posters on their doors with **poetic verses** on them. They also **put up** pictures of Chinese New Year on their walls and **decorate** their homes with Chinese **lanterns**. **Fireworks** are **set off** in the evening to **cast out** any **bad luck** and bring **good luck**. It is a family festival. Children are given 'luck' money, **drums** are **beaten** and there are **dragon** and **lion** dances in the streets. It is also a **public holiday** in China.

Valentine's Day

(14th February)

Now to a **romantic** special day. Valentine's Day, also known as **Saint** Valentine's Day, as one **expects**, was **originally** to **honour** Saint Valentine. **Nowadays** it is a more **cultural** and commercial celebration.

From about the 18th **century** it developed into an **occasion** when people **in love** started giving each other flowers, chocolates or sending cards. Some people send their cards to somebody they are secretly in love with. ⟫

grape	Traube
to toll	läuten
happiness	Glück, Zufriedenheit
▸ happy	glücklich
to head	gehen
to approach	annähern
evil ['i:vəl]	böse
lentil	Linse
wealth [welθ]	Reichtum
to serve	anbieten, auftischen; bedienen
ocean ['əʊʃn]	Ozean, Weltmeer
health	Gesundheit
lunisolar	vom Lauf der Sonne und des Monds abhängig
calendar	Kalender
spring festival	Frühlingsfest
poetic verse [pəʊˌtɪk 'vɜ:s]	poetische Lyrik
to put up	aufhängen
to decorate	schmücken; tapezieren, anstreichen
▸ decoration	Schmuck *(für die Wohnung)*, Dekoration
lantern	Laterne
fireworks	Feuerwerk
to set off	entzünden
to cast out	vertreiben
bad luck	Unglück, Pech
good luck	Glück
drum	Trommel
to beat [bi:t], beat [bi:t], beaten ['bi:tən]	schlagen
dragon	Drache
lion ['laɪən]	Löwe
public holiday	gesetzlicher Feiertag
romantic	romantisch
saint	Heiliger, Sankt
to expect	erwarten; schätzen, annehmen
originally [ə'rɪdʒnli]	ursprünglich
to honour	ehren
▸ in honour of	zu Ehren
nowadays	heutzutage
cultural	kulturell
century ['sentʃəri]	Jahrhundert
occasion	Anlass
in love	verliebt

cd5bca2

Other people write fun poems in their cards that have sweet rhymes in them: 'Roses are red, violets are blue, honey is sweet and so are you.'

More recently, this day has developed further and cards are sent to friends and children. The card industry and florists really love this day, as their profits are very good.

Easter

(March/April)

Now to a religious festival, that again is celebrated in different ways in different regions in the world.

Easter has no fixed date every year. It is celebrated on the first Sunday after the first full moon on or after 21st March, when spring officially begins. Therefore Easter is always between 22nd March and 25th April.

The lead up to the Easter weekend is very important. It starts on Shrove Tuesday (or Pancake Day), which is the last day before the period of Lent starts on Ash Wednesday. In some countries Shrove Tuesday is also known as Mardi Gras (literally meaning 'fat Tuesday'). This is a carnival day and, as it sounds, a day of gorging before Lent starts.

Ash Wednesday gets its name from the blessed ashes from the previous year's Palm Sunday, being placed on the heads of churchgoers on this day, to help them remember and believe in God.

A lot of people fast in the period of Lent; they don't eat meat or sweets or drink alcohol. It is the 40 days before Easter, well actually 46 days, but the six Sundays are not included as they are not fasting days. It was always a time of fasting, but it has been adapted to modern times when you look at what people don't consume – like not using their smartphones or using their smartphones less. Churches are not decorated with flowers at Lent and the church altar is kept very plain.

The Sunday before Easter Sunday is called Palm Sunday and is the sixth Sunday in Lent. The week before the Easter weekend is called Holy Week. It includes Maundy Thursday, the day of the Last Supper, and Good Friday, the day that Jesus was crucified. Most people think it ends on Easter Sunday, but this is actually the beginning of the Easter season which lasts seven weeks.

poem ['pəʊɪm]	Gedicht
rhyme [raɪm]	Reim
‣ to rhyme	reimen
honey	Honig
more recently	in jüngerer Zeit
industry	Industrie; Wirtschaft, Branche
florist	Blumenhändler(in)
profit	Gewinn, Profit
fixed	fest, nicht variabel
officially [ə'fɪʃli]	offiziell
therefore	deshalb; also
lead up	Zeit
Shrove Tuesday	Faschingsdienstag
period ['pɪəriəd]	Zeitraum, Dauer
Lent	Fastenzeit
Ash Wednesday	Aschermittwoch
Mardi Gras [ˌmɑ:di 'grɑ:]	Fasching, Karneval
literally	wortwörtlich
carnival	Karneval
to gorge [gɔ:dʒ]	schlemmen, sich vollessen
blessed [blest]	gesegnet
ash	Asche
previous	vorhergehend
churchgoer	Kirchgänger(in)
to fast	fasten
alcohol	Alkohol, alkoholische Getränke
to adapt sth to modern times	etw. an die moderne/heutige Zeit anpassen
to consume	zu sich nehmen, verbrauchen, konsumieren
altar	Altar
plain	einfach, schlicht
Palm Sunday [ˌpɑ:m 'sʌndeɪ]	Palmsonntag
holy	heilig
Maundy Thursday	Gründonnerstag
the Last Supper	das Abendmahl
Good Friday	Karfreitag
crucified ['kru:sɪfaɪd]	gekreuzigt
season	Jahreszeit

cd5bca2

Easter is celebrated in different ways. Some people **attend** Easter **church services**; for other people it is another **excuse** for a family **get-together** as it is a **long weekend**. Easter eggs made of chocolate are given as presents or hidden for children to find. Houses are decorated with **colourful** eggs. In gardens there are **daffodils** and **tulips**, and it is **generally** a time of **awakening** after the long winter months.

So spring has arrived. The next special day is celebrated on different days in different countries, but what can it be?

Mother's Day

(fourth Sunday in Lent, UK; second Sunday of May, USA/AUS)

Mother's Day or Mothering Sunday is a modern special day in honour of mothers, **motherhood** and also the **influence** mothers have on **society**. It is celebrated on different days in different countries, but is usually in March or May. It started in the USA in the early 20th century. Usually cards are sent; mothers are visited and presented with flowers, chocolates or other presents and are generally **spoilt**. Younger children make their presents at **playschool** or school.

The most important thing about this day is that you shouldn't forget it - or your mum.

Father's Day

(third Sunday in June, UK/USA; first Sunday in September, AUS)

The same as Mother's Day, Father's Day is in honour of fathers, **fatherhood** and the influence of father's on society. Again presents are given, sometimes **handmade**, and fathers are spoilt by their **loved ones**. Again, it is not a good idea to forget this day, especially if you want your dad to **give you a lift** or help you.

Independence Day

(4th July, USA)

In the USA the 4th July is a very special day. On this day America celebrates the **signing** of **the Declaration of Independence** in 1776. At this time the **inhabitants** of the 13 **colonies** of the east coast were at war with Great Britain because they felt that they were not being **dealt** with **fairly**. The **colonists** soon **realised** they were really fighting for their independence from Great Britain. The declaration **signed** by the leaders of the colonies was the first **official document** in which the name 'The United States of America' was used.

Today it is a family day of **barbecues**, picnics and **patriotic** parades, concerts and firework displays. You can see the American flag with its **stars and stripes flying** everywhere. It is also a national holiday in the USA.

to attend	besuchen
church service	Gottesdienst
excuse [ɪk'skjuːs]	Entschuldigung, Ausrede
get-together	Beieinandersein, Zusammentreffen
long weekend	verlängertes Wochenende
colourful	bunt, farbig
daffodil	Narzisse, Osterglocke
tulip	Tulpe
generally ['dʒenrli]	im Allgemeinen, generell
awakening	Erwachen, Aufbruch

motherhood	Mutterschaft, Muttersein
influence	Einfluss
society [sə'saɪəti]	Gesellschaft
to spoil sb [spɔɪl], spoilt [spɔɪlt], spoilt [spɔɪlt]	jdn. verwöhnen, jdn. verziehen
▸ spoilt child	verwöhntes/verzogenes Kind
playschool	Kindergarten

fatherhood	Vaterschaft, Vatersein
handmade	handgemacht, handgerfertigt
loved one	Nahestehende(r), Angehörige(r)
to give sb a lift	jdm. eine Mitfahrgelegenheit geben, jdn. mitfahren lassen

signing ['saɪnɪŋ]	Unterzeichnung
the Declaration of Independence	Unabhängigkeitserklärung
inhabitant	Einwohner(in)
colony	Kolonie
to deal with sb	mit jdm. umgehen
fairly	anständig, richtig
colonist	Kolonist(in), Siedler(in)
to realise	begreifen, erkennen
to sign [saɪn]	unterzeichnen, unterschreiben
official document	amtliche Urkunde, offizielles Dokument

barbecue	Grillfest; Grill
patriotic	patriotisch
stars and stripes	Sterne und Streifen
to fly [flaɪ], flew [fluː], flown [fləʊn]	fliegen

cd5bca2

Labor Day

(first Monday in September, USA)

It's the Americans' turn again, and on the first Monday in September they have another public holiday, this time to celebrate Labor Day. Labor Day honours the American labor **movement** and the things that workers have done to **strengthen** the **well-being** of the USA. It is a day when most people don't have to work and it is the Monday of the Labor Day Weekend which is **considered** the **unofficial** end of summer.

On Labor day there are parades and festivals, as well as **speeches** made by important people. It also **marks** the beginning of the **fall** sports season, and lots of **leagues** have their first **match** of the new season in the week following Labor Day. In other sports, finals of the previous season are held on Labor Day Weekend, **for example** car races.

Halloween

(31st October)

Now get your **costumes** and your **frightening make-up** out. Halloween is on the 31st October, which is the **eve** of **All Saints Day** on 1st November. It is a very **ancient** festival, although today, it is more for children, and it is very **commercialised**.

People usually **dress up** on Halloween as **witches**, **ghosts** or other scary **characters**. There are lots of **fancy dress** parties and people go trick-or-treating. This means they visit their neighbours, ring the **doorbell**, say "Trick or treat!" and hope for a **treat**, of usually sweets, so that they don't have to **play a trick**.

Houses are decorated with orange objects, **skulls**, **skeletons** and other scary things. **Jack-o-lanterns** are made from **pumpkins** with a candle **burning** in them. These are placed on **verandas**, **porches** and **doorsteps**. People have bonfires, play games like **apple bobbing**, visit **haunted places**, tell scary stories or watch **horror** films.

movement ['mu:vmənt]	Bewegung; Beweglichkeit
to strengthen sth ['streŋθn]	etw. stärken
well-being	Wohlbefinden
to consider	erwägen; überlegen
unofficial	inoffiziell
speech	Rede
to mark	bezeichnen
fall [fɔ:l] *AE* = autumn *BE*	Herbst
league [li:g]	Liga, Spielklasse
match	Spiel
for example	zum Beispiel

costume	Kostüm
frightening	furchterregend, beängstigend
make-up	Schminke
eve	Abend des Vortags, Vorabend
All Saints Day	Allerheiligen
ancient ['eɪnʃnt]	uralt
commercialized [kə'mɜ:ʃəlaɪzd]	kommerzialisiert
to dress up	sich verkleiden
witch	Hexe
ghost	Geist
character ['kærɪktə]	Charakter; Eigenschaft
fancy dress	Verkleidung
doorbell	Türklingel, Türglocke
treat	Leckerei, Süßes
to play a trick	einen Streich spielen
skull	Schädel
skeleton	Skelett
jack-o-lantern	Kürbislaterne
pumpkin	Kürbis
to burn [bɜ:n], burnt/burned [bɜ:nt/bɜ:nd], burnt/burned [bɜ:nt/bɜ:nd]	brennen
veranda	Veranda
porch [pɔ:tʃ]	Vorbau, Vordach *BE*; Veranda *AE*
doorstep	Stufe vor der Haustür
apple bobbing	Spiel, bei dem man versucht, mit dem Mund einen Apfel aus einem mit Wasser gefüllten Behälter zu holen
haunted places	Orte, an denen es Geister geben soll, verwunschene Orte
horror ['hɒrə]	Horror

cd5bca2

Bonfire Night

(5th November, UK)

Now some people think this is a **strange** day to celebrate, and it is only celebrated in the UK: Bonfire Night or Guy Fawkes Day. As the name **suggests**, bonfires are lit in the evening and it has something to do with a man called Guy Fawkes. But what is it all about?

In 1605 there was a plot by a number of people, including Guy Fawkes, to **blow up** the **Houses of Parliament** in London. They had hidden lots of **barrels** of gunpowder in the **cellars beneath** parliament. **Fortunately**, when Guy Fawkes was hiding the last barrels, he was caught and **arrested**. He was **tried for treason**, found **guilty** and **hanged**. The English celebrate Guy Fawkes and his friends for not being **successful**.

Nowadays there are big firework displays organised by towns and cities, and there is usually a huge bonfire in the middle of an **open area**, and a **guy** is placed on top and is **set fire to**. The guy is to remember Guy Fawkes and his friends' **failure**. People make guys using old clothes that are **stuffed**, and then they place them on top of the bonfire before setting it on fire. Children sometimes collect money and **donate** it to **charities**.

Thanksgiving

(fourth Thursday in November, USA)

Now we have to do a **brief** visit to the USA for this special day. Thanksgiving is an American special day celebrated on the fourth Thursday in November. Originally it was the **harvest festival**, giving thanks that all **crops** have been safely harvested and everyone has enough to eat in the long winter months. The first Thanksgiving was celebrated by **the Pilgrims** after their first harvest after arriving in **the New World** in 1621.

Nowadays **the poor** are often provided with food at Thanksgiving. **Communities** collect **packaged** and **tinned** food which is **distributed among** the poor. Traditional food on Thanksgiving tables is **stuffed turkey** (**roasted** or **baked**), **mashed potatoes**, sweet potatoes, cranberry sauce, **gravy** and pumpkin pie.

There are well-known parades in many American cities like New York, Chicago, Philadelphia or Detroit. You can see **floats**, **marching bands**, large **balloons** and often **celebrity guests**. Usually the parades are also shown on TV. As on Labor Day, there are also many **sporting events**. American football matches and college basketball games are held, and also fun events like the Turkey Trot take place, where people dress up as turkeys and run between a mile and a marathon. ⟫

strange [streɪndʒ]	seltsam, eigenartig
to suggest [sə'dʒest]	andeuten; vorschlagen
▸ suggestion	Andeutung, Vorschlag

to blow up [ˌbləʊ'ʌp]	in die Luft jagen, sprengen
Houses of Parliament ['pɑ:ləment]	das (britische) Parlament
barrel ['bærl]	Fass
cellar ['selə]	Keller
beneath [bɪ'ni:θ]	unterhalb, unter
fortunately ['fɔ:tʃnətli]	glücklicherweise, zum Glück
to be arrested	verhaftet werden
to be tried for treason	wegen Verrats angeklagt werden
guilty ['gɪlti]	schuldig
to hang [hæŋ], hung [hʌŋ], hung [hʌŋ]	hängen
successful [sək'sesfl]	erfolgreich

open area	öffentlicher Platz
guy [gaɪ]	männl. Puppe, die Guy Fawkes symbolisiert
to set fire to sth	etw. anzünden
failure ['feɪljə]	Misserfolg, Versagen
to stuff	ausstopfen; füllen
to donate	spenden
charity	Wohltätigkeitsorganisation

---

brief	kurz
harvest festival	Erntedankfest, Erntefest
crop	Feldfrucht, Ernte
the Pilgrims = the Pilgrim Fathers	Die Pilger
the New World	die Neue Welt

the poor	die Armen
community	Gemeinde
packaged ['pækɪdʒd]	abgepackt, verpackt
tinned	in Dosen, Dosen-
to distribute among	verteilen an
stuffed turkey	gefüllter Truthahn
roasted	gebraten, Brat-
baked	gebacken
mashed potatoes	Katoffelpüree, Kartoffelbrei
gravy	Bratensoße

float	Festzugswagen, Umzugswagen
marching band	Marschkapelle, Blaskapelle
balloon	Luftballon
celebrity guest [səˌlebrəti 'gest]	eine berühmte Persönlichkeit als Gast
sporting event	Sportereignis

cd5bca2

The President of America traditionally **pardons** a turkey at the White House. He **picks** a turkey that won't be **slaughtered**, instead it gets sent back to a turkey farm, not always the one it came from.

Christmas

(24th to 26th December)

Possibly the **best-known**, and maybe for some people (children) the **best-loved**, time of year brings us to the end of our journey through the year of special days: the Christmas season.

Christmas, although celebrated on Christmas Eve (24th December), Christmas Day (25th December) and Boxing Day (26th December), also includes the time **leading up to** Christmas called **advent**, which starts on the fourth Sunday before 25th December. Christmas is **a time of** decorating houses, buying presents, sending **greetings cards**, putting up Christmas trees and ... eating lots. It is a lot of work but usually **results in time off** of work over the three-day **festive period** for most people.

In Great Britain and the USA, on Christmas Eve, **stockings** are hung, if possible on the **mantelpiece**, for **Father Christmas** or **Santa Claus** to fill with **brightly wrapped presents** - if you have been good.

The **feast** is on Christmas Day bringing families together to eat **roast turkey with all the trimmings** and **plum pudding**. Presents are exchanged, and in the UK many people watch the Queen's speech on TV at 3 o'clock. Christmas **crackers** are pulled, paper hats are worn, and silly **jokes** are also told.

Boxing Day was given its name as it was the day that the **servants** always used to get their Christmas presents in boxes from their **employers**, as they were working on Christmas Day. It is a day to visit family and friends or just **relax** and eat **leftovers**.

Christmas is also celebrated to remember the **birth** of Jesus Christ and the journey Mary and Joseph took to Bethlehem. The story is often **performed** in schools in the time before Christmas. There are lots of **roles** as **shepherds**, kings, **angels** and even sheep, so everyone can take part in the **nativity play**.

Well, I hope you enjoyed my **explanations** and even learnt a few things you didn't know. Maybe you will also think about different things on these special days in the **future** or look at how you celebrate them.

to pardon sb	jdn. begnadigen
to pick	aussuchen, auswählen
to slaughter ['slɔ:tə]	schlachten
possibly	möglicherweise, wahrscheinlich
best-known	bekannteste
best-loved	beliebteste
to lead up to	vorangehen, auf etw. hinführen
advent ['ædvent]	Advent
a time of	eine Zeit für
greetings card	Grußkarte
to result in sth	zu etw. führen
time off	arbeitsfreie Tage/Zeit
festive period	Feiertage
stocking	Strumpf
mantelpiece ['mæntlpi:s]	Kaminsims
Father Christmas *BE*	Weihnachtsmann
Santa Claus *AE*	Weihnachtsmann
brightly wrapped presents	bunt eingepackte Geschenke
feast	Festmahl
roast turkey	Putenbraten
with all the trimmings	mit allem Drum und Dran
plum pudding [ˌplʌm'pʊdɪŋ]	Plumpudding *(Weihnachtsnachtisch in Großbritannien)*
cracker *BE*	Knallbonbon
joke [dʒəʊk]	Witz
servant	Bedienstete(r), Dienstmädchen
employer	Arbeitgeber(in)
to relax	sich entspannen
leftovers	Essensreste *(vorheriger Mahlzeiten)*
birth	Geburt
to perform	ausführen
role	Rolle
shepherd ['ʃepəd]	Schäfer(in)
angel ['eɪndʒəl]	Engel
nativity play	Krippenspiel
explanation	Erklärung
future ['fju:tʃə]	Zukunft

cd5bca2

11 Skills – phrases and words

Tips for writing letters

1. Write your name, address and other contact data, e.g. your telephone number and/or e-mail address on the right or left (before the name and address of the person you are writing to) at the top of your letter.
2. Write the name and full address of the person the letter is to on the left at the top of your letter.
3. Write the full date under the address of the person you are writing. Leave an empty line between the end of the address and the date.
4. If you don't know the person's name you are writing to, write 'Dear Sir or Madam,' or 'To whom it may concern,'. If you do know their name write 'Dear Mrs (last name),/Dear Mr (last name),/Dear Ms (last name),'
5. Write an appropriate subject line. This can either come before or after number 4. It can be in CAPITAL LETTERS, in **bold** or <u>underlined</u>.
6. The first word in a letter always has a capital letter.
7. Next comes the main part of your letter including why you are writing, any questions you want to ask and any information you want to give the recipient.
8. The last sentence should bring your letter to a positive and polite close.
9. End your letter with one of these phrases:

   An informal letter:

   - Best wishes,
   - See you soon,
   - Write soon,

   A formal letter:

   - Yours faithfully, (if you started your letter 'Dear Sir or Madam,')
   - Yours sincerely, (if you started your letter 'Dear Mrs, Mr or Ms …,')
10. Type your name leaving enough space for you to sign your letter above your typed name.
11. If you are sending enclosures, e.g. a photo or a list of information, make a list of what you have included. It helps you check you have sent everything and the recipient can check they have everything.

Informal letters/emails

The following example uses the layout of a written letter. If you are sending an e-mail you just need to use the part from Dear …, to the end of the letter. You can leave out the addresses and date. The style of writing is the same for a letter or an e-mail.

Introducing yourself

Richard Smith
7 Station Lane
Stamford
Somerset TA33 4RR

David Beispiel
Hauptstraße 32
D- 12345 Hauptstadt
Germany

England
10th June 2016

Dear Richard,

I have been given your name and address by my English teacher as she said you were looking for a German penfriend.
My name is David and I'm 12 years old. I live in Hauptstadt, which is in the north of Germany, with my mum and dad and my brother (he's 8) and my sister (she's 15). We have two cats and a dog. I'd like a rabbit or a guinea pig too, but they are too much work. My favourite food is pizza. My hobbies are playing computer games, reading detective stories and I play handball twice a week. Most of my friends play football, but I prefer handball as we play it inside. That is a short summary of me. There wasn't much information in your letter about you. Can you tell me what sports you like and your hobbies and if you have any pets?
Me and my family are coming to England in the summer. Maybe we could meet up; I don't know how far you live from where we are staying. We are going to Essex I think.

Write soon,
David

Saying thank you

Hi Rich,

What an amazing holiday we had in England. It was brilliant that we managed to meet up too and a real surprise.

Thank you for talking to your parents and persuading them that we should meet up at the Harry Potter Studio Tour. I know it was a long journey for you and I couldn't believe how much it cost to get it. It was a great day out though and my family really got on well with yours – it was so cool.

I have attached some photos of us all having fun. I have to go now as I have a handball match. I'll write more later, I just wanted to say thanks and send you the pics.

See you,

David

Formal letters/emails

Asking for information

Happy Days Leisure Centre
111 Main Road
Maintown
Essex MA13 4AZ

Eric Beispiel
Hauptstraße 32
D- 12345 Hauptstadt
Germany

England
20th July 2016

Dear Sir or Madam,

We are planning our holiday to England in August 2016 and our friends have recommended your leisure centre.
Unfortunately, they could give us no information about your prices and opening times. We will be in Maintown from 15th to 20th August. Can you please send me your opening times for this period and also tell me about your prices? We are a family of five, two adults and three children aged 15, 10 and 8.
I look forward to hearing from you soon and visiting your leisure centre in August.

Yours faithfully,
Erica Example

Writing a complaint

Happy Days Leisure Centre
111 Main Road
Attn.: Mrs Smith
Maintown

Eric Beispiel
Hauptstraße 32
D- 12345 Hauptstadt
Germany

20th September 2016

Dear Mrs Smith,

We visited your leisure centre on 17th August 2016. We paid extra money in order to be able to use the special slides into the pool. Nobody told us at the entrance that our youngest child, aged 8, would not be allowed to use two of the slides as he isn't tall enough. This also meant we could not get full use of the pool and its slides as a family, as one of us always had to stay with David, not to mention how upset he was.
On leaving the leisure centre we tried to speak to you but you were busy and we were given your business card and informed we should complain in writing. Firstly, we are annoyed that we couldn't enjoy all the facilities as a family, but also that I now have to spend more time writing to you. I would just like to recommend that you inform your staff that it is important they pass on the information to visitors on the different height restrictions for the slides, so other families aren't as disappointed as we were. The rest of your leisure centre was clean and the staff were friendly.

I look forward to hearing your opinion of our experience.
Yours faithfully,

Erica Example
Encs.
A copy of our entrance tickets from 17th August 2016

A letter of application

Check out the letter of application in the World of Work chapter on page 68.

8 steps for writing a text

1. Think about the text you have to write. What type of text is needed?
2. What will it be about? Which information should be in the text?
3. What special features does this type of text have? What does it look like? (A letter doesn't look the same as a review.)
4. Make a plan for your text. Make sure that your plan includes all the points that will be in the finished text.
5. Which key words go with this topic? That is where *this book* is helpful.
6. Write a first copy of the text. If you write your text by hand, leave a line between each line so that you can correct your text.
7. Ask a friend to read the first version of your text. Did they understand it? Listen to what they say about your text and improve it. Use the checklist for written texts to get rid of as many mistakes as possible.
8. Write the text again in a 'clean' version.

Useful phrases for writing ...

An opinion

I agree with ...	Ich stimme ... zu.
I disagree with ...	Ich stimme ... nicht zu.
I really liked ...	Mir hat ... sehr gefallen.
I didn't like ...	Mir hat ... nicht gefallen.
In my opinion ...	Meiner Meinung nach ...
According to ...	Zufolge/Gemäß ...
On the one hand ...	Einerseits ...
On the other hand ...	Andererseits ...

A story

Once upon a time ...	Es war einmal ...
Then ...	Dann ...
After that ...	Danach ...
Suddenly ...	Plötzlich ...
At the same time ...	Zur selben Zeit ...
... because ...	... weil ...
... but ...	... aber ...

A diary entry

I'm really happy/excited ...	Ich bin wirklich glücklich/aufgeregt …
I'm sad/annoyed/worried ...	Ich bin traurig/verärgert/beunruhigt …
I saw/met/heard …	Ich sah/traf/hörte …
I want to …	Ich will …

A biography

She/He was born in (place) in (year).	Sie/Er wurde (*Jahr*) in (*Ort*) geboren.
She/He went to school in …	Sie/Er ging in … zur Schule.
She/He left school in …	Sie/Er verließ die Schule im Jahr …
She/He invented …	Sie/Er erfand …
She/He was famous for …	Sie/Er war berühmt für …
It was made of …	Es wurde aus … gemacht/hergestellt.
She/He visited …	Sie/Er besuchte …
She/He died in (place) in (year).	Sie/Er starb (*Jahr*) in (*Ort*).

A review

The actors are …	Die Schauspieler/innen sind …
It is a comedy/drama/romance.	Es ist eine Komödie/Drama/Liebesfilm.
The start/ending is …	Der Anfang/Das Ende ist …
The story is about …	Die Geschichte handelt von …
The location of the film is …	Der Film spielt in …
It was one of the best/worst …	Es war eine der besten/ schlechtesten …
Give it a miss!	Nicht empfehlenswert!/Nicht anschauen!
Go and see it!	Geh auf jeden Fall hin!
I really enjoyed / didn't enjoy it.	Ich fand es gut / nicht so gut.
I give it X stars.	Ich würde X Sterne geben.

About a survey

This was a survey about …	Dies war eine Umfrage über …
The survey group were …	Die befragte Gruppe waren …
The first/second question is about …	Die erste/zweite Frage betrifft …
First of all, the grid shows that …	Zunächst zeigt die Tabelle, dass …
Very few people chose …	Sehr wenige Leute wählten …
Almost no students …	Fast kein(e) Schüler(in) wählte …
Secondly, the chart shows that …	Zweitens zeigt die Tabelle, dass …
… was more popular than …	… war beliebter als …
… was the most popular.	… war am beliebtesten.
So the results show that …	Die Ergebnisse zeigen, dass …

Checklist for written texts

Spelling

Have you spelt all the words correctly? Pay attention to:

- Letters that are written but not spoken (walk)
- Words that sound the same but are spelt differently (sea/see)
- The correct ending of a word (stop → stop**ped**, easy → eas**ily**)

Questions marks, full stops, etc.

Does each sentence end with a full stop?

Does each question end with a question mark?

Don't forget your speech marks when you use direct speech ("The train was late," Sarah explained.)

Capital letters

Do all your sentences start with a capital letter?

Do the following words start with a capital letter (and only these words)?

- Months (January, February, …)
- Days of the week (Monday, Tuesday, …)
- People's names (Tom, Sarah, …)
- Place names (London, Germany, …)
- Nationalities (English, German, …)

Grammar

Have you used the right tense?

Have you used the correct plurals where necessary?

Tips for a presentation/an oral exam

Getting ready

- Choose a topic that can be presented in the given time.
- Collect material about your topic from different places. Don't forget to make a note of your sources.
- Decide which main points you want to deal with. Choose a few other points that are also interesting or funny to keep your audience listening.
- Prepare the visual material you are going to use: maps, diagrams or pictures. Summarize key facts in a computer presentation or on a poster to give your audience something to look at. Make sure the writing is big and clear enough so that even the people at the back of the room can read it. Don't include too much information, you want your audience to listen to you.

- Write your notes on cards. Use one card for each point and only write down important words and facts. Do not write complete sentences.
- Put the cards and computer presentation in a logical order and number your cards.
- Make a handout and enough copies for everyone to get one. Don't give your handout to your audience until the end of your presentation so that they still listen to you.
- Practise your presentation. Use your cards, but speak freely. Check how long your presentation is. If necessary, shorten it or make it longer.

Presentation

- Speak loudly and clearly and not too fast. Change your voice now and again so that your presentation doesn't sound boring.
- Remember to look at the audience when you are speaking. You should only need to have a quick look at your cards if you have practised enough. After looking at your card, look up and speak freely to your audience.
- Use words that you know.
- At the end, thank your audience for listening, and ask them if they have any questions.

Useful speaking phrases for ...

Describing a picture or photo

At the top/bottom ...	Oben/unten ...
In the middle/centre ...	In der Mitte/Im Zentrum ...
On the left/right ...	Links/rechts ...
In the foreground/background ...	Im Vordergrund/Hintergrund ...
In the lower left/right corner ...	In der unteren linken/rechten Ecke ...
In the upper left /right corner ...	In der oberen linken/rechten Ecke ...
Next to/opposite/between ...	Neben/gegenüber/zwischen ...
Behind/in front of ...	Hinter/vor ...

Asking for and giving directions

Excuse me please, can you help me?	Entschuldigung, können Sie / kannst du mir bitte helfen?
Where is the ...?	Wo ist das ...?
Turn left/right.	Biege / Biegen Sie nach links/rechts ab.
Go straight on.	Gehe / Gehen Sie geradeaus.
Take the first road on the right.	Nehmen Sie / Nimm die erste Straße auf der rechten Seite.
Cross the road.	Überqueren Sie / Überquere die Straße.

Giving a presentation

My presentation is about ...	In meiner Präsentation geht es um ...
This slide shows ...	Diese Folie zeigt ...
The next slide shows ...	Die nächste Folie zeigt ...
Thank you for listening.	Danke fürs Zuhören.
Any questions?	Haben Sie / Hast du / Habt ihr Fragen?

Making a phone call

Hello. Can I speak to ..., please?	Hallo. Kann ich bitte ... sprechen?
My name is ...	Ich heiße ...
I'm calling from Germany.	Ich rufe aus Deutschland an.
Can you put me through to ..., please?	Können Sie mich bitte zu ... durchstellen?
I'm sorry, ... isn't here right now.	Es tut mir leid, ... ist zur Zeit nicht da.
Could you take a message, please?	Können Sie bitte etwas ausrichten?
Can I take a message?	Kann ich etwas ausrichten?
I'll call again later.	Ich rufe später noch einmal an.
Thanks/Thank you. Goodbye/Bye.	Danke. Auf Wiederhören/Tschüss.

Deciding where to go or what to do

Where would you like to go?	Wo würdest du gerne hingehen?
I like the mountains/beach ...	Ich mag die Berge/den Strand ...
How can we get there?	Wie können wir dorthin kommen?

Going shopping and in a restaurant

May I help you?	Kann ich Ihnen helfen? / Was darf es sein?
Excuse me, have you got any ...?	Entschuldigung, haben Sie ...?
Can I have ..., please?	Kann ich bitte ... haben?
I'd like ..., please.	Ich hätte gerne ...
How much is / are ...?	Wie viel kostet / kosten ...?
Do you sell ...?	Verkaufen Sie ...?
Sorry, can you say that again / repeat, please?	Entschuldigung, könnten Sie / könntest du das bitte wiederholen?
Where can I try it on?	Wo kann ich das anprobieren?
The changing room is over there.	Die Umkleidekabine ist da drüben.
Do you have a larger/smaller size?	Haben Sie das in einer größeren/kleineren Größe?
Yes, of course. What size are you?	Ja, natürlich. Welche Größe haben Sie?
I'll take it.	Ich nehme es.
Here's your change.	Hier ist Ihr Wechselgeld.
You can keep the change.	Behalten Sie den Rest.
a kilo of/a bag of/a packet of ...	ein Kilo/einen Beutel/eine Tüte ...

Travelling

Could you tell me the time of the next train/bus, please?	Könnten Sie mir die Abfahrtszeit des nächsten Zuges/Busses sagen?
Do I have to change trains?	Muss ich umsteigen?
What platform does it leave from?	An welchem Bahnsteig fährt er ab?
What time does it arrive?	Wann kommt er an?
How long is the journey/flight?	Wie lange dauert die Reise/der Flug?
Where can I buy a ticket?	Wo kann ich eine Fahrkarte kaufen?
How much is a one-way ticket to ...?	Was kostet eine einfache Fahrt nach ...?
How much is a return ticket to ...?	Was kostet eine Rückfahrkarte nach ...?

A job interview

I'm still at school.	Ich gehe noch zur Schule.
I left school early.	Ich habe die Schule abgebrochen.
I did my final exams some time ago.	Ich habe vor einiger Zeit meinen Abschluss gemacht.
I'm interested in the job because ...	Ich interessiere mich für den Job weil ...
I like working outside / with computers.	Ich arbeite gerne im Freien / mit Computern.
I like working with people/in a team.	Ich arbeite gerne mit Menschen / in einem Team
I'd like to train to be a/an ...	Ich würde mich gerne als ... ausbilden lassen.
I'd like to work with animals.	Ich möchte gerne mit Tieren arbeiten.
I'd like to work abroad/in ...	Ich würde gerne im Ausland / in ... arbeiten.
My hobbies are ...	Meine Hobbys sind ...
How much will I be paid?	Wie hoch ist mein Lohn/Gehalt?
When will I have to start work?	Wann ist mein erster Arbeitstag?
How much holiday do I get?	Wie viele Urlaubstage habe ich?

Talking about strengths and weaknesses

I think ...	Ich denke ...
I'm reliable/creative/practical.	Ich würde sagen, ich bin zuverlässig/kreativ/praktisch veranlagt.
I find (don't find) it easy to meet people.	Es fällt mir (nicht) leicht neue Menschen kennenzulernen.
I find it easy to learn new skills.	Ich lerne recht schnell.
I'm good/not so good at ...	Ich bin (nicht so) gut im Umgang mit ...
I prefer ...	Ich ziehe es vor, ...
I don't like ...	Ich mag ... nicht.

At a hotel

I would like to make a reservation, please.	Ich möchte ein Zimmer reservieren.
Do you have any rooms available?	Haben Sie freie Zimmer?
I would like a single room with a bath.	Ich hätte gerne ein Einzelzimmer mit Bad.
I would like a double room with a shower.	Ich hätte gerne ein Doppelzimmer mit Dusche.
I would like a twin room.	Ich hätte gerne ein Doppelzimmer.
How much will the room cost?	Wie viel kostet das Zimmer?
Is breakfast included in the price?	Ist das Frühstück mit im Preis inbegriffen?
I'd like a non-smoking room, please.	Ich hätte gerne ein Nichtraucher-zimmer.
What time is breakfast?	Um wie viel Uhr gibt es Frühstück.
All our rooms have en suite bathrooms.	Alle unsere Zimmer sind mit Bad.
The room will cost XX per person per night.	Das Zimmer kostet XX pro Person und Nacht.
The light bulb is broken.	Die Glühbirne ist kaputt.
The TV isn't working.	Der Fernseher funktioniert nicht.

Saying how you feel

That's fantastic!	Das ist fantastisch!
I'm really enjoying it.	Ich genießes richtig.
I'm looking forward to ...	Ich freue mich auf ...
I'm glad that ...	Ich bin glücklich/froh, dass ...
I feel hopeful that ...	Ich bin voller Hoffnung, dass ...
I've never felt so good.	Ich habe mich noch nie so gut gefühlt.
What a nice idea!	Was für eine gute Idee!
That makes me happy.	Das macht mich glücklich.
How terrible!	Wie furchtbar!
I'm really frustrated.	Ich bin sehr frustriert.
What happened is really sad/awful ...	Was passierte ist sehr traurig/schlimm...
That makes me angry.	Das macht mich wütend.
I'm worried about ...	Ich mache mir Sorgen um ...
I feel guilty because ...	Ich fühle mich schuldig, weil ...
I wish I could help.	Ich wünsche ich könnte dir helfen.
I'm sorry to hear that ...	Es tut mir leid zu hören, dass ...

Prepositions

The smallest words in most languages are the ones that cause the most problems. The words below are prepositions and come in front of other words usually to describe where they are. Unfortunately, their meaning changes depending on what comes after them. It is best to learn these phrases by heart.

at

at my house	bei mir
at 3 o'clock	um 3 Uhr
at the top/bottom	oben/unten

for

for breakfast	zum Frühstück
for fun	aus Spaß
for me	für mich

from

from Germany	aus Deutschland
from 3 o'clock	ab 3 Uhr
from ... until	von ... bis
from David	von David

in

in the middle	in der Mitte
in time	rechtzeitig
in turn	der Reihe nach

on

on foot	zu Fuß
on the right/left	links/rechts
on the table	auf dem Tisch
on time	pünktlich
on average	im Durchschnitt
on purpose	absichtlich

by

by train/car/bus/boat	mit dem Zug/Auto/Bus/Boot
by 3 o'clock	bis 3 Uhr

Adjectives

Here are some adjectives which are useful if you want to desribe what someone looks like, what their character is, or if you want to talk about their feelings.

Describing someone's character and qualities

brave	mutig, tapfer
calm	ruhig
careful	vorsichtig
careless	unvorsichtig, leichtsinnig
charming	charmant, bezaubernd
clever	schlau, klug
confident	selbstsicher, selbstbewusst
creative	kreativ
cruel	grausam, herzlos
curious	neugierig
(un)fair	(un)fair
(un)friendly	(un)freundlich
generous	großzügig
helpful	hilfsbereit
honest	ehrlich
kind	freundlich, nett
laid back	entspannt
lazy	faul, träge
likeable	liebenswert, nett
nervous	nervös
optimistic	optimistisch
patient	geduldig
pessimistic	pessimistisch
pleasant	angenehm, nett
polite	höflich
proud	stolz
rude	unhöflich
shy	schüchtern
stupid	dumm, blöd

Describing what someone looks like

bald	kahl, glatzköpfig
beautiful	schön
blond-/fair-haired	blond
curly-haired	mit lockigen Haaren
dark-haired	dunkelhaarig
fat	dick
good-looking	gut aussehend
overweight	übergewichtig
pretty	hübsch
slim	schlank
small/short	klein
smart	schick, flott
straight-haired	mit glatten Haaren
tall	groß
thin	dünn
ugly	hässlich
well-dressed	gut angezogen

Describing someone's feelings

angry	wütend
annoyed	verärgert
awful	schrecklich
bored	gelangweilt
cool	ruhig, gefasst
crazy	verrückt
depressed	deprimiert
disappointed	enttäuscht
embarrassed	verlegen
excited	aufgeregt
funny	komisch
glad	froh
happy	froh, glücklich
horrible	schrecklich
lonely	einsam
pleased	erfreut, zufrieden
surprised	überrascht
terrible	furchtbar
tired	müde
unhappy/sad	traurig
worried	besorgt

Prefixes and suffixes

Prefixes are two or three letters that can be added to the front of certain verbs (or some adjectives) and they usually make the meaning of the verb change to the opposite meaning.

'dis-' at the beginning of a verb

to dislike	nicht mögen
to disappear	verschwinden
to disagree	nicht einverstanden sein

'mis-' at the beginning of a verb

to misread	falsch lesen, falsch verstehen
to miscount	sich verzählen, sich verrechnen
to misunderstand	falsch verstehen

'un-' at the beginning of a verb

to undo	öffnen, aufmachen
to unlock	aufschließen

'un-' at the beginning of an adjective

unhappy	unglücklich
unusual	ungewöhnlich
uncomfortable	unbequem

'in-', 'im-' or 'il-' at the beginning of an adjective

incorrect	falsch, fehlerhaft
impossible	unmöglich
illegal	illegal, gegen das Gesetz

Suffixes are two or three letters that can be added to the end of certain verbs which makes them into adjectives. Depending which suffix you use, you can make a verb into two adjectives that mean the opposite.

'-ful' at the end of a verb

careful	vorsichtig
helpful	hilfsbereit

'-less' at the end of a verb

careless	unvorsichtig, leichtsinnig
helpless	hilflos

Irregular plurals

Usually you just add an 's' to a noun to turn it from its singular form into its plural form. There are nouns that have different plural forms.

The plural is spelt different to the singular

singular	plural	German
man/woman	men, women	Mann, Frau
child	children	Kind
die	dice	Würfel
mouse	mice	Maus
tooth	teeth	Zahn

The plural form is the same as the singular form

singular	plural	German
sheep	sheep	Schaf
information	information	Information
fish	fish	Fisch
news	news	Nachricht

You add 'es' to the singular form to make the plural form

singular	plural	German
sandwich	sandwiches	belegtes Brot
bush	bushes	Busch
tomato	tomatoes	Tomate
potato	potatoes	Kartoffel

With nouns that end in '-f' or '-fe' replace the '-f' with '-ves'

singular	plural	German
leaf	leaves	Blatt *(von Pflanzen)*
shelf	shelves	Regal
life	lives	Leben

Exception: belief → beliefs

'a' or 'an'?

When you are talking about one thing in English you can use either 'a' or 'an'. It is the **sound** of the first letter of the word that follows that is important. You use 'an' for things that begin with a vowel and 'a' for things that begin with a consonant.

'a'	'an'
green apple	apple
European	egg
uniform	umbrella
machine	MP3 player
house	hour
yellow umbrella	ice-cream
sofa	orange sofa

'much' or 'many'?

Just learn the rule and you will never have a problem with 'much' and 'many'. They are both mostly used in questions and negative sentences.

'much' is used for things in the singular and if you can't count them.

- How much money have you got?
- We haven't got much food for the party.
- We haven't got much homework.
- How much flour do we need for the cake?

'many' is used for things in plural and if you can count how many of them there are.

- How many people live in Germany?
- We haven't got many eggs.
- How many friends have you invited?
- I haven't got many sweets left.

Present simple – 3rd person singular

He, she, it das **‚s'** muss mit, aber auch bei **David, Sarah** und **sports kit.**

He likes the rain. – **David** likes the rain

She walks to school. – **Sarah** walks to school.

It smells horrible. – **The sports kit** smells horrible.

American English – British English

Most words are the same in British English and American English, but there are a few exceptions. Some words are just spelt differently so you can recognise them if you know the British English word, and others are completely different words.

Different spellings

British English	American English	German
centre	center	Zentrum
colour	color	Farbe
favourite	favorite	Lieblings-
grey	gray	grau
neighbour	neighbor	Nachbar(in)
to practise	to practice	üben

Different words

British English	American English	German
autumn	fall	Herbst
chips	French fries	Pommes Frites
crisps	chips	(Kartoffel)Chips
film	movie	Film
flat	apartment	Wohnung
headteacher	principal	Schulleiter(in)
holiday	vacation	Ferien
lift	elevator	Aufzug
lorry	truck	Lastwagen
queue	line	(Warte)Schlange
rubbish	trash/garbage	Müll/Abfall
shop	store	Laden
taxi	cab	Taxi
toilet	restroom/bathroom	Toilette
town centre	downtown	Stadtmitte
trousers	pants	Hose

Same sound - different spelling/meaning

The more English words you learn, the more you might get confused. This could be because sometimes you will hear two (or even more) words that sound the same, but they have completely different meanings. What makes it even worse is that the words may sound the same, but they have different spellings. These words you really do have to learn well.

to (zu, an, nach)	**two** (zwei)	**too** (auch)
there (dort, da)	**their** (ihre)	**they're** (sie sind)

flour (Mehl)	**flower** (Blume)
for (für)	**four** (vier)
here (hier)	**hear** (hören)
meet (treffen)	**meat** (Fleisch)
past (Vergangenheit)	**passed** (bestanden)
practice (Training)	**practise** (üben)
red (rot)	**read** (gelesen)
see (sehen)	**sea** (Meer)
sun (Sonne)	**son** (Sohn)
witch (Hexe)	**which** (welche)
wood (Holz, Wald)	**would** (werden)

Same spelling - different sounds

Another group of words that make learning English tricky are words that are spelt the same but sound different and have different meanings. Again this group of words will get bigger the more English you learn.

live – [lɪv] (leben)	**live –** [laɪv] (live)
read – [ri:d] (lesen)	**read –** [red] (gelesen)
use – [ju:s] (Nutzung)	**use –** [ju:z] (verwenden)
produce – [prə'dju:s] (herstellen)	**produce –** ['prɒdju:s] (Produkte)
present – [preznt] (Geschenk)	**present –** [prɪ'zent] (präsentieren)

False friends

False friends are words which look the same or very similar in German and English. They don't have the same meaning though. The best thing to do to find out if a word is a false friend or not is translate the word and see if it fits in the context of the sentence. The best thing to do is learn some of the most common false friends (listed below) so you don't make mistakes.

Different meanings

to become	werden
brave	mutig, tapfer
chef	Koch(in)
chips	Pommes Frites
gift	Geschenk
eventually	schließlich
fabric	Stoff
meaning	Bedeutung
mobile phone	Handy
note	Notiz, Zettel
prescription	Rezept
receipt	Quittung
sensible	vernünftig
stadium	Stadion
sympathetic	mitfühlend

Different spellings in British English

address	Adresse
calender	Kalender
career	Karriere
carnival	Karneval
catalogue	Katalog
colleague	Kollege
guitar	Gitarre
kilometre	Kilometer
litre	Liter
model	Modell
per cent	Prozent
photo	Foto
rhyme	Reim
second	Sekunde
wonder	Wunder

Index

B

D

S